Writing for tl

A Practical Gui

Cynthia L. Jeney

Missouri Western State University

PEARSON

Prentice
Hall

Upper Saddle River, New Jersey
Columbus, Ohio

Library of Congress Cataloging-in-Publication Data

Jenby, Cynthia L.
     Writing for the Web : a practical approach / Cynthia L. Jenby.
          p. cm.
     Includes bibliographical references and index.
     ISBN 0-13-119236-1
     1. Web sites—Design. 2. Technical writing. I. Title.

TK5105.888.J46 2007
005.7'2—dc22   2006043195

Brief Contents

Contents

SECTION II

WRITING STYLES FOR THE WEB

This book is dedicated to Barry Maid, Keith Miller,
John Ramage, Duane Roen, and David Schwalm,
who got me started.

And to Deborah Hanline,
who kept me going.

Preface

This book began with a phone conversation between myself and Brandy Dawson, Prentice Hall Humanities & Social Sciences Director of Marketing. Brandy had called my office to chat about textbooks I was planning to use in my upcoming classes, including a relatively new course called "Web Authoring." I voiced some of my frustrations about the difficulty I was having in finding a satisfactory book that dealt specifically with *writing* for Web sites and online environments, so Brandy asked me what I would like to see in such a book. As I rapidly listed the issues and topics I wanted my students to read about, she said I had the makings of a Table of Contents—would I be interested in submitting a proposal? Yes, I was interested.

That proposal became this book, because I believe that it is important for people—not just technical writers and journalists, but all citizens of the world—to become stronger and clearer online writers. Responsible teachers of writing and online communication will ask students to stop and consider the historical moment in which we live. *For the first time in the history of the world, mass communication is possible for any individual, living anywhere on the planet.* This new age of turbocharged information technology is not like any previous age, for in contrast with the advents of print, radio, and television, Internet technologies allow the common person, anyone with even a small number of communications skills (basic literacy, and a few digital software user skills), to communicate with vast numbers of other people *without being filtered, edited, or "weeded out" by anyone.* It is impossible to exaggerate the implications of this technological capability. True, such communication capabilities seem an almost natural technological evolution to Americans and to citizens of other countries in which freedom of speech and communication are prized and encouraged. But to the millions of people who live in sectors of the world where mass communication has traditionally been controlled, the development of the Internet has caused interesting changes. Before the 1990's, the wide dissemination of information, whether for good or for ill, was controlled by layers of corporate and government editors, fact-checkers, public relations personnel, and information specialists. But now all of those controls have been weakened by the sheer openness of Internet technologies.

The Internet has created an urgent need for strong writing skills in the workplace, the community, and even in the arts and entertainment fields. With so many messages and sales pitches spinning around in networked communication spaces and places, it is the good writers—the powerful, ethical communicators—who are needed in every aspect of our lives.

Writing for the Web: A Practical Guide introduces students to writing for Web sites and for other forms of online documentation. Because most of the writing done for professional Web sites is technical and information-based, the approach to writing in this book is rhetorical. Students are asked to prioritize audience and learn strategies that optimize Web site readability *and* usability. The assignments and exercises were developed from practical situations and ideas that evolved in classes I've taught and in Web projects I've worked on over the years.

WHO SHOULD USE THIS BOOK

Writing for the Web: A Practical Guide is an introduction to writing effectively for common types of Web sites. I wrote it selfishly, with my own Web writing course in mind, but with the knowledge that many of my colleagues are also teaching similar courses. The book addresses beginning technical writers, but I believe it will work very well for any college writing course that emphasizes online projects and Web writing assignments. I would even encourage instructors of technology-oriented technical communication courses to consider using this book for beginning Web content development courses.

The information and assignments in this book are intended for beginning technical communicators, although advanced technical writers who have little or no Web experience might find the book useful. The book is not a reference work or handbook, although a useful glossary of terms is provided in Appendix C.

THE PURPOSE OF THIS BOOK

The purpose of the book is to help students and instructors focus intensively upon the *writing* situations and requirements of typical Web projects. Students will learn about developing writing styles and approaches that create identity, clarify documentation and support, assist usability, complement visual design, facilitate commerce, encourage originality and creativity, and organize information for optimum usability.

This book deliberately foregrounds writing as a critical element of communication on the World Wide Web. It does not teach computer programming, Web coding, digital graphics, or database management. However, it should be easy to incorporate this book into courses that do teach one or more of these Web development skills. The purpose here is to help students wear a "Web writer's hat" and focus on elements of human communication necessary to achieve the desired results on the Web. The assignments and exercises were specifically developed to give students opportunities to put a variety of writing styles and strategies to work. Exercises in each chapter help students practice skills and strategies such as captioning photos, establishing corporate (or institutional) identity, incorporating links, writing FAQ pages, and answering online visitors' complaints. The assignments can be completed whether or not the course teaches Web design and/or programming.

ASSIGNMENTS, EXERCISES, CASES, AND ASSESSMENT

The exercises and assignments in this book provide opportunities for students to practice typical Web writing tasks. This book asks writers to take time to plan, organize, strategize, and *think critically* about the motives and purposes behind different kinds of Web writing. While most of the activities in the book allow breathing room for teacher creativity and course adaptation, the assignments are, primarily, rhetoric-driven. Therefore I would recommend that student work be evaluated on its rhetorical virtues and its practical merits. Students should gain from this book a working familiarity with the concepts of identity, content development, and emotional appeal. They should also begin to gain a sense of planning, organization, and style. Along the way, students should begin to understand the value of identifying and targeting *exigency*—the need or desire that brings visitors to a Web site. And of course they should begin to test their own writing choices against *purpose*—the aims and motives that drive their own Web sites. As they work through rhetoric-based Web writing assignments and projects, students should gradually develop confidence in their own answers to the questions "Who wants to know?" and "What is the best way to write and organize this for online visitors?"

Projects in the book can easily be used as either individual writing projects, or as cooperative/collaborative student projects. The book's exercises and assignments also can be used in service-learning and/or applied learning course components. Keep in mind that evaluation of assignments and exercises should be based upon the criteria and skills being emphasized in the course.

THE PHILOSOPHY UNDERLYING THIS BOOK

This book takes its theoretical underpinnings from classical and modern rhetoric, and from critical thinkers in the fields of writing pedagogy and online communication. I agree with Kenneth Burke, John Dewey, Charles Peirce, and others who have described the English language as an intricate, breathing, complicated phenomenon that takes a lifetime to begin to understand. There are different approaches (and sciences and logics) to understanding it, and writing anything powerful enough to really reach people, to touch someone's mind or heart, is hard work. But it can be done, and it starts with us, the writers, and what we're trying to accomplish. In the world of professional and technical writing, this is called "getting results."

Getting results is a tough job, no matter what kind of writing we're doing, or what kinds of writers we want to be. Writing is human thought and desire pushed through attitude, into action. It is messy, complicated, weird, and unruly; and wherever it goes, it takes the baggage of centuries of meanings and shades of meaning with it. As Jacques Ellul has pointed out, language is not a direct and easily deciphered "code" so much as it is the symbolic transmittal of human desires and attitudes all mixed up with motive and zapped onto the page in hopes of getting something we want or need from another symbol-using animal. Writing at its best is a piece of our *selves* on the page and on the screen. The flashing buttons and swirling video images on a Web site are fine and dandy, but they are usually just window dressing that often masks a sad lack of real content and purpose. Effective and exciting Web sites (by this I mean sites that attract many visitors who return often and spread the word to others who also pay repeated visits) keep our attention largely because of good writing. Language connects us to each other and works to satisfy our desires. It brings details and viewpoints into perspective, in ways that pictures or video clips cannot do on their own. This book, while down-to-earth and practical in style, is based upon the idea of the "citizen orator"—that all members of the global community should be able to articulate and communicate in professional, effective, and creative ways. The Internet has brought the Global Village into being, and now it is time for us all to participate in critically responsible and productive ways. So let us begin.

ACKNOWLEDGMENTS

Writing for the Web: A Practical Guide was a challenging book to write, and I want to thank all who helped make it happen.

I owe a debt of gratitude to my colleagues in several academic communities, including the scholars and teachers who attend the annual Conference on Computers & Writing, and the many past and present members of MegaByte-U, ACW-L, TechRhet, ATTW-L, and WPA-L online discussion lists.

I am grateful to Brandy Dawson, Director of Marketing at Prentice Hall's Humanities & Social Sciences Division, for getting me started on the book. Many thanks go to my editor at Prentice Hall, Gary Bauer, and to his assistant, Jacqueline Knapke, for holding my hand and helping me through all of the technicalities as the book worked its way into print. My gratitude goes, as well, to the reviewers who provided so many helpful comments and suggestions during the manuscript stages of the book: Douglas Gray, Columbus State Community College; Erin Karper, Niagara University; Ann Jennings, University of Houston – Downtown; Michael Johanyak, University of Akron; Thomas Lowderbaugh, University of Maryland; Michael Morgan, Bemidji State University; Daniel Royer, Grand Valley State University; and Madeleine Sorapure, University of California – Santa Barbara.

Special thanks go to my friends and colleagues, especially Deborah Hanline, Wayne Chandler, Barry Maid, John Walter, Kaye Adkins, Stacia Bensyl, Trish Donaher, Kate Coffield, Mary Fieber, Margaret Pella, and Thea Ide for keeping the coffee hot, making sandwiches, brainstorming with me, reading through drafts, testing my pages for clarity, pointing out errors, and making me *think*. Additional thanks go to my parents, Esther and Karl Harnack, my sister Karla Bonora, my brother Thomas Harnack, and my dear friend Jean Sowa, for believing in me. Finally, thanks to my furry family of four cats, one horse, and the best golden retriever in the whole world, who always lend their moral support and comic relief no matter what the endeavor.

Introduction to Writing for the Web

Glossary Terms
(See Appendix C for definitions of glossary terms)

ARPANet	Internet
Bit	Internet Relay Chat (IRC)
Browser	ISP
Bulletin board system or service (BBS)	Local area network (LAN)
CERN	Operating system
Client	Packet
Codex	Rhetorical purpose
Connectivity	Server
Data stream	TALK
Download	URL
Genre	Upload
Gopher	Usenet
Graphical user interface (GUI)	Web site
Human-computer interface (HCI)	Web surfing
Hyperlink	World Wide Web
Icon	WYSIWYG
Information management	

INTRODUCTION

This book is about writing for the Internet. Specifically, it's about writing for that part of the Internet called the World Wide Web. For although the two terms are often used interchangeably, the Internet includes a number of computer network capabilities, including e-mail, file sharing, local area networks, multi-user dungeons, instant messaging, gaming networks, chat, bulletin board systems, electronic data transfer, and so on. The Web refers specifically to Internet files called up from various electronic servers by a Web browser and displayed as screen pages on our computers. This book is about writing for the Web in professional, informed ways, so that Web site users will get what they need and what they want. This book is designed to help you improve the writing on your own Web site, your company's Web site, and your clients' Web sites, so that the sites will deliver on their promises in efficient and pleasing ways.

If you are using this book for a class, your teacher may have also selected one of the many good books on Web design, graphics, and/or programming. This book should supplement your work with those important elements of Web-site building. If you have selected this book on your own, or if you are taking a class focused on writing (a course, that is, without Web design or programming components), then you may wish to browse through the "Suggested Further Reading" section in Appendix D to find books on digital graphic design and programming architectures for the Web. It is a good idea for writers to explore methods of design, markup, layout, programming, and site architecture.

Although this book focuses on strategies and styles for writing on the World Wide Web, that doesn't mean Web writers see words and images as completely separate or unrelated elements. You have probably already explored the Web enough to know that the most successful Web sites include textual, graphical, and dynamic elements that are integrated and thematically coordinated. This book is about writing—but gives writers ideas and exercises to help them develop a sense of writing as part of a technical team. Web writers work closely with digital artists, graphical interface designers, programmers, database administrators, and information managers. Even when writers are developing Web sites independently, they need to realize that sites no longer exist in a vacuum. Sites need to function compatibly with many different kinds of computers, platforms, and browsers.

Writing for the Web should also be about making the right promises, giving the right impression, setting up expectations, and then meeting them. Visitors want to be delighted and pleased, and they will revisit sites that give satisfaction. Possibly, you've experienced enough of the Web to have noticed that the writing on many Web sites promises one thing, while the site actually delivers something else (or possibly nothing at all). This is often the result of writing that is either poorly planned or deliberately misleading. Some call this "crass commercialism." But bad marketing and dishonest business practices have flooded the Web, and in an attempt to create "professional" Web sites, beginning Web developers sometimes imitate these poor examples of commercial writing.

This book gives writers (1) a helpful glossary of terms; (2) a concise, rhetoric-driven introduction to the situations, contexts, and technologies within which Web writing is situated; (3) an organized reference and tutorial tour of the genres and categories of conventional webs and Web page types; (4) an example-driven catalog of stylistic approaches Web writers can use; and (5) assignments that replicate problem-solving and composing tasks faced by Web writers.

The first chapter is an overview of the Internet as a technical writing and publishing situation. For that is what the Internet is, from a writing standpoint. It is important for writers to have a basic understanding of the Internet, how it conveys messages and information, and what its size and scope mean to professional writers. On the Web can be found all kinds of writing styles, genres, approaches, and techniques, both good and bad. News Web sites feature journalistic writing. Commercial Web sites feature marketing-style writing. Support-group Web sites feature nurturing, "self-help" styles of writing. Media and broadcast-affiliate Web sites feature contemporary "media-speak" (choppy, sensational, sentence-fragment style) writing. Chapter 2 discusses the Web as an opportunity for technical writers to wear many different "hats." Chapter 3 introduces writers to common principles and conventions for developing, organizing, and presenting written content for the Web. Chapter 4 emphasizes formats and documents that have become standard fare on the Web, some of which have made transitions (for better or worse) from common print formats, and some of which are "in transition," often formatted and reformatted for both print and electronic storage and transmission. In Chapter 5 writers have a chance to practice different approaches to style, including rhetorical, grammatical, and structural schemes and patterns from which various effects can be created, using professional writing techniques that satisfy the reader's desires and needs. Chapters 6, 7, and 8 concentrate on purpose-driven kinds of Web sites and the typical writing strategies that go along with each. Chapter 6 focuses on writing for commerce-driven sites, including business, database, and marketing styles. Chapter 7 discusses information-based sites, including academic, scientific, help-file, and journalistic Web sites. Finally, Chapter 8 explores approaches to writing for creative Web sites, including personal, humorous, satirical, and literary writing styles. Some case-based Web writing assignments are given in Appendix A. Appendix B lists basic HTML tags, Appendix C is a glossary of terms for Web writers, and Appendix D offers suggestions for further reading. *Writing for the Web: A Practical Guide* was written to provide writers of all kinds with basic principles and a "toolbox" of writing strategies for accomplishing goals and creating dynamic appeal on the World Wide Web.

GOING ONLINE: WHAT IS THE "NET"?

In the latter part of the twentieth century, personal computers were isolated units of computational functions and data storage. For the home computer hobbyist, **connectivity** was limited to dial-up modem connections that logged a computer into a single **bulletin-board system (BBS),** a place to post and read messages, play text-based games, or trade bootleg copies of proprietary software and chunks of programming code. In the 1990s, industry and government backing combined to open up technologies that had once been designed for the U.S. military. Strategists wanted "self-healing" routes of communications during the event of nuclear war. Thus **ARPANet** was created by engineers determined to ensure that vital data and codes could be transmitted among critical systems during nuclear simulations. When one vital communication center went down, packets of digitized information were automatically rerouted so that they still arrived at their destinations. With a few coded adjustments, programmers could also send plain text messages to each other, either in real time or in stored file systems where they could be collected by the intended recipients later (the precursors of chat and e-mail). When the researchers at **CERN** (Conseil Européen pour la Recherche Nucléaire: the European particle physics laboratory in Geneva, Switzerland) added hypertext transfer capabilities to the mix, the **World Wide Web** became possible.

Today, we use the **Internet** (the "Net") for both personal and professional communication without thinking much about the amazing amount of inventiveness and determination that went into its initial creation. These common message-transmittal systems are based on technologies that are astoundingly stable and resilient, primarily because their inventors envisioned the most nightmarish of worst-case scenarios: nuclear annihilation of major regional communications conduits and power sources. Then they piggybacked their computer-generated data streams on top of the impulse-carrying network of telecommunications cables, transmitters, satellites, switching stations, and fiber optics already in place. All that remained to open up these computer-mediated communications technologies to the general civilian public was a way to package and sell them.

As early as the late 1980s and into the early 1990s, companies such as CompuServe, Prodigy, and America Online understood that most people were not willing to learn complicated, tedious lines of computer code in order to use their computers for information-processing and communication purposes. The text-based interface was useful for transmission of alphanumerical data, and some of the programs available were very well written, but initially the text-based screen was *opaque*—users could not tell just by looking at the screen how to initiate or complete tasks. For computer programmers, these new Internet communications environments—**Usenet, Gopher, TALK, Internet Relay Chat (IRC)**, bulletin board systems (BBSs)—were natural offshoots of their own messaging systems within **local area networks (LANs).** But for the everyday nonprogrammer, the text-based interface proved daunting. As philosopher Philip Bereano has pointed out, that black screen with strange letter-number combinations often frustrated people upon whose desks these new computing machines had landed. (See Figure 1.1.)

The early proprietary database programs created for industrial and institutional use were strictly text-based, capable of displaying only alphanumeric symbols. The new symbol-and-code–based information storage systems were unfamiliar and strange to office workers and managers who nevertheless were eager to employ them. Thus trade schools across the country offered certification and technical degrees in "data entry." Television advertisements promised that their school could, in just a matter of months, turn you into a "Data Entry Specialist," at which time you could command an astronomical salary at any large business. In reality, these jobs

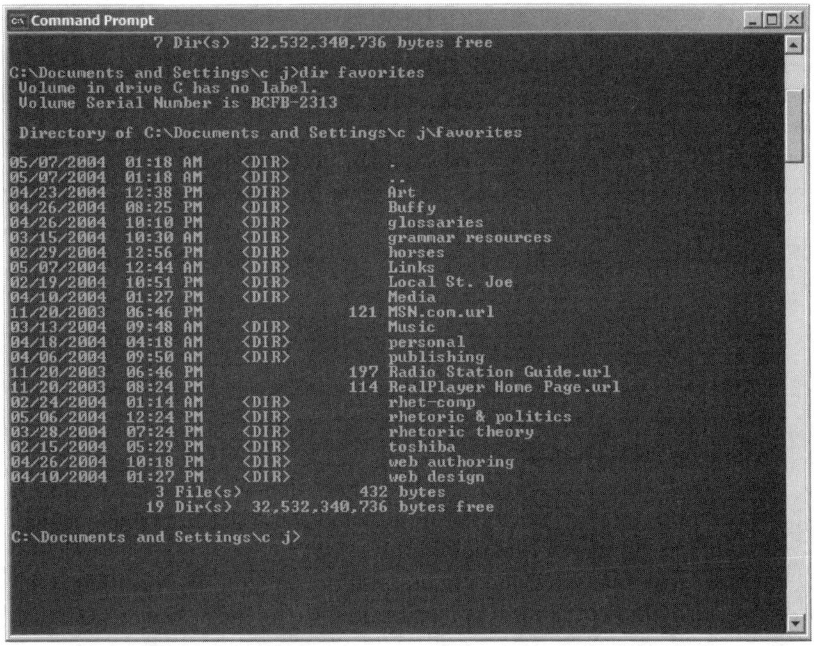

```
                    7 Dir(s)  32,532,340,736 bytes free

C:\Documents and Settings\c j>dir favorites
 Volume in drive C has no label.
 Volume Serial Number is BCFB-2313

 Directory of C:\Documents and Settings\c j\favorites

05/07/2004  01:18 AM    <DIR>          .
05/07/2004  01:18 AM    <DIR>          ..
04/23/2004  12:38 PM    <DIR>          Art
04/26/2004  08:25 PM    <DIR>          Buffy
04/26/2004  10:10 PM    <DIR>          glossaries
03/15/2004  10:30 AM    <DIR>          grammar resources
02/29/2004  12:56 PM    <DIR>          horses
05/07/2004  12:44 AM    <DIR>          Links
02/19/2004  10:51 PM    <DIR>          Local St. Joe
04/10/2004  01:27 PM    <DIR>          Media
11/20/2003  06:46 PM              121  MSN.com.url
03/13/2004  09:48 AM    <DIR>          Music
04/18/2004  04:18 AM    <DIR>          personal
04/06/2004  09:50 AM    <DIR>          publishing
11/20/2003  06:46 PM              197  Radio Station Guide.url
11/20/2003  08:24 PM              114  RealPlayer Home Page.url
02/24/2004  01:14 AM    <DIR>          rhet-comp
05/06/2004  12:24 PM    <DIR>          rhetoric & politics
03/28/2004  07:24 PM    <DIR>          rhetoric theory
02/15/2004  05:29 PM    <DIR>          toshiba
04/26/2004  10:18 PM    <DIR>          web authoring
04/10/2004  01:27 PM    <DIR>          web design
                3 File(s)           432 bytes
               19 Dir(s)  32,532,340,736 bytes free

C:\Documents and Settings\c j>
```

FIGURE 1.1   Text-based screens were often daunting to first-time computer users.

tended to be speed-typing jobs, located in corporate worker-pools, large rooms filled with computer terminals and telephonic headsets, where workers sat at their stations all day long typing insurance or banking account numbers and billing invoices into credit card company databases.

A popular expression describing the limits (and in a sense, the logical beauty) of computers in the early 1980s was GIGO: "Garbage In, Garbage Out," a summary of the principle that garbled input results in garbled output. Already computer users were consciously reminding themselves and each other that computers only perform the processes they've been programmed to perform, and they can only process the data that have been entered into them. In an attempt to make computers more "user-friendly," hardware and software developers worked to improve the **human-computer interface**—the physical point at which the computer user and the machine meet. They designed operating systems that display not just alphanumeric symbols on a blank background, but visual spaces and "windows"—graphical representations of files and directories, buttons and menus, toolbars and data entry fields—on full-color pixilated monitors (see Figure 1.2).

Today, computer screens are capable of breathtakingly beautiful graphical displays. In place of cumbersome, nonintuitive lines of file-directory commands, the **operating systems** we use have "**icon**-based" graphical displays. Operating systems developers soon settled on the "desktop" metaphor, around which these icons have clustered—folders, pages, "clipboards," and so on—to help ease the transition that office workers around the world were making from a "paper-based"

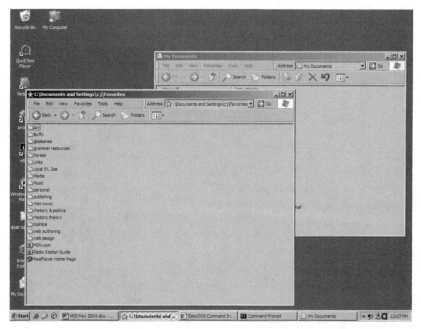

FIGURE 1.2   Graphical interfaces are much more intuitive than text-based screens. Workers adapted easily to the pictures and icons they could select using a mouse or touchpad.

information management system to digitized systems. Still, running underneath the software we use today, these lines of code are busily moving **bits** of information and data around.

The same is true of Web page development. When Web developers first began working with hypertext markup language (HTML), they had to "code by hand" all of the tags and script lines in plain-text editors, so that these hypertext documents could be handled by the average home computer's Web browser application. Nowadays, Web designers can choose from a number of programs that display text and images in the format they have planned for Internet users to see. Usually these programs also display lines of source code as well, so that Web pages can be fixed or tweaked.

SERVERS, NETWORKS, PACKETS, AND DATA STREAMS

Industry has gone Internet-crazy. During the 1990s, a common assumption was that the Internet was going to blow the top off the business world as we all knew it. It was going to change the face of commerce forever. And in many ways Internet technologies *have* changed the way most business is done. Therefore, as these technologies grow and change, it becomes more important for technical writers—and all business communicators—to have at least a working understanding of the fundamental principles of electronic communication.

For many of us, the Internet is a kind of mysterious, wonderful resource, a sort of computer-screen gateway to information, entertainment, retail, and communication. We don't really think much about how the information gets from one place to another—and we don't really have to. Internet companies have invested a great deal of money and expertise to make it as easy, seamless, and (we hope) painless as possible for the average person to use. But when we become Internet communicators ourselves, we may be surprised to discover that the media we access through our computers is stored and moved around in structured and orderly ways.

Most Internet usage for business purposes (some estimates go as high as 80%) is done behind the scenes, in encrypted form. Encrypted information has been transformed into undecipherable code by a computer program that uses algorithms. Theoretically, this keeps sensitive or proprietary information secure because only the sender and the intended recipient have the electronic "keys" to crack the code and read the information. In contrast, information available openly on the World Wide Web is stored on **servers**—computers that are set up to store and deliver information and software requested over a **network** connection (see Figure 1.3). Even though the digital files of information appear effortlessly on our computer

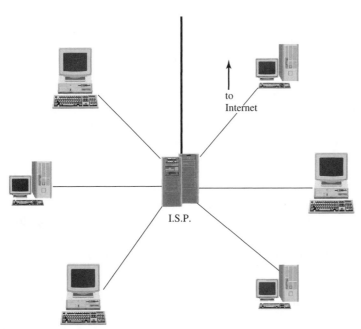

FIGURE 1.3 ISP server and PCs. Your computer is one of the machines in the outer circle; your Internet service provider (ISP) runs a machine with software that connects you to every other computer that is online via a system of servers, routers, telephone lines, satellite beams, and switching stations. These hardware technologies comprise the infrastructure upon which the Internet was built.

screens with the click of a mouse, most of the time there are several layers of software and equipment that come into play, sending blocks of electronic data in units sometimes referred to as **packets** at unimaginable speeds through a variety of network conduits. There are even layers of programming and equipment in our own desk computers that transform these fast-moving digitized packets into symbols, sounds, and images we can use. When these packets are traveling by the millions at blinding speed over uninterrupted global networks, we can think of the Internet as one of those artsy time-exposed photos of Los Angeles freeways in which beams of light whoosh along in intricate patterns, rarely colliding and always moving from one point to the next. Some data are even transferred in continuously flowing connections known as **data streams**. Historically speaking, our home computers, when compared to computers of the not-so-distant past, are extremely powerful machines capable of downloading, storing, displaying, and transmitting impressive amounts of information.

BROWSERS AND NETWORKS

Web pages are nothing more than bundles of digitized data that have been "called up" onto the computer screen and displayed on the screen by means of a program known as a Web browser.

When you "go on the Internet," you use a program called a **browser** that sends signals out to the "addresses" of servers, large data-storage computers that hold files you want to look at. These files are organized and designed to display on your personal computer screen—usually they are called **Web sites**.

A Web browser is a software application that displays digitized files you have **downloaded** via the Internet. When you open your browser, a window appears on your screen and you can type an Internet address called a **Uniform Resource Locator (URL)** directly into the field provided (Figure 1.4). When you type a URL and click "Go," you are sending a coded signal across the Internet that searches for a particular designated file (Figure 1.5). The URL supplies a domain and address for a particular machine that is storing the files, and provides the name of the directory of specific files that are located on that machine (Figure 1.6).

Think of Web sites for a moment as physical documents and media stored in solid paper file folders. Imagine the folders are located in a building downtown, in a musty old file room, in a cabinet locked away in a closet that nobody ever wanders into, until you ask for them. Your Web browser acts as an assistant who requests that a file clerk in the building go directly into the file room, locate the documents you want, and send them to you. Of course, since the "file clerk" is actually a machine, it can only locate the exact file you asked for and any files or packets of information that are coded to appear along with it. The relationship between your machine and the server storing the files is often referred to as a **client-server** relationship. The browser on your machine is a kind of "client" that logs into a server to get files for you.

In client-server environments, your computer is running a software application, but the data you want to view and possibly work with are not on your computer;

This prefix indicates that the type of information transfer is called "hypertext transfer protocol"	Indicates the "staff" Web server located on the MWSU campus	The "dot" divides elements of the URL domain (server) address	Registered domain name of Missouri Western State University	Identifies this domain as a registered postsecondary (college or university) server	Slash indicates a division between directory and subdirectory of files stored on the server	Tilde (~) indicates a (sometimes password-protected) "home directory," in this case the folder is mine	Subdirectory, in which Web files are stored for retrieval via a Web browser	Filename of a Web page, usually called an "html file"	File extension, indicating that this type of file can be opened by any application that recognizes hypertext markup pages
http://	staff	.	missouriwestern	.edu	/	~jeney/	writing/	style	.html

FIGURE 1.4 The Uniform Resource Locator (URL) provides specific kinds of locator-information that helps your computer's browser find the exact Web site files you are looking for. Each part of the URL provides a discrete type of information necessary for the call-up and download to be completed.

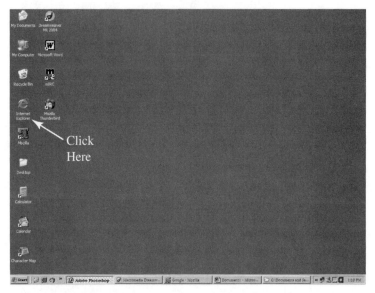

FIGURE 1.5   Once a computer is connected to the Internet, the computer can download files using a Web browser application such as Internet Explorer, Mozilla Firefox, Opera, Mosaic, Lynx, or Netscape.

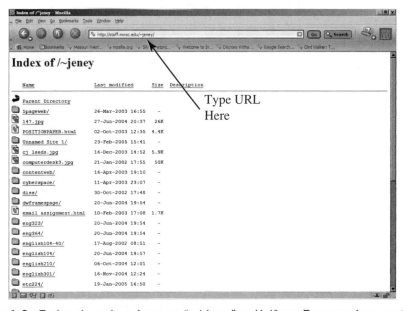

FIGURE 1.6   Typing the unique Internet "address" or Uniform Resource Locator (URL) of a Web site calls up files from remote servers.

the data are somewhere else. The client runs on your PC, while the server may be a program that is running on a mainframe or other large multiuser computer acting as a repository for large amounts of information. The fact that the information resides somewhere other than on the computer you are using is "transparent"—that is, your computer's graphical interface (which includes the icons, windows, and symbols on the screen) does not bother you with the details of how it is operating and where it is sending signals that call up the files and data you are viewing.

This transparency often creates the illusion that information and media are simply "appearing" on the screen, transmitted in much the same manner as television signals are transmitted to your TV. However, each file must be somehow "translated" visually for the user by means of various software applications. This is why users occasionally have trouble viewing various sound or video files—their computers are not equipped with programs that are associated with those particular kinds of files. There are even different kinds of text-based files that must be opened and displayed by various computer programs. Web browser developers have cleverly managed to integrate their software with a number of program applications in order to make downloading and viewing/listening easier. There is every reason to believe that such evolution of software development and integration will continue.

EXERCISE 1.1

Call up some of your favorite Web sites, or sites that your instructor has selected for you to view. In your Web browser, find the View Source Code command and look at the programming that has created the site. Answer (or discuss) the following questions about each Web site (you may wish to use the HTML reference chart in Appendix B):

1. How complex does the code appear to be?
2. What kinds of different *tags* do you see?
3. Do you see lines of commands for scripting languages such as JavaScript or Perl?
4. What are some of the purposes for the codes and tags that you see? (Refer to the HTML tag reference chart in Appendix B.)
5. On your computer, use various tools and menu bars in your browser or operating system options to try to change background color, text sizes, and resolution quality of Web pages you are looking at. Does this affect the look and feel of the Web sites you have downloaded? In what ways? Have the Web designers tried to control the page design and text layout so that there will be little or no change? Or do changes in your browser settings create a very different effect on the textual layout of your screen?

INFORMATION MANAGEMENT

The term **information management** can refer to any means of handling any kind of information by altering it or moving it from one place to another. Technical writers especially must keep updating their familiarity with methods of information management used in their own companies as well as the standards of information management followed in their industry. Information management is also what you are doing when you organize and classify the files stored on your computer and on various other storage devices such as CDs, jump drives, and floppy disks.

EXERCISE 1.2

If you own a computer, look at your document folders and ask yourself the following questions:

1. Is there a single principle by which I have organized my folders?
2. If so, could I state that principle in one phrase or sentence?
3. Does this principle (or logical set of principles) make it easier for me to find and retrieve files quickly, when I need them? Could another user easily navigate through and locate files in my computer?
4. If there does not seem to be a logical principle (or set of principles) ordering my document files, does my system (or lack thereof) ever cause confusion when I want to retrieve a document?
5. What could I do to better organize my files and folders?
6. What kind of principle or principles might I develop for organizing my document files and folders?

Professional Web writers must develop good habits for organizing and visualizing relationships among files and documents that will be stored on their own computers, and ultimately on a server. Whereas paper documents display information in a *linear* fashion—ideas and information follow one another in sequenced patterns—Web sites often integrate the powerful complication of *hyperlinked* information. **Hyperlinks** allow readers to click and **"surf"** for what they hope will be manageable, discrete units of nonlinear but nevertheless helpful additional materials. The most common error made by inexperienced Web designers is poor management and organization of the site's HTML documents and media files. Frequently, there is no organizational planning *at all*. Novice Web creators simply tack on page after page, until the original plan (if plan there was) is lost in a tangle of broken links and empty folders. When that happens, it is time to start over, preferably from scratch, and completely reorganize the Web site and its contents. Most Web professionals say that it is much easier to begin a new Web site from ground zero than it is to reorganize a hopelessly tangled one.

Role of the Writer

Writing for the Internet can be seen as a **genre**—or more correctly, a set of genres—that convey information and ideas in ways that are "screen-friendly." Even when print text is simply **uploaded** and displayed online in a form that closely resembles its **codex** (print) form, readers have to deal with hardware and interface issues that do not exist when they read books, documents, or manuscripts.

Internet Web pages are not often created with the intent simply to replicate print documents. Web designers know that Internet users approach a site with some different reading strategies from those they would use to read a book, magazine, or reference volume. People tend to "surf" when they use the World Wide Web, clicking on one link and then another, visiting dozens, sometimes a hundred different sites per day in search of news, information, images, and commentary relevant to their personal and professional needs.

Many of the good practices adopted by technical print communicators and journalists are also effective when writing for Web sites. Technical writers and reporters are required to pack as much information as possible into limited space, while preserving and clearly communicating all of the required content. Creating content for the World Wide Web requires, at the very least, that the writer acquire the following skills:

- Information and file management
- Command of a forceful, precise, crisp style
- Mastery of sophisticated vocabularies
- Subject matter expertise in one or more areas of knowledge
- Document design
- Editing
- Working familiarity with HTML, XHTML, XML, DHTML, Perl, JavaScript, and other Web coding systems
- Ability to identify and quickly appeal to specific audiences
- Sense of **rhetorical purpose**—knowing why the Web site exists and what its visitors expect/desire
- Research strategies
- Documentation styles and formats
- Flair for originality

HYPERTEXT MARKUP LANGUAGES

How much should Web writers know about computer code, such as the various "markup" languages used to format and display text and images for the Web? The answers will vary, depending upon your interests, the degree of your involvement in Web design, and possibly your knowledge of online database management. This book is not designed to turn you into a Web programmer. Technical writers often are excited and fascinated with the programming that goes into online document and Web site management, and it is a very good idea for writers to get as much knowledge and experience as possible, so that they understand how their materials will be organized, formatted, and displayed.

There are many wonderful courses and books on Web programming and design available for anyone from the beginning Web writer to the advanced technical communications information management specialist. Only you can decide what level of programming expertise will feel "right" for you. Many people are amazed at their own interest level when they finally decide to learn, say, XML, or start to work with some database elements and active server pages (ASPs). Most large industrial or corporate Web sites are not created and maintained by one person, but by a team of "Web developers" in charge of various elements of the site. Technical writers need to understand the basics of markup languages and at least some fundamentals of Web coding so that they can clearly and accurately communicate with programmers, database managers, and Web administrators with whom they are working. Web programmers often justifiably fall back upon standard methods and patterns of organizing information if the writers in charge of the content do not step up and explain how the information-bearing parts of a particular Web site should be organized for optimum usability and readability. More than one Web writer has expressed frustration with the awkward organization of a Web site's page layout and overall design, when their own input was not sought during the initial development stages. Learning the important concepts and programming elements of Web design can help to get a technical writer invited to those initial meetings and brainstorming sessions. Good things happen when the programmers themselves understand the most important special requirements of the particular content, audience, and purpose of a Web site.

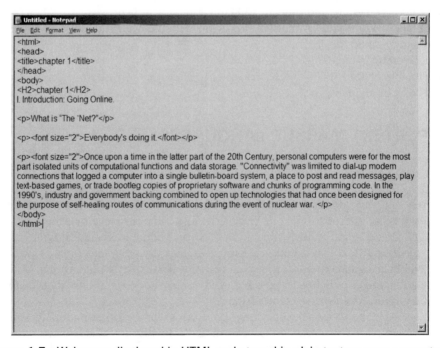

FIGURE 1.7 Web page displayed in HTML code typed in plain text on your computer.

WYSIWYG EDITORS: USABILITY AND THE GRAPHICAL USER INTERFACE

WYSIWYG (pronounced "wizzy-wig") means "What You See Is What You Get," and refers to software that is used to create Web pages by means of a **graphical user interface,** or GUI (pronounced "gooey"). Most Web developers prefer to use powerful WYSIWYG editing software in which they can view both the Web page layout *and* the HTML code. One reason for this is the nature of hypertext documents and of the various settings and features available on popular Web browsers. Even looking at the examples in Figures 1.7 and 1.8, we can see that the symbols, letters, and abbreviations within the angle brackets (for example, <p><font size="2">), known as **tags**, are visible and aesthetically distracting when we view the source code of a Web page. But unless pages are carefully coded for layout and formatting, they become unwieldy and uncomfortable for readers. Powerful WYSIWYG software can be the key to building Web pages and full-blown Web sites that are both attractive and functional.

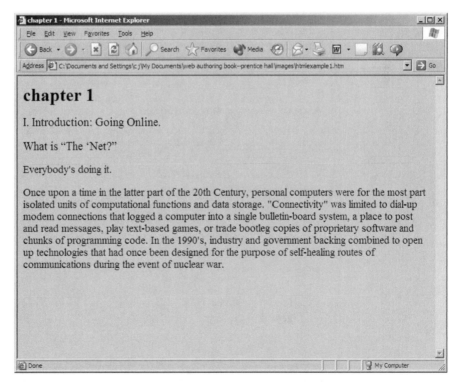

FIGURE 1.8 The same document, saved as hypertext, then opened and viewed with a Web browser.

EXERCISE 1.3

Create a simple HTML template:

1. Open a plain text editing program on your computer (on a PC using the Windows operating system, this is usually a program called "Notepad"; on a Macintosh, it is "SimpleText").
2. Type the following in the plain text editor window *exactly as it appears below*. Do not save your work until instructed to do so:

```html
<html>
    <head>
    <title>title of my web page</title>
    title of my web page
    </head>
    <body>
    <h2>This "heading" appears in a larger font</h2>

    The web page has a bulleted (unordered) list:<br />

    <ul>
    <li>Apples</li>
    <li>Oranges</li>
    <li>Pears</li>
    </ul>

    And it also has a table:<br />

    <table width=250 cellspacing=0 cellpadding=5 border=1>
    <tr>
    <th>Column 1 Header</th>
    <th>Column 2 Header</th>
    </tr>
    <tr>
    <td>Row 1, Column 1</td>
    <td>Row 1, Column 2</td>
    </tr>
    <tr>
    <td>Row 2, Column 1</td>
    <td>Row 2, Column 2</td>
    </tr>
    </table>
    </body>
</html>
```

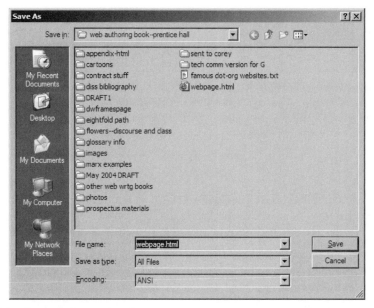

FIGURE 1.9   Type: webpage.html.

3. When you are finished, click on File → Save As and select the disk drive, USB drive, or share drive in which your instructor prefers that you save your own work. Create and enter a folder for your practice work.

4. In the "File Name" field, type "webpage.html" (leave out the quotation marks; see Figure 1.9).

5. Click "Save."

6. Open a Web browser and go to File → Open → Browse.

7. Locate the file that you just saved, titled "webpage.html," select it, and open it.

8. Note the appearance of the page you just created. Compare it to Figure 1.10. What appears in the title bar at the top of the browser display window? How did each angle-bracketed tag or set of tags affect the layout of the text?

9. Play around with your Web page in the plain text editor, making text changes and trying out different kinds of HTML tags (refer to Appendix B). Save your changes, always remembering to use the "Save As" function, keeping the ".html" file extension at the end of the filename.

10. Use the "refresh" button on your Web browser to view changes in your page.

Note: If your school has made Web-server space available for students who wish to post Web pages, your instructor may ask you to save your Web page to your public Web folder and to view other students' pages as everyone makes changes.

Assignments

1. Write about or discuss the kinds of errors and bugs that occur when HTML tags are typed incorrectly, or when other kinds of HTML coding errors occur.
2. Write about or discuss the reasons that programmers refer to HTML tags and values as the "skeleton" of a Web page or Web site.

NOTE:

The code used in the exercise is actually XHTML, a combination of HTML 4.01 with XML rules that has been developed as a fix for various web design problems. XHTML is really not much differrent from HTML, but it is good to remember the following:

- XHTML elements have to be "nested" properly (opening and closing tages must appear in the correct order)
- XHTML tag names are typed in lowercase
- All XHTML elements must be closed (must end with a </> tag). End tags that must appear alone (such as the <br> line break tag) must now have an extra space and a slash mark <br />.

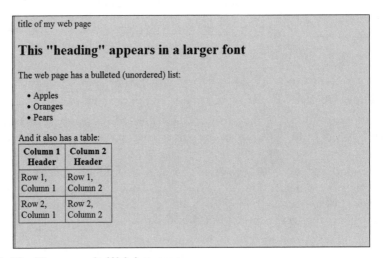

FIGURE 1.10   View page in Web browser.

Planning and Identity

2

- Identity: Who Am I . . . and What Am I Doing on Your Screen?
- Some Theories About Internet Use: Identity and the "Televisual Gaze"
- Planning with Purpose: Commerce, Information, Community, Entertainment
- Planning for Audience: Primary, Supervisory, Secondary, and Peripheral audiences
- Planning for Design and Images
- Planning for Readers and Readability Issues
- Branding or "Branded"?
- The "Economy of Attention"

Glossary Terms

Chunk	Feature creepism
Data	Intellectual property
Discourse community	ISO
Driver	Layout
Electronic data transfer (EDT)	Reflective cognition
Experiential cognition	Wide area network (WAN)

WHO AM I . . . AND WHAT AM I DOING ON YOUR SCREEN?

Historically speaking, it makes sense that in a capitalist economy, many "early adopters" of a new medium will be those who have commercial interests. In order to sell their products, marketers have to get our attention. Newspapers, radio, and television grabbed the attention of advertisers and marketing companies *fast*—and now the Internet has *definitely* gotten our attention! Unfortunately, soon after Americans began to be attracted to the novelty and the convenience of owning desktop computers and connecting to the Internet, almost every business, large and small, rushed online to get the attention of consumers—some using programming tricks to "push" their way into search engines in interesting and sometimes aggressive ways. Many businesses were in such a rush to "go online" that they did not take the time to plan their Web presence, and they often created Web sites that were redundant, incomplete, and unhelpful. Unplanned, slapdash sites tend to disappear as quickly as they appear.

On the other hand, a large part of the Internet's bandwidth is occupied by signals that are not open to the general public but are encrypted for use by specific commercial, industrial, and institutional data transfer systems. Companies have found that the Internet is a perfect conduit for **electronic data transfer (EDT)**, which they employ to manage everything from "just in time" inventory tracking to payroll, scheduling, shipping, and billing. Because computers are extremely good at calculating and organizing huge amounts of quantitative **data** at lightning speeds, they have become the hottest business management tool since the invention of money. With the addition of **wide area network (WAN)** and Internet technologies, networked computer systems have become standard equipment in virtually every place of business in every corner of the developed countries of the world.

Web sites with staying power have substance and originality: People are attracted when a site has something to offer and when they can easily get what they want from it. To accomplish this, Web writers and designers spend as much time, or even more time, *planning and preparing* the site as they do programming and assembling it. Smart Web builders take EDT systems as their model for planning: They assume that the traffic of communication and commerce will be more complicated than just one-way "hard sell" messages and images, and they assume that a Web site may require expansion and upgrading at any time in both predictable and unpredictable ways.

SOME THEORIES ABOUT INTERNET USE: IDENTITY AND THE "TELEVISUAL GAZE"

Canadian scholar Marshall McLuhan argued in the 1960s that "the medium is the message," while at the same time Harvard's psychedelic chemical guru Timothy Leary was declaring that the *actual* message of the latter half of the twentieth century was "Tune in, turn on, and drop out." Millions of Americans, he said, are happy simply to sit in front of their television screens, passively ingesting every image and sound—including advertising messages.

Today, theorist Kathleen Welch hypothesizes that Americans have been *conditioned* by the very nature of our media culture to stare happily, numbly, at electronic video screens. She calls this almost-hypnotic phenomenon the "televisual gaze." Welch argues that whether most people admit it or not, we live vicariously through the images that move across the television screen, and it should be no surprise that we have easily and willingly made the transition, both in the home and in the workplace, to the almost mesmerizing, continuously changeable computer screen. Some of the most vivid images on our computer screens have been created by the multitrillion-dollar gaming industry. Characters, scenes, and action come stunningly alive with animation and sound.

In contrast, the look and feel of computer programs we use in the workplace tend to be generic, impersonal, faceless, industrial, and almost identical. This is not coincidental, of course. Despite the wide range of tasks they are designed to accomplish, most software applications are created according to international standards (known as **ISO** standards) that produce a remarkably identical look and feel from one application to another. The good news about these consistent features on our computer screens is that we can often move seamlessly from one task to another in the workplace, without having to spend too much time relearning the visual layout of the workspace in front of us. The bad news for Web designers is that, given this tendency for computer programs to adhere to ISO standards, it can be difficult to establish an *identity* within that square window on the computer screen, to make a first impression that attracts attention and invites Internet surfers to come to your site, spend time with you, and take advantage of all that your site has to offer.

The less a computer user is forced to *actively engage* with the elements on the screen, the more likely she is functioning on the level of what psychologist Donald Norman calls **experiential cognition** (Figure 2.1). When we engage in activities that are familiar and comfortable to us, we tend to function experientially; that is, we naturally move from one subtask to another without consciously focusing on the small decisions necessary to complete the job. Tasks that we have taught ourselves to do repeatedly, such as serving a tennis ball, parking the car, or making coffee, simply do not engage our problem-solving, higher-order cognitive skills (which, of course, is not to say that we cannot choose at any point to focus more intensely and make a *better* cup of coffee, or *improve* our tennis serve). But when we take on tasks that are unfamiliar, or when we must translate familiar kinds of tasks from a

FIGURE 2.1 Experiential cognition at work. The "Coffee Talk" home page features an ordered structure that employs transparent, familiar organizational patterns. Visitors' expectations are anticipated, so they can passively skim the links and click—no surprises here!

FIGURE 2.2 Reflective cognition required. The "Surreal Dreams" home page employs evocative expression. An opaque, unfamiliar organizational "structure" invites visitors to engage actively, imaginatively, to find links and explore strange artistic images and expression.

familiar context into an unfamiliar one, we are essentially *forced* to function at the level of **reflective cognition** (Figure 2.2). Thus, when Web designers create a visual environment within an already established environment (i.e., the browser window), they must constantly test their designs for the level of engagement the Web site visitor will have to employ.

> The database is in principle similar to the filing cabinet but with a level of automation and speed that made radically different textual practices possible. On the physical level, the surface of reading was divorced from the stored information. For the first time, this breaks down concepts such as "the text itself" into two independent technological levels: the interface and the storage medium. On the social level, huge texts could be browsed, searched, and updated by several people at once, and from different places on the globe, operations that only superficially seem to resemble what we used to call "reading" and "writing." Armed with a good search engine and a digital library, any college dropout can pass for a learned scholar, quoting the classics without having read any of them.
>
> *Espen Aarseth, Cybertext: Perspectives on Ergodic Literature (10–11)*

In any case, few of your goals will be accomplished if you take a hit-or-miss, scattershot approach to the site. No matter what your ideas and theories about Web users may be, *planning* is the key to controlling your site's themes, its look and feel, its file structure, and its writing style.

PLANNING WITH PURPOSE: COMMERCE, INFORMATION, COMMUNITY, ENTERTAINMENT

The first thing Web managers and writers must do before designing and launching a site is to answer the question everyone who visits the site will be asking: What is this site *for*? Except for those personal sites launched by techno-narcissists who have no real aim other than to fiddle around with Web technologies, we can begin to answer the question of purpose for the writer who must supply content and some principles for organization by considering the four general categories of Web writing:

Commerce: Commercial Web sites focus on buying, selling, trading, product information, customer service, billing, and investment.

Information: Information resource Web sites provide news, scientific data, statistical research, advice, product testing and evaluation, archived articles, and online scholarly journals and indexes.

Community: Community-based Web sites include membership building, interactive technologies, chat boards, discussion forums, questionnaires, group newsletters, Web logs, events calendars, and social activities.

Entertainment: Internet users want stories, jokes, games, music, film, and images—but they also want to read about artists and entertainment products and personalities. As a writer, it's important to know the difference between entertaining readers and reporting on the "entertainment scene."

Most Web sites—especially larger corporate or institutional domains and *portals*—are multipurpose, of course. Technical writers, journalists, copy editors, and other "content providers" who supply text for these sites have to work closely with designers and Web managers so that they can write to the *purpose* of each area of the site.

Just as Web site owners have different purposes for putting their resources and materials online, people who visit Web sites have different purposes and tasks in mind when they log on. With any luck, the relationship becomes mutually beneficial: Web managers ask users for feedback, respond to that feedback by improving the site, and enjoy increased traffic as a result. The feedback-improvement-feedback process should be ongoing. It is your job as a writer to be inside that loop, to know what visitors to the site are saying when they contact the Web owners, and to help the Web teams produce changes and revisions that make sense.

The important thing to remember is that the reader's "purpose" in using a Web site is not the same as the writer's. It might be more helpful to you as a writer to think of the reader's *desires,* and how you as a writer can fulfill those desires. In many cases your goals must be consistent with the visitors' desires. To meet those desires, writers must employ thoughtful techniques and sufficient knowledge to get the task done.

Reader's Desire	Web Writer's Goal	What It Takes
Medical information	■ Technically accurate and correctly cited information ■ Short, concise chunks of textual information; clinical style ■ Consistent formatting; searchable data bank of information retrieved from accredited sources	■ Medical background; knowledge of the conventions of medical writing ■ Ability to translate medical jargon into "plain English" ■ Technical support from licensed practitioners ■ Understanding of patients' rights and your liabilities if the site will be open to the general public
Scientific data	■ Reliable documented information organized within a searchable database for fast, efficient access ■ Properly formatted and captioned charts, graphs, and tables ■ Professional, unbiased reporting	■ Background in science and science writing ■ Familiarity with the particular branch of science you are writing about ■ Identifying the specific user groups you are writing for
Social connection	■ Friendly invitation to participate ■ Clear, enthusiastic community identity ■ Prompts and encouragements to help users connect and find each other ■ Prompt and patient responses to members' requests for help	■ Deep knowledge of discourse community ■ Connection and clear line of communication with community leaders and members ■ Affiliation with reputable community organizations and commercial interests ■ Interpersonal communication skills ■ Light touch and ability to be unbiased when conflicts and flame wars arise
Fun reading	■ Original stories, jokes, poetry, song lyrics ■ Clearly cited permission to use all copyrighted materials that are not your own	■ Talent, style, ability; willingness to share your own creative property with the world ■ Realization that the better your material is, the more likely you will find it reproduced anywhere and everywhere, without your permission
Retail products	■ Product information and technical specifications ■ Pricing ■ Ordering information ■ Delivery information	■ Close work with sales and marketing teams ■ Close work with design architecture and programming teams

(continued)

Reader's Desire	Web Writer's Goal	What It Takes
Retail products (continued)	■ Help files ■ User-friendly search capability ■ Intuitive organization ■ Humane, "boilerplate" e-mail response text	■ Firsthand familiarity with product lines and pricing structures ■ Close work with ordering, shipping, and help desk personnel

PLANNING FOR AUDIENCE: PRIMARY, SUPERVISORY, SECONDARY, AND PERIPHERAL AUDIENCES

When rhetoric and language expert Walter Ong made his famous 1975 claim that "the writer's audience is always a fiction," he did not mean for writers to throw up their hands in despair and quit trying to appeal to particular groups of readers. What he was trying to tell us is that when we create public texts (such as those released onto the World Wide Web), we cannot make smug assumptions about readers and their reactions to (or understanding of) our writings. We *can* learn about the people we are targeting. Not every Web site is for everyone, and most have a particular subculture or **discourse community** in mind as primary users and readers.

> "Learning is social." Most understanding is socially constructed. Through conversation and dialogue, children come to their own understanding of an experience. This is true for adults as well. Learning organization theorist Peter Senge argues forcefully that learning within organizations tends to occur in teams.
>
> *Donald Tapscott, Growing Up Digital: The Rise of the Net Generation (137)*

We cannot *assume* that without actually getting to know them better, we can persuade, inform, appeal to, and create a connection with people. We must acquire more than a shallow impression of them. And even more important than becoming familiar with our readers, we must respect them as fellow human beings. The moment we lapse into the sloppy misuse of terms, disorderly thinking, needless repetition, or self-indulgent sarcasm, we signal a lack of concern or understanding for their needs and for their reasons for coming to our sites in the first place.

> *About the only thing we can assume about the audience for a Web site is that each visitor is probably sitting in front of a computer.*

There are many questions we can ask about our audience in order to know them better. But before we begin to inquire into their preferences, needs, and attitudes, it will help to realize that there are different kinds of audiences in the workplace for everything we write, and it will solve a number of problems if we first organize our understanding of their perspectives, regardless of our purpose, mission, or subject.

Primary Audience

The *primary* or *target audience* of a Web site is the direct audience the site must address. This is the group (or groups) of people to whom the site is most meant to appeal. As a writer you expect these visitors to be intrinsically motivated to visit your site. They are looking for a riding lawn mower, or hoping to meet other trap and skeet shooters in their town. They have found your site by word of mouth, a recommendation from a fellow member of an e-mail discussion list or newsgroup, from a print or television ad, or perhaps they have typed "lawn mower" or "trap shooting" into a Web search engine. They want what you *say* you have to offer, and it's your job once you've got their time and attention to keep them happy, to keep them coming back, and to make them want to recommend your site to other members of your target audience. These are the people who must follow your instructions, download and use your documents, and rely upon you for help when they are trying to use your site to complete their own tasks on the job.

The better you know this target group, the easier your decisions about content will be. When other Web team members make decisions that could make the Web site less convenient or appealing to targeted visitors, the information you have collected can support your suggestions. Learn as much as you can about your primary readers by means of interviews, surveys, and other research into this discourse community so that you can help when programmers or graphical designers ask for your advice about audience appeal and content.

Supervisory Audience

The supervisory audience is a familiar one to professional technical writers. This reader is often a manager, project director, account executive, or team head who has given you, the Web writer, the writing task in the first place. Although you are writing *to* your primary audience, the supervisory reader is the castle gate through which your writing must pass before it gets to the other audiences. If your text must be approved by a supervisor—or a group of superiors on up the chain of command—then it is important to know their expectations. Writing for your personal Web site can feel like the ultimate autonomous experience. For a nation of individualists, the Web provides the quintessential democratic writing experience. But in the workplace, *content providers* must answer to Web managers, supervisors, clients, and other members of a Web development team. The *supervisory audience* comprises all of the people who must answer for the content of a Web site, including vendors or suppliers whose merchandise or services may be represented or available for order from your site.

Trying to please and satisfy the primary audience and the supervisory audience at the same time can sometimes be tricky. But once again, if you have done your homework about the primary (target) audience for a Web site and have listened to and understood what the Web owners and managers are trying to accomplish, it will be easier to defend your writing choices to managers, programmers, and clients.

Secondary Audience

The *secondary audience* is made up of readers who must act upon the written materials you have created. For example, a writer working on a company Web site is told to include summaries of new safety policy proposals. The proposals are addressed to the board of supervisors (the primary audience), and the Web team coordinator (the supervisory audience) hands her the documents to summarize. The secondary audience includes the employees of the company who will need to start making changes in order to comply with these new policies. Or consider the writer who must describe powerful file management software that has many useful capabilities, including a handy subapplication that copies, organizes, and saves music files quickly and easily. She knows that the primary audience for this feature will be people who like to download and swap music via the Internet. The problem is that her secondary audience can include the legal department of her Web development company, whose responsibility is to warn her that the reproduction and distribution of copyrighted **intellectual property** (other people's works of art) is illegal. When developing your text for the Web and for local area network environments, it is important to tune in to those important secondary audiences. When, for instance, you compose page footers with contact information, *listen* to the client's support team members (who comprise part of your secondary audience) so that they can inform you about the methods of communication they can use most efficiently to help their customers. If they find it easier to provide help via telephone and do not have time to develop e-mail help messages, then you should make sure that users can easily find the toll-free help line number, while explaining briefly to customers the reason they are encouraged to call rather than e-mail the company.

Peripheral Audience

Peripheral audiences are the readers we don't always expect (or even imagine) will be affected by the materials on our sites. When you are charged with writing about the background of a company, keep in mind that organizations are part of communities, and that you are having an effect on their corporate identity both locally and globally. During the final shakedown period before a site is launched, you may be called upon to consider just what kinds of peripheral readers might be affected by your site, both positively and negatively. Obviously, controversial celebrities such as gossip columnists, talk radio personalities, and political muckrakers will rub—or even scrape—peripheral readers the wrong way. Rush Limbaugh relishes the opportunity to offend the liberal left and feminists. Political humorist Bill Maher often calculates his barbs to intentionally zap powerful figures in government. Arianna Huffington, who appeals to left-wing liberals, gleefully slings challenges in the face of politically conservative groups. Each celebrity engages in potentially offensive discourse, but he or she knows this and does it with full awareness about the peripheral groups who find their messages less than palatable.

Writers may need to make some difficult or even controversial decisions where the peripheral audience is concerned, but they should never make stylistic or content decisions in a vacuum. Web content providers can't afford to ignore the peripheral impact that the content of their Web sites will have. Militants in Iraq claimed that it was the appearance in print and on the Web of Iraqi prisoners being degraded by American military personnel that inflamed them. According to their statements, these Web sites caused them to kill a young American civilian and post a video file of the execution on an Islamic Web site. Although this may be a tragically extreme example of McLuhan's principle of the medium being the message, it is a cautionary tale about the possible unforeseen consequences of posting various types of potentially controversial materials on a Web site.

Your site on the World Wide Web is accessible to the world—but as a writer you make choices about with whom you connect, and how you go about doing so.

PLANNING FOR DESIGN AND IMAGES

Many people organize their lives in the world, creating a pile here, a pile there, each indicating some activity to be done, some event in progress. Probably everybody uses such a strategy to some extent. Look around you at the variety of ways people structure their rooms and desks. Many styles of organization are possible, but the physical arrangement and visibility of the items frequently convey information about relative importance. Want to do your friends a nasty turn? Do them a favor—clean up their desks or rooms. Do this to some people and you can completely destroy their ability to function.

Donald Norman, The Design of Everyday Things

If a picture is worth, as they say, a thousand words, a Web writer's job is to weed through those thousand words and choose the ones most relevant to the purpose of the Web site. Web writers are frequently tempted to replace textual information with images, but it is important to remember that images are usually static and nonhierarchical in nature, whereas the human mind prefers structure and hierarchy. We can think of many famous images that convey far more than words can manage.

Frequently when we are writing for the World Wide Web, data and information represented by photographic or illustrative images alone will be incomplete. Consider, for example, the problems Web shoppers encounter when they see nothing but a screen image of a computer printer they might consider purchasing, with only a model number and a blurb that assures them this is a "terrific all-purpose color desk jet PC printer." Shoppers want prices, and where printers are concerned, they want to know what the average cost of replacement cartridges will be, as well as the type and availability of the ink cartridges. They want to know how sharp and detailed

their printed images will be (not cryptic resolution numbers that only the manufacturer or distributor would be able to decipher). They want to know if they have to
buy a full multicolor cartridge every time one color runs out, or if they can buy each
color cartridge separately. They want to know how much space the footprint of the
printer will take up on a cramped office desk. They want to know the speed of the
printer, and how difficult or easy it will be to install the program (called a **driver**)
that will run the printer from their own computer.

Designing pages for the Web includes the use of company logos, headers, background colors or images, text fonts, quantitative graphical images (i.e., charts,
graphs, and tables), image maps, animation, original art, and photos. In the "old
days" of print page design, the term for organizing all of these elements was **layout**
because commercial artists would in fact "lay out" columns and blocks of text, headlines, cut-out pieces of clip art, and half-tone processed photographs on "blue line"
paper (paper graph-lined in a shade of pale blue that literally disappeared when reproduced by offset print cameras).

Instead of leaning so hard on images and trying to make them do our work for
us, writers need to choose images and design elements wisely so that they fit the purpose and message of a Web site, make its elements easy to read and use, and provide
a pleasing, aesthetically professional "look and feel" to the pages on the screen.

Tips for integrating written and graphical elements:

- Embrace the obvious: Use captions to clearly identify images. Not everyone
  knows that "Don and Mary" are the company founders.
- Use thumbnails: Image files can take a long time to download and display.
  Smaller versions of your digital photo images, known as *thumbnails,* can give
  users the option of looking at the full-sized images. Warn users in captions
  about the size of the larger image files.
- Beware of property issues: Before going image-happy and uploading every
  pretty picture that you consider relevant to your purpose, be aware of basic
  copyright laws pertaining to photographic images and other multimedia repro-
  ductions of other people's artistic works. There are general rules for placing images on your Web site:

  1. Get written, signed permission to display the photo or illustration from any-
     one whose face clearly appears in the image.
  2. Get written, signed permission from the photographer who took the picture
     or the artist who created it.
  3. Get written, signed permission from anyone who hired the photographer
     and paid for the photographic image. Get permission from anyone who
     commissioned a portrait or illustration you wish to use, as well.
  4. Get written, signed permission from any owner or curator of publicly or pri-
     vately owned collections to which the image belongs (example: "Used by
     permission of the Tate Gallery, London").

The elements of *visual rhetoric* that you incorporate into your Web site are just
as important as your written text, but they are not a substitute for written content.

Importing images from other sites on the Web can leave you open to legal action, and also presents the danger of boring your visitors, who may have already seen those pictures on other Web sites.

On the other hand, when you have carefully selected exciting or relevant images, your site can come alive. For example, adding a picture of the company's founders to the "About Our Company" page or providing an exploded diagram of the printer that shows its cartridges and points to important features can make the difference between customers who surf around for a better deal and customers who are pleased at your thoughtfulness. Many museums and art galleries provide tour schedules, calendars of upcoming events, and helpful maps or diagrams for their patrons and prospective visitors. Keep design in mind, but make sure that your site's visual elements support and supplement the text, rather than substitute for a lack of anything helpful or interesting to say.

EXERCISE 2.1

1. Fill in a "back story" for one of the pictures (Figure 2.3, Figure 2.4, or Figure 2.5). Write for 5 or 10 minutes.
2. Working from your back story, create a caption for the picture in 25 words or less that explains satisfactorily the content of the image.

FIGURE 2.3

FIGURE 2.4

FIGURE 2.5

PLANNING FOR READERS AND READABILITY ISSUES

> Clear thinking becomes clear writing: one can't exist without the other. It is impossible for a muddy thinker to write good English. He may get away with it for a paragraph or two, but soon the reader will be lost, and there is no sin so grave, for he will not easily be lured back.
>
> *William Zinsser, On Writing Well*

More than any other medium, the Internet requires that writers not waste space, and that they know specific, interesting, and effective ways to maximize impact while minimizing reader impatience. Because of the malleability and high level of reproducibility of Web sources, even the most original writer will struggle to maintain a reputation for avoiding clichés and worn-out phrases. A writer can slave for hours to find just the right way to bring an idea, opinion, or feature story to life, only to find her own materials reproduced in dozens of "Check this out!" electronic mailing lists and interest-group Web sites the next day. *This is not an excuse to shrug and give up.* Indeed, this is an exciting time for writers. Dynamic, skilled writers will be sought. Why? Because if the writing on a Web site is weak, readers will not return—they have too many other choices available. Although some news and entertainment Web sites will probably always be able to attract attention by simply providing large numbers of photo images, Internet users will continue to seek out the most textually useful and pleasing sites when they are through gazing at pictures and hungry for information and ideas.

What Web Readers Want

- Key terms and phrases should be at the top of the screen or prominently set off with boldface, italics, underlining, highlighting, or bullets. Give readers easy, instant access to the vital elements of the subject matter.
- Consistent terminology is crucial to user happiness. Make sure you have an up-to-date glossary or dictionary of proper jargon and current usage for the subject you are writing about.
- Print-friendly documents make life easy for users. Providing an HTML version of the text that prints all at once will save time and usually will produce a continuously paginated hard copy.
- A clear, complete table of contents at the top of text-heavy Web pages can be linked to sections further down the page.
- Clearly marked links that open in a separate window make Web surfing easier. Both internal and off-site links should be labeled (annotated) correctly, giving readers sufficient information about the resource to decide whether it's worth their time to click and access that source.
- Clean, succinct, active-voice sentences make information, ideas, and narratives easy for readers to understand and process. Sentences should do the work of conveying information and ideas; they should not make readers work too hard to get the content.
- Paragraphs should "chunk" information, organizing information logically into main topics or claims, supported by further ideas, information, and arguments.
- Use all of the elements of good writing, but tighter, leaner, and richer. Good Web writers cut out the clichés, "babyish" oversimplified generalizations, and tired old truisms. What's left is the "beef"—information and ideas that Web users can't get anywhere else.

Why "Less" Is Best

Why should writers spend time planning the textual content of a Web site? In the first draft of any written project, writers are thinking about a large number of elements.

But a first draft should be seen only as a framework. The content of a first draft has been organized, composed, constructed, and argued around information and ideas the writer is wielding for the first time. Even the most fascinating topic tends to have its adherent clichés, homilies, broad assumptions, and stereotypes—and these elements tend to be the first that come to mind as we work to create meaning while we write. A writer's job is to cut out these first ramblings and too-obvious lumps of matter, and sculpt a text that is packed with substance.

Internet users, more than any other readers, are not willing to stare for long periods at an unbroken field of text with no real "payoff"—they are looking for hard data; substantiated facts; new developments; stimulating, original ideas; punch lines; and controversial arguments. They often call up "**chunks**" or "objects" that contain discrete units of written information, organized around their own needs or systems of use. They want to be able to find primary and secondary facts that they can use to get their work done, or that they can ponder and talk about with their peers. The Web is no different from any other media resource when it comes to attracting and keeping an audience. People visit and revisit a Web site that is

- full of useful and interesting information,
- easy to read,
- well organized (even customizable),
- and well crafted.

When they get what they want, people tend to save URLs and pass them along in e-mail or newsgroups to their friends, family, co-workers, and various discourse communities to which they belong. When that happens, a Web site is on its way to becoming successful.

Planning Useful Patterns for Reading and Writing

Readers expect to encounter strong, clear sentences in which the subject is an agent that is doing something, and the verb describes that action. They understand such sentences more easily than sentences in which the subject is a phrase or an abstraction:

1. The manager (simple subject) altered (transitive verb) the records (direct object).
2. The facilitation (abstract subject) of the altering (prepositional phrase) of the records (prepositional phrase) was enabled (passive verb structure) by the manager (reflexive object).

Sentence 2 is obviously a bloated (and bad) attempt to sound more formal—but it is not a better sentence. Before adding five-syllable words ("facilitation") or allowing awkward syntax ("the altering of the records was enabled") to remain in our text, we should first ask if such constructions are going to add anything useful. Before we can upload written text for a wide audience of impatient and hungry Web surfers, we have to put ourselves in the reader's place and admit that allowing a sentence like "The facilitation of the altering of the records was enabled by the manager" is a clumsy, thoughtless waste of someone's time.

If the manager altered the records, she altered them, and there is no need to "fancy up" the fact. When revising text that you have written for a Web page, *just say it,* and say it as tightly, precisely, and directly as possible. Then move on.

Planning Word Choices

Consider the following exchange:

Nursing student: I hate the anatomy and physiology class! All that memorization makes my head hurt. I hate learning all those terms. I'll never get a grade higher than a C in there!

Engineering student: (teasing) Gee …I don't want to be admitted to the hospital where *you'll* be working. I want to be treated by someone who knows where all the body parts are, someone who knows how to take care of them!

The nursing student is still thinking like a *student,* but not like a *nurse.* The engineering student, however, is thinking like a future patient. This might have been the first time this nursing student has ever considered that his level of knowledge and expertise is actually going to affect others when he becomes a medical professional in the "real world."

Novice technical writers can suffer from the same kind of tunnel vision in the way they envision their work. They produce what is called "writer-based" material, doing the very least amount of work that seems to satisfy the specifications of the task. But just as good registered nurses must master all of the knowledge and tools of their profession before they go out into the medical world, good writers must be ready to take command of language skills and get the job done so that others can use the information, ideas, stories, and opinions in their texts.

Planning to Be Precise

Suppose circumstances surrounding the "altered" records in the previous example sentences were complex and not actually as suspicious-sounding as the bare statement might indicate. Perhaps the manager was new, and the records she inherited were jumbled and incomplete. In this case, the "alteration" didn't really constitute a deceitful act and was never intended to harm the business or the books. The Web writer had written "the facilitation of the altering" during the initial drafting process in an attempt to soften the blunt, accusatory tone of "The manager altered the records." Adding multisyllabic Latinate words or rearranging the sentence in a clumsy way is not the answer (although we frequently see corporate and bureaucratic statements that include such language strategies in an attempt to disguise or "soften" otherwise disappointing or possibly alarming news).

Often, in the initial drafting stage, writers attempt to paste qualifying phrases and affixes to the initial text in order to clarify the facts, when what they really need is to replace vague or unclear terms with more precise and vivid language.

Stating events and facts accurately is a matter of choosing verbs and nouns much more carefully than we would do in an ordinary conversation. For example, we may think that words like *man* and *dog* are accurate, clear terms. And in a first draft, it is important that we get basic elements of the information correctly positioned and logically identified. The old newspaper cliché about sensational headlines that sell papers shows how the basic facts are crucial:

"Dog Bites Man" is not a sensational headline.
"Man Bites Dog" will probably catch readers' attention.

But by substituting language that is even more specific, we can further change readers' perception:

"Chihuahua Bites Linebacker."
"Rottweiler Bites Senator."
"Baby Bites Newfoundland."

Simply replacing each noun with a more specific one creates an accurate and vivid statement of fact, without lengthening or otherwise cluttering up the sentence. Choosing nouns carefully can even result in opportunities for wordplay: "Boxer Bites Boxer."

Another way to clarify what happened to the dog (or to the man) is to choose a more precise verb. We can combine "what happened" and "how it happened" by working hard to find the best possible verb, one that evokes the kind of image we hope to convey.

Consider changes we can make in readers' perception by altering the verbs in our headlines:

"Chihuahua Nips Linebacker."
"Rottweiler Nibbles Senator."
"Baby Gums Newfoundland."

Without the added "weight" of adjectives and adverbs, each headline has changed the events first indicated in the less specific "Dog Bites Man" or "Man Bites Dog."

Likewise, there is no need to add fluffy, redundant terms or phrases. "The small toddler" is no more clear than "the tall giraffe" or "the long, scaly snake." Toddlers by definition are small children, just as giraffes are tall and snakes are long and scaly. Trust your reader to have a reasonable vocabulary. English, after all, far exceeds all other languages in the number of words it employs. And while some writers may see this as a license to add more words to their sentences, smart writers realize that the vast lexicon in the English language provides the opportunity to be more selective. Restaurant critics know that people don't just "drink wine": They sip Cabernet, snort Champagne, gulp Merlot, knock back Chablis, or indulge in a lovely dessert Port. Automotive column writers know that people don't just drive cars: They race Porsches, zoom around in Toyotas, road test Mustangs, maneuver their Saturns, and roll down the highway in their GMC Sierra extended-cab, short-bed, four-wheel-drive pickup trucks.

Readers are unwilling to stare at glowing computer screens for extended periods of time, but writing for the Web is not about saying less in order to keep their attention. Writing for the Web is about saying just as much as you would in print form, but doing it in fewer words whenever possible. When poets say that "less is more," they do not mean that one should convey less meaning—they mean that writers should craft logical sentences, choose words carefully, and make each word and phrase count for more.

Consider two ways of depicting a scene. First, in haiku:

> Gray wisps on pillows;
> Her last words, "I love you too."
> Even the moon weeps.

Now consider the same scene told in prose form:

> *The last time I saw my grandmother, she was lying on a hospital bed with tubes and IVs connected to her frail arms. She was only vaguely lucid, looking at me, her beloved only grandchild, but not recognizing me until I sat close and called her name, reminding her who I was. I held her hand as tenderly as I could, it was so fragile and bruised from so many needles, and I told her I loved her. Before falling asleep, she said to me, "I love you too." I watched her doze off as my grandfather returned to her side, then escaped into a deserted hallway to cry.*

The haiku tells a reader almost as much about the event in 15 words as the prose passage does in 109. But the poet has planned ahead to accommodate her message to a very restricted space; she has allowed herself the time to go back through her text and choose specific words that accumulate into an image that she hopes will provide iconic meaning and at the same time evoke emotional responses. In the spirit of the ancient Japanese art form, she reaches for words that are symbolically powerful. There is no need for her to state the obvious when the four words "Even the moon weeps" indicate the scope and depth of her sorrow. While some readers, such as those who enjoy finding fiction and prose works on the Web, may find satisfaction in the longer version, the deceptively compact haiku is an example of a traditional art form that aims, like the Web writer, to pack meaning into a small space.

Condensing textual meaning is not a mysterious art form—the key is to explore and study the subject and purpose of your Web site so that you can be confident that, like a sculptor, you have given yourself ample material to work with, before you skillfully cut away all of the superfluous language that is not a part of what you are trying to say or what you are trying to accomplish on the screen for yourself and for your readers.

BRANDING OR "BRANDED"?

Breathtakingly beautiful graphics and exploding animations grab attention quickly. They lend appeal and attractiveness—what we have come to call "coolness"—to a Web site. But once we have their attention, people *like* to connect with a personality.

They like to feel that there is a human element behind all the flashy technology, not just a familiar mark burned into their visual memory. Established companies and organizations know this and work hard to develop images that project personality, sometimes called a *corporate identity*—an image that tells the public what it is that sets the company apart from the others in its class.

Of course, most consumers are not fooled by the smiling clowns and dancing cartoon animals that represent hamburger chain restaurants. They tend to ignore (or think they have ignored) the TV public relations messages from oil, natural gas, and electric companies. Public relations in the mass media arena has become a cynical game. Corporate conglomerates tell us they are deeply concerned about our communities and our lives, while we nervously anticipate their next big oil tanker spill, core meltdown, or inflated price hike. We may shake our heads and chuckle, but at the same time the saturation of their repeated messages has an interestingly powerful subliminal effect. Companies know that these messages don't tend to attract new customers, but they do make their current customers feel good about buying their products and services.

The entire field of industrial psychology was built upon the corporate, bureaucratic desire to use our natural thinking processes to control and condition the attitudes of workers and consumers. According to Robert Cialdini, we have automatic ways of responding to particular kinds of triggers in our environment that can be mimicked by marketers, public relations specialists, and other "compliance professionals."

THE "ECONOMY OF ATTENTION"

The World Wide Web has become so cluttered with commercial and informational sites that it seems we can't get to what we want without the aid of radio and television. Broadcast commercials and public service announcements all seem to have responded to a ubiquitous memorandum declaring that listeners and viewers are simply *desperate* to know the URL for their Web sites. Banks, credit unions, insurance companies, car dealerships, bookstores, brokerage houses, investment companies—everyone wants us to visit their Web site. Web writers really can trust that old perfume commercial slogan:

"If you want to get someone's attention ... whisper!"

Usability studies have shown that visitors to Web sites tend to ignore pictures and banners when they initially log on and prefer to read headings, captions, and well-organized, "chunky" informative text first. Although some Web designers prefer to code in specific font sizes and use frames and tables to place textual and graphical elements precisely on the page, writers need to keep in mind the **feature creepism** of programmers. Every time Web designers find a way to control the visual elements of a Web page display, browser developers find ways to give back to users the choices about text size, typeface styles, element placement, and image resolution on their own computer screens. Therefore, good Web writers know that *the written content must satisfy the visitors*. Writers cannot rely too heavily on boldface type or flashy design elements.

Once visitors have arrived at your site, the way to get and keep their attention is to:

- Be organized. Allow users to find all of the features of your site quickly and easily.
- Be concise. Provide popular and most-requested information up front. Put elaboration and long-winded explanations on a linked page.
- Be excellent. Treat users with respect and warmth. To err is human, but to show decency and courtesy is humane.
- Be correct. Proofread, edit, and double-check every passage of written text and every fact, figure, and unit of data.
- Be pleasant. Work to incorporate programming strategies that customize, personalize, and organize the information on your site for your frequent and heavy users.
- Be original. Provide products, information, ideas, community connections, creative works, and opportunities that users *cannot get anywhere else.*

Especially be sure that you have not created a site that is simply redundant, one that has collected materials already available elsewhere on the Web. Remember: If you have copied and pasted someone else's text, you are simply moving information around, like a file clerk (and you're probably plagiarizing, too). Your site will get the attention of your target audience, and perhaps more importantly, you will *keep* their attention if you create something original, useful, detailed, and relevant to their interests.

Assignment

Create a preliminary description of a special-interest Web site that you might like to plan, design, and create. Use the following questions as a worksheet to propose a workable site plan.

Purpose Analysis:

1. How many other sites can you find that resemble yours or serve the same function?
2. What will your site do that is similar to other related sites?
3. What will your site provide or do that is different from other related sites?
4. Why will people prefer your site over those already uploaded to the World Wide Web?
5. Why will you want to keep maintaining your site for at least two years?
6. Who might want to be involved in helping to run and maintain your site? Why? For how long?
7. How many people do you expect to be "hitting" your site regularly?
8. Why will they visit your pages?
9. What will keep them coming back?

Audience Analysis:

1. Age:
2. Gender:
3. Income:
4. Ethnicity:
5. Geographic location(s):
6. Religion:
7. Reason they will use your site:
8. Controversies they are interested in:
9. Number of times per week/month each user will visit your site:
10. Ways in which users can interact with you on your site:
11. Ways in which users can contribute to your site:
12. Ways in which users can interact with each other on your site:
13. Reasons your site will remain viable and useful for at least two years:

Developing Content

3

- Content: Where's the Beef?
- Seven Smart Rules for Developing Web Site Content
- Property, Permission, and Ownership
- Downloads and Product Presentation
- Menus: Creating Roadmaps for Readers
- Site Maps
- Reader-Oriented Sites: Tips for Text-Heavy Content

Glossary Terms

Bandwidth	HTML
Branding	Hypertext
Byte	Menus
Directory	Meta tags
Folder	Search engine
Frames	Site map
Host	

A lot of designers think that Web design is about the interface, and that content is what's added on later, or else it's "the client's problem." I've seen designers argue that the content must be changed to fit the way the site was designed. This only represents the designer's failure.

Phil Brisk, writer and art director, *http://www.webdesignfromscratch.com*

CONTENT: WHERE'S THE BEEF?

It's no accident that people are calling the Internet the "New Home Shopping Network": commercial corporations have scrambled to make use of its **bandwidth** in order to stay competitive. Of all the possibilities of pan-global communications and instantaneous international data transfer possible, of all the "revolutionary" innovations that the new Internet technologies seem to hold, the disappointing fact that many Web developers have found is that those who most desperately wish to have a "Web presence"—a site for commerce and information exchange on the Web—are often the least prepared to provide the most important element of any Web site: content. To begin approaching the somewhat daunting work of information management, there are a few basic rules that can help writers proceed in a confident and organized way as they begin a new Web writing project.

SEVEN SMART RULES FOR DEVELOPING WEB SITE CONTENT

Rule 1: Offer Something

Good Web pages are rich with information, ideas, products, resources, social connection, and opportunities to interact or extract something people want that they cannot get anywhere else. A Web site that offers nothing unique or desirable is a nothing Web site. Although there are no rules or laws about what you must have on your personal Web site (thank goodness!), there are many copyright and intellectual property laws in the United States that govern the use of images, information, and ideas owned by individuals, corporations, or institutions—materials that you may not use legally without obtaining permission. The urge to copy and paste material from other Web sites and published resources (books, CD-ROMs, magazines, etc.) may be overwhelming at first: Those empty Web pages you are working on can look, well, dauntingly empty. But the question to ask when creating a Web site is this: What *original* materials, products, and resources do I want to offer on this Web site? If the answer does not come easily, it's time to back up a step and begin to collect or create the materials that you want to display on the World Wide Web.

Professional Web sites are frequently packed with material previously generated by an in-house technical writing team at a company or organization. The same technical writing and information team may be in charge of creating and maintaining both print documents and electronic materials for the company Web site. Sometimes companies hire Web designers to come in and work with one or more of the local tech writers. Occasionally an organization hires a Web management company to do all of its Web site design and management; this is especially necessary when a company has no permanent on-site technical communications expert.

In each instance, the writers and designers have to sort through the available materials, create materials and elements that are needed, and prepare everything digitally in a way that projects the company's image and delivers what Web site visitors want and need. Web writers understand that a professional Web site is a public communication space in which all of the digital elements must come together and deliver some kind of value, both for the site **host** and the site's visitors.

Frequently, professional Web sites are about meeting expectations:

- Web designers expect clients to have something to "push" on their sites—merchandise, messages, services, or even an elusive commodity known as **branding**: a corporation's or institution's marketable identity.
- Web writers expect companies and clients to have a reasonably substantial body of data and information they can write about, organize, rework, and edit.

- Programmers expect designers, writers, content experts, and customers to have a clear idea of the scope and functions of the entire site.
- Visitors to the site expect to find something they can use, think about, enjoy, interact with, or buy.

Rule 2: Get Organized

Web sites are made up of digitized text and image files that must be organized in sensible and intuitive ways both for users and for Web managers. A page misfiled is a page lost, and therefore it is much easier to build a new Web site from an organized map than it is to reorganize and upgrade an old one. Web sites quickly can become extremely large, incorporating dozens of pages that must be updated and maintained.

Figure 3.1 shows some of the ways that units of information interconnect on one Web site. On the "back side," or the computer-server end of the project, a Web site looks simply like a collection of folders and subfolders that open to lists of Web pages and image files (see Figure 3.2 and Figure 3.3).

Many Web sites could use a few tips on file management! All over the world there are Web servers storing millions of file **directories** much like the one pictured in Figure 3.4, containing **hypertext**-linked, readable documents. On the server where the Web site owners and designers are storing pages, the site simply appears as folders full of documents, or as records in a database program. In the Web designers'

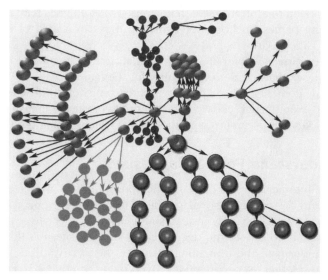

FIGURE 3.1 Pages on a Web site and the hyperlinks between them, showing how the information is designed to interconnect. How would you plan changes and updates for something this size? Web designers and writers face these challenges every day.

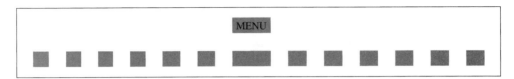

FIGURE 3.2 Wide-and-shallow site architecture.

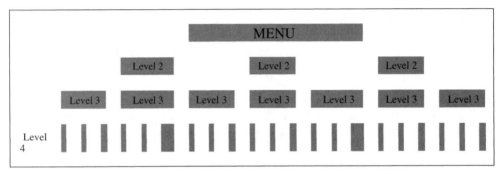

FIGURE 3.3 Narrow-and-deep site architecture (sometimes called *N-tier structure*).

plans, however, the site may be linked *structurally* in ways that encourage visitors to navigate in various directions.

Given the immense size and apparent chaos that is the Internet, the job of simply helping visitors find our Web sites is daunting. The most important tool for this has, of course, been the Internet search engines. These engines tend to have clever, playful-sounding names (in hopes of attracting those in search of fun, cool Web sites), such as Yahoo!, Google, and Ask.com.

A **search engine** is a computer program that "crawls" the Web looking for keywords and phrases that users are searching for. Organized Web sites contain programming and content that will help search engines find them fast. Web programmers use embedded codes called **meta tags** to make it easy for search engines to match keyword searches with their site's content headings.

Rule 3: Understand Formatting Issues

Although most Internet users understand the conventions of Web site organization, many times (and for many reasons) people will not enter your site through the "home" or portal page. They may instead surf around another site or search for specific topics that link to one of the deeper layers of your site. For this reason, Web writers must understand the formatting structures necessary to best transmit messages and data. Internet users coming to a Web page, whether it is a home page or some other part of the Web site, should at the very least be given the means to navigate their way to the main pages (or home page) of the site. When in doubt, Web writers and designers frequently refer to established forms that readers have come to expect: headers and footers that provide basic information about the site such as

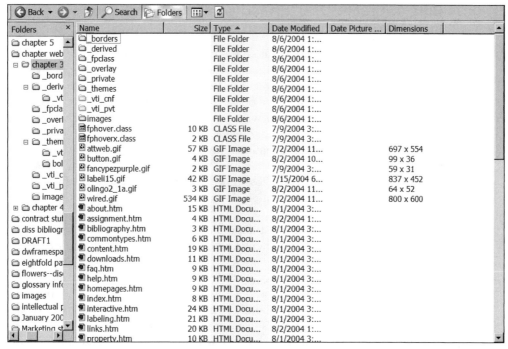

FIGURE 3.4 File directory management for one small Web site. Developers may perceive a different kind of pattern in the organization of a Web site, depending upon the arrangement of links. When links to pages in a site do not work, managers have to seek out specific filenames and check the coding in their navigational links on the site. File organization and logical naming structures are key components for maintaining and updating a site.

copyright ownership, publication date (or *upload date*), and navigational links that lead to the head or home pages of the site.

Style sheets, **frames**, active server pages, and other Web-management tools have become popular. Using these (and other) programming solutions, designers can create formatting that appears uniform and seamless on every page of the Web site, giving the site a consistent "look and feel." These tools can clearly display site information and "identity" on each page, so that users don't have to explore the site just to figure out who owns it and what its main purpose might be. Page elements that commonly appear on all Web pages on well-developed sites include:

- Title of the Web site
- Name of the Web site owners
- Copyright or date when the page (or site) was last modified
- Link to site map or site index
- Link to home page

Rule 4: Create User-Friendly Patterns and Clusters of Information

Once the file structures are created, the work of organizing the Web site is still not finished. Databases and **HTML** files are the "back end" of your content management (the "behind the scenes" file structures that visitors to the Web site don't see). The "front end" (what the visitor sees on the screen) must be visually represented in intuitive and sensible ways. Web writers need to "chunk" information into patterns that are easy to access and digest quickly.

Most people also prefer minimal advertising clutter (although the search engines we use every day for free have still got to make a living). When someone has a specific need, it simply takes less time to type a search term and press the Enter key than it takes to visually search through dozens of unrelated topics on a busy screen.

Chunking is one of the most important skills Web writers use to organize information. Readers can find and interact with information best when they can see patterns or clusters of information logically arranged at a glance. Technical writers usually work closely with subject matter experts, chunking the information for easy, at-a-glance reference. For print documents, writers typically use bulleted lists, graphs, charts, diagrams, alphabetic (or numbered) indexes, outlining, or other visual tools that guide the reader's eye to the desired information.

The need for visual help is doubled when references to large amounts of information are placed within the limited space of a computer screen. Using familiar patterns will "push" information across to visitors more comfortably than simply jumbling up the screen with written copy. The following patterns are common:

- Alphabetical
- Numerical
- Chronological
- General-to-specific
- Priority-driven
- Cause-to-effect
- Problem-solution
- Geographical
- Size
- Cost
- Shape
- Color-coding

Each of these ordering systems has its advantages and its drawbacks. Retailers, for example, have to make decisions about organizing merchandise on the pages of their online catalogs. One merchant may wish to push more expensive items by placing them at the top of the screen, and another may hope to attract volume by placing less expensive items first. A third may have programmed its site so that visitors can choose the price range of items displayed. Writing for such sites means chunking information for each item so that it can stand alone or blend in when surrounded by variable contexts, including related merchandise, limited-time offers, special instructions, financing terms, and payment methods.

Whatever organizational pattern you choose, it's a good idea to have your layout tested for usability *before* the site goes online, and to provide a way for site visitors to comment on its strengths and weaknesses *after* the site becomes active. That way, when the site is updated you can use visitor input to guide improvements.

Rule 5: Use the Correct Formatting and Programming

Technical writers need to acquire at least a working familiarity with issues of information management and Web programming architectures. With that working knowledge, a writer can participate in all phases of a Web site's development. Simple Web pages are easy to construct and revise. Small Web sites that contain only a few (or even a couple dozen) pages linked together can be constructed as a few .html files collected within a single **folder**. They are easy to organize and maintain. But if your online Web pages are numbered in the hundreds and your digitized data is measured in *gigabytes* (approximately one billion **bytes**, or 1,024 **megabytes**), it's time for a powerful database.

You may have noticed that when you use an information-heavy Web site that allows you to do fairly complex searches, the letters "php" appear in the browser address window. PHP stands for Parser Hypertext Preprocessor, which is a server-side, HTML-embedded scripting language used to create dynamic Web pages— pages that are created "on-the-fly" by a program that runs on its own server. Because PHP is executed on the server, the code is hidden from the average user visiting the site. The strength of using a scripting language such as PHP lies in its compatibility with many types of databases.

Many Web sites are portals for thousands of *objects,* or units of digitized information stored in database systems. Often large Web sites preserve archives of constantly changing information, such as online news publications, government documents, and academic journals. The managers of these sites must be especially prepared to construct, organize, and "grow" various stored-file environments over an indeterminate length of time. News articles and company updates can quickly take up huge amounts of file-server space. At that point the site needs a powerful way of pointing to the objects that users want to retrieve.

Web writers need to learn something about the databases and their front-end and back-end interfaces so that they can format and construct information in ways that make sense. Some writers have begun to refer to this kind of writing as "database style"—writing in such a way that chunks of text, sometimes referred to as *objects,* can be organized logically and displayed for users in ways that will be useful and not incompatible or chaotic. Writers sometimes have to think in terms of creating seamless chunks of text that adhere to a consistent style so that object-oriented programs can handle these objects and tile them together on-screen in an infinite number of combinations and permutations that will be readable and make sense to users (see Figure 3.5).

Another issue that Web developers have to deal with is Section 508 of the Rehabilitation Act. A major addition to the federal Americans with Disabilities Act (ADA), Section 508 includes documents that are guidelines which must be followed by federal agencies so that all Americans with disabilities will have total access to the government's electronic and information technology. Although the ruling strictly applies to electronic data managed by federal agencies (and any organization that receives federal funding), the guidelines are considered the standard that most large corporate and institutional entities will want to follow. Writers must often make adjustments and add alternate text to pages when usability testers check for ADA compliance.

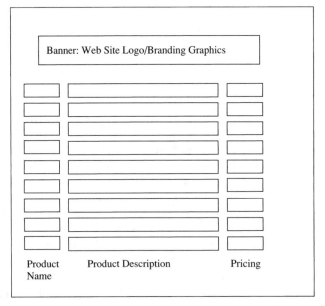

FIGURE 3.5 Each box represents an "object" or "chunk" of information the Web writer has prepared for the database. Web pages that assemble themselves "on-the-fly" are programmed to "call up" each object and display it in the correct placeholder on the screen. Each object might be written separately, updated at different times, or even written by different departments or teams on a project. But they still have to make sense when assembled together on the screen or page.

Rule 6: Edit for Perfection

When a professional Web site is launched, it may be visited by thousands or even millions of users. The writing must be error-free and stylistically clean. Think of a Web site as a published text that cannot be sprinkled with embarrassing mistakes and uneven patterns of usage. In a commercial context, writing errors are seen as evidence of weak or sloppy thinking. This in turn reflects upon the company or institution that owns the site. Using a word processor's spell-check feature is not enough. Writers need to have a strong understanding of sentence structure, grammar, and style.

Rule 7: Create a Realistic Maintenance Schedule

A site that is maintained well and kept up-to-date is alive and attractive to users. When visitors encounter dead links, outdated information, unavailable merchandise, broken scripts, and lost or malfunctioning pages, they simply leave. A site that often offers new features, upgraded capabilities, and prompt replies from the site owners when they are contacted by visitors is a site that will be recommended by word-of-mouth.

Keep in mind the "shelf life" of the site you are writing for. If you don't know how long the site will be kept online in its current form, ask someone. A large part of a technical Web writer's job involves talking with content experts, programmers, designers, and customers about their expectations and needs. Ideally, writers are included from the outset, when the site's initial design and architecture questions are being posed and answered. And just as ideally, writers will be able to contribute to the long-range planning of a Web site by making suggestions and asking questions about the methods that will be used to keep the site living and breathing for years beyond the initial launch date.

PROPERTY, PERMISSION, AND OWNERSHIP

In the United States and many other countries, ideas, information, artistic creations, formulas, inventions, and designs can be owned and protected as intellectual property. Laws governing intellectual property fall under four general categories: copyrights, patents, trademarks, and trade secrets. The simple rule for professional Web sites (and, frankly, for personal ones, too) is this:

Do not offer images, downloads, text, sound, or video files without permission.

Owners of personal Web sites often argue that "off-linking" to sites that hold images or other media files they want to share can result in dead links and frustrated visitors. Their purpose in copying images or sound files, they say, is to preserve access, not to steal anyone's property. But the simple fact is that we do not have the right to control access to other people's intellectual property. As technical writers whose important supervisory audience is the employer or client who pays for the Web site, we have a clear responsibility to ensure freedom from liability for the materials on the site. In order to avoid liability and risk where copyright issues may be concerned, the best way to handle text, image, sound, video, and software files is to make sure you have followed guidelines that aim for the highest degree of safety (see the discussion of planning the site's photo and graphic images in Chapter 2).

Adhering to intellectual property guidelines may sound excessively cautious, but it is the best set of rules to follow for two reasons:

- First, by following these rules, Web managers can respond to any letter of complaint challenging their right to use the material.
- Second, these guidelines will remind Web managers that all elements of a site should, to the greatest extent possible, be original.

A faxed copy of the signature (or set of signatures) granting permission to use the media in question is, in many instances, the best answer to any complaint about reproduction rights. But there are exceptions, especially when ownership is in question for complicated legal reasons. Thus, the best approach to Web media is to create our own multimedia and design elements.

A company's original logos, images, sounds, text, and video accomplish more than just brand-name recognition and safety from legal challenges concerning intellectual property rights. Creating unique designs and media that accompany the textual and interactive elements of the site guarantees a certain amount of Web traffic simply by obeying the basic principle of supply and demand. When there is something interesting or comment-worthy on a Web site that cannot be found elsewhere, the curious will arrive, if only to window shop or take a look. And remember, when we're talking about the overall customer base who browse and shop on the World Wide Web, we're talking about *billions* of people. In many complex, interesting, and dynamically shifting ways, offering something unique tends to funnel a surprising number of visitors directly to an original Web site *simply because it is original.*

Text and Intellectual Property

It should go without saying that reproducing other writers' works should not be done without permission. If you are quoting from the following types of written and/or published materials, always remember to properly cite and give credit to the source and its author.

- Books
- Magazines and online 'zines
- Play scripts for radio, television, film, and stage
- Manuals
- Documents

- Letters
- Web sites
- Interviews
- Original manuscripts

Sometimes the ease of moving text and images around from one window to another tempts us to just grab catchy quotes and other written materials that have been previously published. But unless you have the permission of the copyright owner, other writers' materials should be respected.

Technical writers frequently describe what they do as "moving chunks of information around" or "combining already-made information" into new forms and documents. But what they really mean is that they are constantly taking company information and data and revising, shaping, and adding to it for specific practical purposes. When putting information on the Web, technical communicators learn to develop a good sense for the kinds of texts they can and cannot plug into their pages. Generally, we can feel safe if we are working with materials generated in-house and placing them in company-published forums and publications. If we find ourselves surfing outside our own company's or institution's Web site and grabbing chunks of text written and owned by outsiders, we need to review copyright rules and ethics so that we know how to properly quote and cite these texts.

EXERCISE 3.1

Alone or with a partner, search the Web for 5–10 "text-heavy" sites such as news publications, academic articles, Web 'zines, white papers, interviews, and stories. Evaluate the reader friendliness of the Web site.

1. Is there a "print-friendly" version of the text?
2. Can readers easily scroll down the text of the article on one page, or must they click their way to each section that is continued on another page?

3. Copy and paste a sentence from the text and run it through a search engine. How many other sites have copied (or "mirrored") this exact text, word for word?
4. With news publications, mirrored text usually signals a wire story generated by a news service. What are some other instances of articles and other works that have been reproduced on two or more Web sites?
5. Can you find sites that seem to have used text from another Web site (and possibly even from a printed source) without permission?
6. What are your conclusions about the level of respect for intellectual property on the World Wide Web today?

DOWNLOADS AND PRODUCT PRESENTATION

When a Web site offers software or other types of files that can be downloaded by visitors, programmers will want to write scripts and create interfaces that make it easy for people to get what they want from the site. They want their programmed features to provide seamless access, fast downloading, and easy access to help files and other materials that users might want. Various design features are created to bridge what design expert Donald Norman calls the "gulf of execution" and the "gulf of evaluation."

The gulf of execution is created when users take some action (such as clicking on a link or button), but receive no visual or textual feedback telling them that the desired operation has begun. The gulf of evaluation is created when users initiate some operation (again, they have clicked or keyed a command), and while they can see that a process has begun, they cannot determine how far along the process is or how much longer they will have to wait until it finishes. Designers, often with the help of technical writers, try to create messages and visual animations to inform users that the operation has begun as a result of their actions. For example, if a user clicks on a link titled "Download Yahoo! Messenger now," a pop-up window may inform the user that execution has begun (bridging the gulf of execution), while a status bar moves to indicate the progress of the operation (bridging the gulf of evaluation).

Web programmers use various kinds of pop-up windows, dialog boxes, and other kinds of images that appear on-screen to let the visitor know that an operation has been initiated. A safety message may appear, for example, telling the user that a program or file is about to be downloaded to some folder or directory on the user's machine, often asking the user to click "OK" before the process can begin (usually this also allows visitors to click "cancel" if they have accidentally initiated an unwanted download or installation). Figure 3.6 shows an example. A moving progress or status bar visually represents the progress made, thus bridging the gulf of evaluation (i.e., showing us the results of executing an action from start to finish).

Most of us take these messages and visual indicators for granted. But when they are not present, users are often left sitting in front of their computers, pulling on their hair and wondering if anything is really happening after they click "Download Now!"

When Web sites feature a large number of downloads, technical writers need to consult with the programmers and server administrators to understand and then

ARE YOU SURE YOU WANT TO DOWNLOAD THIS APPLICATION?

OK   Cancel

FIGURE 3.6 Pop-up menus must be clearly labeled to indicate actions and their results.

clearly explain on the pages the kinds of technology issues that users might have. This helps to avert at least the most common types of problems.

General Guidelines for Download Pages

- Explain prominently (in plain English) the system requirements necessary for completing the download and installing or viewing files on the visitor's computer.
- Make sure that intellectual property and other legal issues are prominently shown so that users understand exactly what ownership issues are in play when they download items from your site.
- Show pricing and terms up front (don't make users click through several menus to get to this crucial information).
- Give something in return for visitors' time. Don't promise news, resources, information, downloads, or merchandise that doesn't really exist.
- Give something in return for visitors' information. Forms and dialog boxes asking users to sign up or subscribe by giving their personal information before they have access to your site should be brief and as noninvasive as possible. Such requests should be accompanied by a link disclosing your information-sharing policies.
- Disclose all important features (and lack thereof) in free demonstration versions of software available for download on your site. (Not doing so can result in a word-of-mouth backlash against your product!)
- Create pleasant, well-organized menus and displays. Avoid pushing new products and ad campaigns so prominently on the screen that visitors cannot find things they need and expect.
- Prominently display all available help and contact information should something go wrong with downloading, installing, and using your product. Visitors should instantly be aware of the level of support available from the site. This commonly includes installation instructions, update information, help files, frequently asked questions, and contact information.
- Provide ethical descriptions, privacy disclosures, ownership, terms, and descriptions of products and files that are available to visitors.
- If possible, briefly ask for feedback (again, don't waste people's time!) so that the site's visitors can request information and suggest features that they would find useful.

EXERCISE 3.2

The following complaints are common when users visit download pages on a company or organization Web site. For each complaint, create a solution you would propose in advance to help avoid the problem. For example:

Complaint: "I signed up and downloaded a demo program from your site. Now I'm getting spam (junk e-mail) in my mailbox from you every other day! Please stop sending ads to my e-mail address!"

Writer's Assignment: Explain a solution that the writer and programmer can use to prevent this type of customer complaint. For example:

Web marketers sometimes assume that "spamming" customers is a good way to sell their newest products. Actually, people dislike spam, find it intrusive, and tend to have negative feelings toward companies who send unsolicited "updates" and advertising. When creating customer information forms for Web site visitors to fill out when they download demos or media files, writers can request that a radio button or check box should be provided, with a clear prompt stating, "Yes! Send updates to my e-mail address." Such options should include what is called a *negative default setting:* It should be turned off so that users must voluntarily check this option to activate it. Another solution is to warn visitors that providing their e-mail address will automatically result in receiving advertisements from the Web site owners.

Complaint 1: "I downloaded the free demo (demonstration version) of the program, but most of the coolest features listed on the Web site were not operable!"

Writer's Assignment: Write a brief, clear message that explains to visitors what features will be available (and what will not be available) for use in the demo version of the software.

Complaint 2: "It said 'Click here to download,' so I did, but nothing happened!"

Writer's Assignment: Explain to visitors the exact steps for downloading and installing the demo software; include some tips about systems requirements and file management.

Complaint 3: "I had to click through three or four pages of promotional information for each separate product and accessory before actually getting to the price of each product available on your site. It was such a hassle!"

Writer's Assignment: Write a memorandum to the Web site host company, explaining why they should not "bury" pricing and shipping information too deeply within the Web site.

MENUS: CREATING ROADMAPS FOR READERS

Organized Web sites are actually made up of hypertext-linked "pages" that have been separated and categorized in some logical manner for the visitors' (and Web managers') convenience. They include menus, indexes, and site maps that function as roadmaps helping visitors navigate the materials on the site. Effective menus should appear on home pages and subsequent main pages around which clusters of documents are organized. Menus tend to be less detailed than indexes and site maps (which should provide visual and linked listings of all available pages or data-objects available on the site).

Effective **menus** greet visitors with a visual representation of the main topics or areas of the site and set up expectations. Good professional writers should seize this opportunity to create anticipation, as well. Creating a home page menu is like making a promise to your visitors: "Look! Here's what we have for you!" Menus also provide the categories and scope of information available on the site. If buttons or menu items are labeled in a pithy or confusing manner, visitors will quickly become frustrated or bored with clicking around a site when they are looking for something specific. The menu in Figure 3.7 is a good first draft for a dog club Web site, but its layout seems vague (and possibly misleading). The links have not been categorized by any familiar organizing principle. Menu links such as "Play Time!" and "More Stuff" are not helpful. They force visitors to click around in the site before finding the information they want.

The menu in Figure 3.8 is an improvement upon the previous draft. Note that topics are labeled more clearly, without necessarily being longer. Web writers usually prefer to keep in mind a plan for using navigation bars, or lists of navigation links, on each page of the site, so that visitors can easily navigate the site as they search for information.

After clarifying the labels for a menu of links within the Golden Retriever Club site, the writer decided that for the home page, she wanted to go one step further and arrange the home page menu into logical groupings of information in a way that would be helpful for both long-time club members and for newcomers (see Figure 3.9). Because the site itself was not large, the writer decided to expand the text of most main menu items while keeping shorter labels for the navigation bar. Note that at this stage, the writer elected not to write a welcoming message or any other extended text for the home page. In the end, it was decided that newcomers could simply click "About OTGRC" to be welcomed and to learn more about the organization, its work in the community, and the Web site itself.

Welcome to the Our Town Golden Retriever Club Web Site			
Who Are We?	Play Time!	Puppies!	Competition
Joining Up	Calendar	Rescue	Local Businesses
Classes & Misc.	Other Golden Retriever Sites	Therapy Dogs	More Stuff

FIGURE 3.7 Working draft of site navigation menu.

Our Town Golden Retriever Club			
About OTGRC	Local Off-Leash Recreation	AKC Breeders	Field Trials
OTGRC Membership	Calendar	Retriever Rescue & Adoption	Grooming & Retail
Obedience & Training	Links	Therapy Dogs	FAQs

FIGURE 3.8   Improved site navigation menu. Experiment with different arrangements and categories of information.

Our Town Golden Retriever Club

Welcome to Our Town (general info for newcomers)

- About OTGRC (who we are)
- FAQ: OTGRC frequently asked questions
- OTGRC Membership (join, pay dues, see directory here!)
- OTGRC Calendar (news, activities, & shows)
- Local Off-Leash Recreation Areas
- Directory of Local Grooming Services and Supplies

Local OTGRC-Sponsored Training & Competition

- Basic Puppy & Obedience Classes
- Advanced Training & Classes
- Gun Dog Field Trials
- Therapy Dog Certification

Puppies & Adoption

- AKC Breeders (be patient, lots of pictures may load slowly!)
- Retriever Rescue & Adoption (adorable dogs who need new homes)

FIGURE 3.9   Find groups and clusters of related information that visitors can easily skim.

Whether a Web site is large or small, the key to a well-designed menu page is to use organizing principles that make sense to visitors. Try some common principles of classification such as

- Alphabetization
- Categorization (using types or subcategories relevant to the main subject of the site)
- Function (buying, selling, learning, subscribing, playing games, day-trading, etc.)
- Order of importance
- Exigency (urgency)
- Geographical location

FIGURE 3.10 Informative, organized, and fun menus make the Rock & Roll Hall of Fame & Museum "Exhibitions" Web page interesting and easy to surf. Used by permission. *http://www.rockhall.com*

Topics and links should be clearly named so that users don't have to guess where each link will lead them. Items with labels such as "More good stuff" or "Here's one I like" may seem cute, but they aren't helpful when visitors are trying to locate (or relocate) something they want. Figure 3.10 shows a fun and yet efficient use of menu and art layout on the Rock & Roll Hall of Fame and Museum Web site.

EXERCISE 3.3

Call up five Web sites, large and small, and evaluate their menu labeling and organization strategies.

1. Can you name one single principle that governs the choice of the home page menu items? Name the principle used for organizing each home page menu (i.e., alphabetical, relative importance, topic-specific grouping elements, etc.).

2. Judging from the menus on the home page, what would you say is the primary purpose (or purposes) of the Web site: selling, entertaining, providing information, propaganda, building community, gathering visitor data, or some other purpose(s)?

3. For each site, give a numerical evaluation of the following features: Which sites scored the highest?

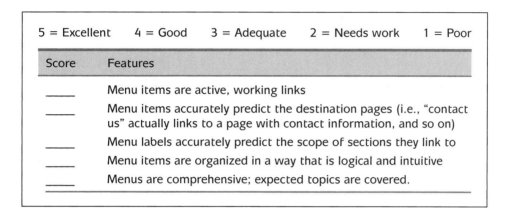

5 = Excellent	4 = Good	3 = Adequate	2 = Needs work	1 = Poor

Score	Features
_____	Menu items are active, working links
_____	Menu items accurately predict the destination pages (i.e., "contact us" actually links to a page with contact information, and so on)
_____	Menu labels accurately predict the scope of sections they link to
_____	Menu items are organized in a way that is logical and intuitive
_____	Menus are comprehensive; expected topics are covered.

4. What can the Web writer do to improve the site's labeling and organization strategies? Be specific, using terms and concepts learned in this chapter.

SITE MAPS

A **site map** is a special page that is designed to visually represent the entire contents of a Web site. It should have a clean, organized layout that helps the searcher understand the site's arrangement. The site map should provide hyperlinks to all other Web pages of the site. Usually an effective site map page displays a hierarchical diagram (or outline) of all the pages on the site. A site map can be sketched on a chalkboard, drawn on paper, or digitally worked out prior to building a site; its structures may or may not mirror the file structure of the Web site, depending upon the requirements for managing the site's information.

Site maps are often confused with site indexes. The index is a comprehensive, alphabetically arranged listing of the site's topics. A site map should be arranged not by alphabetical arrangement of terms the visitors may or may not think to look for, but instead should be arranged logically, with its conceptual organization based upon the subject matter and purposes of the site.

A site map differs from a menu page in that it is, to the highest degree possible, a page that provides links to every single page (or at least every head page of each important subsection) of the Web site. The site map is a tool that Web designers have developed in answer to users' complaints that Web sites, as a resource media, are too opaque for their comfort. That is, when a researcher holds a book in her hand, she can see its scope, length, and breadth simply by flipping through it and by feeling its weight and size. On the Web, however, the size and scope of a site is not tangible. Users usually arrive at a home page or portal and have no way of visualizing (or mentally conceptualizing) the breadth or depth of the information they may be able to access, simply because they are limited to one screen at a time.

The site map provides users with a kind of mental atlas of a Web site. It also provides frequent visitors with a shortcut to the pages and resources they are interested in so that they do not have to click through introductory or welcome pages and menus (provided for new and infrequent users) first.

EXERCISE 3.4

Examine the Web pages of several college or university English departments (or biology, history, etc.).

1. On paper or the chalkboard, try to diagram the entire department Web site and create a site map for it.
2. Evaluate the strengths and/or weaknesses of the site's organization (you may wish to use the chart in Exercise 3.3).

READER-ORIENTED SITES: TIPS FOR TEXT-HEAVY CONTENT

Contemporary wisdom about writing for Web sites holds that textual content should be brief, concise, and "packed at the top" of each screen or page. Usability analysts also agree that navigational tools and overview materials should satisfy readers' desire for brevity and precision. Still, there are many sites that consist of well-written information and ideas, such as news of the world or literary essays and stories. These "text-heavy" sites are an interesting mixture of technical and creative writing. Web writers should be familiar with many styles in order to meet varied expectations from readers who find satisfaction in immersing themselves in longer works. Many of the types of Web sites listed below feature pages that may contain a dozen or more news stories or full-length essays (5,000+ words):

- News
- Academic and scientific articles
- Essays
- Editorials
- Satire
- Web zines
- Literature archives (online libraries)
- Blogs (abbreviation of "Web logs")
- Government documents
- Legal documents
- Technical documents
- Hypertext fiction
- Personal Web sites

- Political Web sites (both official and unofficial)
- Special-interest Web sites

Online readers, unlike folks seeking "quick fixes" or retail purchases, are going to remain logged onto a site for a longer period of time if they plan to read the entire text on-screen. Many visitors to text-heavy sites, however, prefer to print longer works and read them in more eyesight-saving environments.

Some Web designers and writers, mistaking the rules about chunking information onto different hypertext pages by trying to apply them to longer works, actually cause inconvenience for readers who must click and wait each time they come to a new section of the text. Although works of creative hypertext fiction do this on purpose, with the avant-garde intent of disorienting and dislodging conventional reading habits, most textual pieces prepared for the Web can be packaged in painless, usable ways that will satisfy both Web administrators and site visitors.

Providing a print version of an article or story that will be formatted nicely on paper is a courtesy that will bring visitors back again and again, because they can get what they want with minimal eye fatigue. The letters and symbols on a computer screen are made up of tiny illuminated nodes called *pixels.* The images and text on a CRT computer screen, on average, *refresh*—firing hundreds of tiny lighted, unlighted, and multicolored dots at our eyes—at the rate of 100 Hz (100 times per second). This *refresh rate* goes mostly undetected by our conscious perception, but our eyes feel it, and it can be exhausting. The average television refreshes at 60 Hz in a meshed fashion, and we are not usually trying to read and concentrate while viewing television shows. This is why Web readers tend to read short to medium textual pieces online and print longer pieces. Even readers who have LCD screens (that do not refresh the way CRTs do) still want to print longer pieces, because staring at a computer screen exposes their eyes to *direct light,* a much more harsh experience than reading printed matter or viewing *reflected light.*

Assignment

Using a search engine, seek out some of the text-heavy types of Web sites listed above. Evaluate the tools, organizational strategies, and display choices that the Web managers have made from the perspective of visitors whose goal is to spend a significant amount of time reading, rather than surfing or interacting with the site.

1. How interesting is the writing? Is it fresh? Does it keep your interest? Why or why not? What stylistic features do you like? Dislike? Why? (For further discussion on style, refer to Chapter 7.)
2. Is it easy to locate interesting articles of substantial length?
3. What words would you use to describe the intended readers of the site? Why would you describe them that way?
4. How easy or difficult is it to access an entire essay, article, or story all the way through? How many mouse-clicks did it take?

4 Common Page Types

- Home Pages: First Impressions Always Matter
- "About Us" Pages: What's "About" All About?
- Frequently Asked Questions: Helping the Helpers
- Links: Where Do We Go from Here?
- Interactive Pages: Forms, Buttons, Dialog Boxes
- Community-Building Pages
- Help Pages

Glossary Terms

Domain name
FAQ
Flame
HTTP
Image map
Internal link
Mouse over
Navigation bar
Web page

Like it or not, we're stuck with baseball metaphors: Web sites begin at "home." When our pages are visited frequently, we brag about the number of "hits," and so on. Early Internet users latched onto easy metaphors that evoked familiar images as a way of explaining to friends and colleagues the basics of Web site file management structures and hyperlink organization. (See Figure 4.1.) The visual idea of a flat "field," with a "home" and connected "pages" or "nodes," made it easy for Web developers to talk about their sites. The lingo of the Web caught on quickly, and almost overnight people were talking about Web sites they had "surfed," digital images they had "downloaded," and something called "hypertext." Many of the early terminologies are still in use, whether a site is created in simple HTML code or programmed to assemble objects and templates on-the-fly. This chapter focuses on some of the most common types of Web pages, classifying them by their *purposes*—the work they are supposed to do for you and your site visitors. As you begin to explore in detail these familiar types of Web pages,

FIGURE 4.1   Familiar patterns make it easy for visitors to "find their way" around a Web site.

you might wish to discuss ways in which these standard forms can free a writer to explore the aims of different discourses on a Web site. You should also explore some of the ways in which these standardized forms can seem restrictive and oppressive for writers when their purposes don't seem to "fit" one of the common forms.

HOME PAGES: FIRST IMPRESSIONS ALWAYS MATTER

The home page of any Web site usually determines the kind of first impression the site, and possibly its owners, will make (see Figure 4.2). The home page is the hub, the "entrance hall," the introductory page. Its address is the primary URL (usually the **domain name**—see URL diagram in Figure 1.4, Chapter 1) that visitors most likely will remember and bookmark in their browsers. It is the home page that most clients think about when they hire a Web company to help them establish what they call a "Web presence." Web designers know that if company executives are pleased with the home page, then the layout and design—the "look and feel"—established on that page can be carried throughout the site and repeated on all of the rest of the pages and their various components.

For Web writers, the impression made on the home page is crucial. Think about what you usually say when you want to make a good impression upon someone you have just met. It may be difficult to come up with anything original after the

FIGURE 4.2 Your site has to do more than look good—it has to tell visitors *who you are.*

polite phrases "How do you do?" or "It's nice to meet you." Anything more might seem like grandstanding, anything less might seem rude. But for writers, introducing a place, topic, cause, or community is an important job. While the programming and design of a site make a *visual impression* on first-time visitors, the writing *interprets the meaning* of the site's existence.

Main Features of Effective Home Pages

Whether a home page functions as the portal to a huge number of links or is the hub of a small web, keep in mind that it serves as a cognitive "anchor" for visitors as they explore the different areas of the site. It establishes identity and creates expectations. There may be as many approaches to establishing corporate identity as there are ad campaigns. However, writers should keep in mind three important concepts that tend to drive the written and visual elements of the home page: branding, packing, and usability.

Branding

Logos, trademark images, color schemes, and familiar designs associated with a company or organization are prominently displayed on most corporate and institutional Web sites. The writing on the home page must match the corporate (or institutional) "image" that the host has built up over time. Writing copy for a home page requires some background knowledge of the host organization. Does it have famous— or infamous—past ad campaigns? Does it have a certain place in the local community? Does it have a national or even international reputation? Or more importantly, is the organization planning to change its image? All of these questions and more should be on the writer's mind as he talks with the host about the organization's desires for the home page.

Packing

Information most important for visitors should be "packed" at the top of the screen in clean, concise, error-free text and images so that upon arriving at the company's online "home," visitors do not have to scroll up and down to determine what is available on the site. Packed information usually includes a **navigation bar** or menu (featuring an immediate link to a site map), daily messages (known as the "MOTD" or "message of the day"), greetings, identity-reinforcing images, contact links, special offers, news flashes, and if at all possible, a friendly face or two. Home pages are not usually chatty, but they may feature news items. They are usually portals into different general areas of the site. These subareas in turn can be divided into different topics, retail areas, product information, in-depth news reports, and so on.

Usability

Although programmers are tempted to use the latest, flashiest technologies to make Web sites "cool," writers need to understand that not all visitors to the site will be people who have bothered to upgrade their browsers to the latest, greatest new features that can display these groovy new elements. If a home page relies upon flashy animations and other scripting or programming to make it visible to viewers, its creators should take a moment to browse the site from several different computers, especially those using older programs without lots of updated features. If visitors to the site have not upgraded their browser versions in three or four years (this is more common than Web managers like to think!), many will see nothing at all. (See Figure 4.3.) As a technical writer, you may not be able to convince a Web designer or a client to "dumb down" the programming level of the cool home page. In that case, be sure you have written some links and text that visitors can use to navigate their way into the site to find the resources they are seeking. Many corporations and organizations have a "front page" that asks visitors if they want to view the newer, fancier version or a plainer, stripped-down version of the home page. Users frequently choose the simpler, less flashy version, even when they have fast connections and upgraded browsers.

EXERCISE 4.1

Browse the home pages of 10 major corporations and/or organizations whose corporate identity you think of as being famous and familiar to most people. With a partner or on your own, evaluate the effectiveness of each home page, and then choose the least effective home page.

Assignment 4.1

Create a new home page mock-up for the company whose home page you think is weak or has major flaws. Make sure your mock-up includes text, menus, navigation bars, images, captions, color combinations, and design elements that you think would be most effective for the corporate (or institutional) identity and most user-friendly for visitors to the site. Share your mock-up with the class and discuss the stylistic and design choices you have made.

Assignment 4.2

If the class is working with Web design software, use a WYSIWYG program to create a new home page for the company you chose in Assignment 4.1.

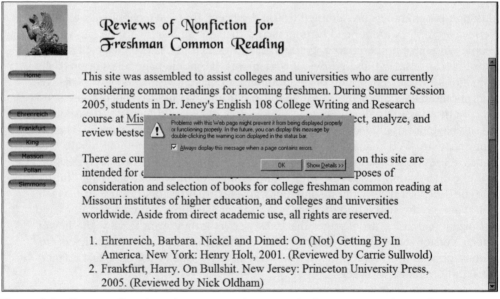

FIGURE 4.3 Beware: Creating a home page that uses the latest, most advanced technologies may result in an unattractive blank page for visitors who have not kept up with all of the latest sotware versions and upgrades—more common than web programmers might think!

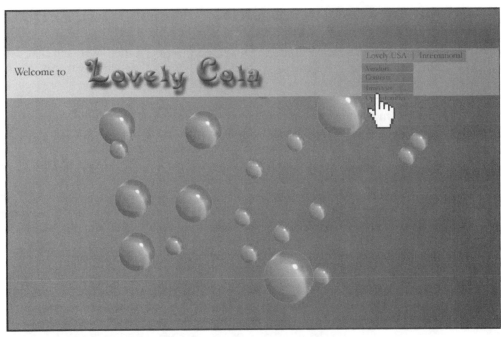

FIGURE 4.4   Product brand-name site: The fictional Lovely Cola Company uses the product logo and sparkly animated bubbles to reinforce its identity for site visitors.

FIGURE 4.5   The fictional Loud Guitars, Ltd. company uses clean, bright graphics to push guitar-shopping visitors directly to the brand-name instruments of their choice.

"ABOUT US" PAGES: WHAT'S "ABOUT" ALL ABOUT?

Most businesses feel compelled to include a page on their Web site that describes the organization. Unfortunately, these pages often are filled with trite, puffed-up language, bogged down in clichés and bureaucratic double-speak for "Hey, look at us. We're great!" (See Figure 4.6.)

The most important questions writers must ask when composing an "About Us" page are: (1) What does this company want Web visitors to learn about it? (2) What will visitors want to know about this company?

Frequently these are drastically different objectives. Companies, organizations, and institutions want to "put their best foot forward" in any public forum. They want the page "about us" to stress their corporate, social, and financial responsibility, while at the same time suggest they are at the head of the pack in their field. These pages are usually so poorly written because the writers are trying to do too many things at once:

- Impress prospective investors, customers, and community leaders.
- Establish credibility and journalistic identity.
- "Puff up" the corporate (or institutional) image.

FIGURE 4.6 "Jim, call the Web team. I just found out what it's all about!"

- Attract top-of-the-line employees.
- Sell products.
- Intimidate competitors.
- Satisfy the company's legal department.
- Flatter the company's upper management (by creating an "ego page").
- Soothe/charm possible skeptics or enemies.
- Tell the history of the organization.

With all of these purposes in mind, it can be impossible for a writer to produce clear, appealing prose that will satisfy everyone. In their heroic efforts to please, Web writers often end up writing fluffy, redundant, bureaucratic, public relations doublespeak.

There is nothing really wrong with the following writing samples, quoted from actual corporate Web sites. But note the self-aggrandizing style typical of such "About Us" web pages.

> Founded in 1946, Fender Musical Instruments Corporation has been an American icon for over 50 years. In that time, Fender's contribution to the evolving sound of contemporary music has been global and continuous. By introducing the first commercially viable solid body electric guitar, the first electric bass and countless classic amplifiers, Fender musical instruments have left their mark on jazz, blues, country, rock and many other styles of popular music.
>
> *http://www.fender.com/resources/companyinfo/history.php*

> BlackBerry is a leading wireless connectivity solution, . . . developed by Research In Motion Limited (RIM), a leading designer, manufacturer and marketer of innovative wireless solutions for the worldwide mobile communications market.
>
> *http://www.blackberry.com*

> Girl Scouts of the USA is the world's preeminent organization dedicated [to helping all] girls build character and skills for success in the real world. In partnership with committed adult volunteers, girls develop qualities that will serve them all their lives, like leadership, strong values, social conscience, and conviction about their own potential and self-worth.
>
> *http://www.girlscouts.org*

> The Coca-Cola Company exists to benefit and refresh everyone it touches. Founded in 1886, our Company is the world's leading manufacturer, marketer, and distributor of nonalcoholic beverage concentrates and syrups, used to produce nearly 400 beverage brands. Our corporate headquarters are in Atlanta, with local operations in over 200 countries around the world.
>
> *http://www.cocacola.com*

Frankly, such self-congratulatory prose often pleases managers and executives. It's the kind of corporate puffery they are accustomed to hearing at motivational gatherings and sales pitch meetings. For the Web writer, the best advice might be to "give 'em what they want," but then make sure the site itself is organized so that customers and other visitors are not bothered with much of it unless they actually seek it out. These PR statements can be shuffled quietly and neatly into a separate section of the site labeled "Our Mission," "About the Flooglehorn Company," or even, "Meet the Flooglehorn Family."

When a client sincerely wants to make a useful, informative statement about the organization and its members, it is the Web writer's responsibility to help achieve that aim. Straightforward, sincere (and brief) statements about the founders or leaders often appeal to people visiting the site. Historical information that is actually interesting should be easy to find and treated in a lively, active prose style.

Consider the following solutions when creating "About Us" text for a Web site:

- Discuss the purposes for the "About Us" section of the site. Ask why this section is there and what it should accomplish. After producing an informed draft, test it against the specific purpose to see whether the writing accomplishes that purpose.
- Consider adding a press release section to the site. If the site's owners frequently generate releases, white papers, public documents, and other materials, the press will appreciate being able to find them easily online. Reporters sometimes prefer to visit a Web site instead of having to play telephone tag with executives for generic statements and information.
- Discuss the reasons why visitors to the site will want information about the organization or about individuals who own the site. Then tailor the text to the visitors' needs and desires.
- Divide more comprehensive "About" sections into several sublinks, each of which may include different kinds of information about the company: corporate history, product history, personnel, sponsors, investors, contributions to the community, and so on. Each of these sections could merit a brief page of its own, which users could access through clearly marked navigational sublinks.
- Avoid repetition and redundancy. If you notice the same text being used on several pages, consider rewriting those pages or cutting them altogether.
- Select interesting and important facts and details. Ask, "Could this paragraph describe any reasonably successful company?" If so, then it lacks specific details that will make the page interesting and worth reading. The more the client insists upon such language, the more the writer should seek to bury puffy text deep in the site, where it cannot waste visitors' time.
- Bury corporate fluff. Mission statements, for example, usually comprise some of the worst corporate prose known to humankind—written by committees, vetted by legal teams, and combed over yearly until they are honed to a perfect, blunt paragraph of nothingness. If a mission statement must be included, bury it several links into the site, so that readers are not put to sleep before they even get a chance to learn about the terrific resources available on the site.
- Make intelligent labels. If the product and the company share the same name, be sure that pages about the company are not just about the product, and vice

versa. Simple labeling and navigation markers can avoid this problem: "About Our Hand-Helds," "About Our Company," and so on.

■ Avoid hyperbole—don't overstate the historic importance of a company or organization. Most visitors will be skeptical when a five-year-old software development company attempts to narrate its glorious corporate history.

■ But do consider writing an accurate, interesting, and richly descriptive "History" page for organizations or companies that actually have earned a place in a nation's or culture's history. The Web sites for Shakespeare's Globe Theatre, the Huntington Library, NASA, and the Santa Fe Southern Railway can and should be expected to provide historical narratives and interesting information about these places and the organizations that keep them open and running for the public.

"About" Credibility

Visitors to a Web site can become skeptical when the sites they visit for information, opinions, or reviews of products and services fail to provide satisfying information about the reviewers and site owners themselves. If a site's primary function is to report or satirize the news, then the "About" page is a crucial piece of information for readers to have. Otherwise, the site becomes just another butt of the old joke, "Of course it's true! I read about it on the Internet!"

EXERCISE 4.2

Either with a partner or on your own, visit the Web sites of 10 major organizations. Choose sites that belong to various kinds of corporations and institutions, both commercial and nonprofit. Usually, these sites can be found by simply typing into a major search engine the name of a commercial, political, social, educational, historical, medical, financial, or artistic organization you are interested in. Find the "About Us" section of each site and read the materials there. Rank the 10 sites in order of the quality of the writing.

1. Discuss or write about the good and bad qualities of the writing on "About" pages.
2. Alone or in a group, rewrite one of the poorly written "About" pages. Discuss the probable purposes for these pages (i.e., what the company is trying to accomplish and what visitors will be looking for on these pages). Use as many resources as possible to find new and interesting information for the revised page, and then discuss ways to sharpen and enliven the writing style. If you are working in a group or with a partner, what is the effect of having more than one person work on the final prose?
3. Discuss the methods you used to gather specific information and the details that you used to bring these pages to life. Discuss the kinds of problems you encountered as a writer when organizing and writing the content for these pages.

FREQUENTLY ASKED QUESTIONS: HELPING THE HELPERS

FIGURE 4.7   What exactly was the frequency of that question?

According to business communications expert Dorothy Leeds (author of *The 7 Powers of Questions: Secrets to Successful Communication in Life and at Work* [New York: Perigee, 2000]), the average four-year-old asks more than 300 questions per day, while the average college student asks fewer than 20.[1] At last search, there are well over 420 million pages of Frequently Asked Questions (**FAQs**) on the Internet. Even if there were only five questions on each page, we're talking about more than 2 *billion* questions that, according to Web sites everywhere, are "frequently asked"! The FAQ (pronounced "fak") page has become a standard fixture on Web sites of all kinds. We can quibble about whose convenience these pages are made for. The FAQ pages of most Web sites are constructed to save the time of help desk workers who hear (or receive via e-mail) the same questions many times per day (Figure 4.7), but the best stance for writers to take stylistically is always to approach the FAQ page as a tool for the site visitor's convenience.

FAQ pages should be treated as the first-level resource for site visitors who need help. Ideally, the FAQ page should develop naturally out of a collection of actual questions that the site owners receive—either online, by mail, in person, or over the phone—on a regular basis. These questions can then be collected by the FAQ page writer, who will also need to be given the answers to the questions. Thus, understanding the interests and background of the typical site visitor is crucial for Web writers. The questions and answers on the FAQ pages must be customized to readers' needs as much as possible.

---

[1]Leeds, Dorothy. "Questions." The Walt Bodine Show. National Public Radio. KCUR, Kansas City, MO. 21 July, 2004.

One common bad practice is front-loading the FAQ page with questions such as "How do I buy the Zippy Flooglemeister today?" or "Can I fill out the Zippy Flooglemeister customer survey?" These types of questions are obviously fake and self-serving, placed on the FAQ page merely to push the sale of a product or direct visitors to an information survey. If the site owners are so eager to hard-sell the Zippy Flooglemeister, the home page menu clearly should have site navigation links or buttons that say "Buy Now!" and "ZF Survey!" The FAQ page should be reserved for visitors' authentic questions and support issues.

Visitors usually click on the site's FAQ page when they are gathering information or when they are hunting a solution to a specific problem. It is safe, then, to consider the FAQ page a place for hunters and gatherers. Web writers need to make decisions about the size and scope of the FAQ page based upon the kinds of answers troubleshooters will be hunting for and the amount of gleanings information-gatherers will be willing to sift through. The following are some common Internet conventions to consider when writing and organizing FAQ pages:

- Internet users expect FAQ pages to be a hit-or-miss resource. Sometimes their problem is not as common as one might think, or it is simply not listed because of space constraints. However, people often browse the FAQ pages before phoning or e-mailing the Web host with a question. Therefore, effective FAQ pages display links to other resources, and if possible provide contact information for visitors who wish to call in or e-mail their questions.
- Frequently asked questions are rewritten for the convenience of Web visitors. Readers understand that many times questions are phrased incoherently or in a confusing way, and that the writers of FAQ pages tend to "clean up" and clarify the questions so that they are clear and focused on one problem at a time.
- Often, the questions most frequently asked are basic, first-time user questions, and to experts they may appear silly or even offensively ignorant. Writers of good FAQ pages treat basic novice questions with the same courtesy, consideration, and patience that they would treat advanced-level questions.
- FAQ pages should be organized for easy browsing and skimming. Sometimes Web writers insist that the questions be listed or "packed" at the top of the page, with internal page links to the answers below. This is a judgment call, since some FAQ pages are fairly short, and linking is unnecessary. However, if there are 10 questions or more, it is easier for "hunters" to seek their own problem quickly when the questions are packed at the top of the page, to be skimmed and read without having to scroll down the screen.
- Questions should be phrased in the voice or persona of the visitor (or customer). That is, as writers we need to put ourselves in the shoes of the person asking the question and use the first person: "How do I change the belt on my Dirt Devil™ Classic Hand-Vac sweeper?"
- Answers should be phrased in a courteous, helpful tone.
- Answers should provide clear, organized, step-by-step instructions for solving the problem.
- Humor is fine, as long as it is helpful and friendly in nature and does not interfere with the process of helping visitors troubleshoot their problems.

EXERCISE 4.3

Compose one of the following FAQ pages for students at your college or university:

1. Frequently asked questions from high school seniors about applying and getting registered
2. Frequently asked questions about choosing and declaring a major
3. Frequently asked questions from seniors about applying for graduation
4. Frequently asked questions from transfer students about applying for admission and registering for classes
5. Frequently asked questions about (insert some student organization)
6. Frequently asked questions about majoring in (insert a specific major or emphasis)

LINKS: WHERE DO WE GO FROM HERE?

One of the reasons the World Wide Web works in such a seamless, efficient, instantaneous way is the hyperlink itself (Figure 4.8). Invented and promoted by Tim Berners-Lee, this capability of connecting and downloading files makes finding, collecting, and saving information easier than it ever has been. Need to know where to get more information? Just <u>click here</u> and go! We could claim without too much of a stretch that it is the hyperlink (or the **hypertext transfer protocol, HTTP**) that makes the Internet the Internet.

Figure 4.9 shows how simple it is to create a hyperlink, from a coding standpoint. The <A HREF=> in the opening tag tells hypertext browsers to look for a hypertext reference or *anchor*. The URL (uniform resource locator, in quotes) gives

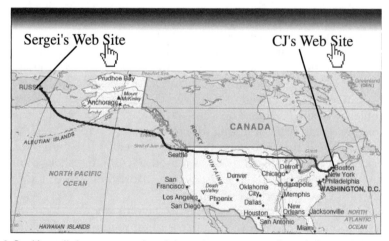

FIGURE 4.8 Hyperlinks connect site visitors instantaneously to information stored anywhere in the world.

> Just <A HREF="http://www.ask.com">click here</A> and go!

FIGURE 4.9 HTML code for text link.

the tag its *attribute,* or a place to find a particular file directory and specific hyper-text file (**Web page**). Between the angle bracket–enclosed tags is the display text, "click here," which will show on the actual page. Text within angle brackets is usu-ally invisible on the browser page; text between tags will display as linked text.

Good Web writers know that people often print reference Web pages full of links for friends or colleagues. Therefore, it is smart to make sure the page actually displays the URL of each linked resource as well as the title of the page, its date, and the name of the Web page owners. Immediately following the display text, which will become the actual linked text, is the closing or *stop tag.* The </A> marks the end of the linked section of text. (Note how it takes a much smaller space to create a hyperlink than it does to explain how it works!)

The links page was developed early and became common in the mid-1990s as a convention on all kinds of Web sites. The coolness factor alone was enough to make early Web designers excited about connecting their visitors instantaneously with other related sites on the Web. Today, most sizeable Web sites have a section devoted to links, although the more commercial sites tend to limit *off-links* (links to "outside" Web sites not owned or operated by the site host) or avoid them altogether. The common assumption is that since it takes hard work to attract visitors to a site, the site owners would prefer not to send people elsewhere—possibly to the com-petition's site.

In order to conceptualize the best way to employ hyperlinks in a Web site, writ-ers first have to be familiar with the different kinds of basic links. There are three major considerations when creating hyperlinks:

1. The linking *styles*, or ways that the links are displayed on the page
2. The linking *destination*, the actual sites or files the link is "pointing to," that is, the specific item that will be brought up when a user clicks on the link
3. The linking *display window* or *target*, the browser window in which the new page should be displayed

Linking Styles

Several different styles of links appear on Web pages, but the two primary types are text and graphic or image map links.

Text Links

The text link is the most common type of hyperlink found on most Web pages. Text links are anchored to text and usually appear either as plain text or as underlined text. Plain text links should only be used if there is some concern that underlining will clutter up the page and when it is obvious that the linked text actually is linked.

In other words, visitors can't find plain text links unless they **mouse over** every section of the text, watching for cursor changes that signal the presence of a link. Most Web writers prefer underlined text links simply so that visitors can see exactly where all linked passages and words are located on the page. This does not guarantee that all users will view the links in exactly the way you have intended them to—most Web browser applications allow users to set their viewing options for "underline links" or "do not underline links." Fortunately for users, links often appear in different colors, especially after they have been visited (bridging the gulf of evaluation: "I can see that I have already visited that link").

Organized on the page as formal lists of Web sites (see Figure 4.10), links pages are sometimes referred to as "Webliographies." Online sources can be listed, annotated, and linked for an academic audience.

Embedded Links.   In the example in Figure 4.10, a "Back to Top" hyperlink takes the reader to a specific location on the same page, in this case back to the top of the same page. Embedded links are useful for helping readers navigate long, text-heavy pages and pages crowded with subheadings and subsections. An embedded link can take visitors to a specified location on a different page, as well.

Inline Text Links.   An inline link is one that occurs within a body of text, rather than appearing in a list or menu. Some examples are shown in Figure 4.11.

Articles on Hypertext Theory and Hypertext Fiction: Text Link

Rationale for Scholarship in Hypertext. Kuhn, Virginia. "A Study--Reading Hypertext Fiction." A Study Investigating the Inclusion of Hypertext Fiction in Literature Classrooms. 29 Nov. 1999.
http://www.uwm.edu/~vkuhn/mastudy.html
An overview of the challenge of teaching hypertext fiction in postsecondary literature course.

Landow, George P. "The Definition of Hypertext and Its History as a Concept." Hypertext: The Convergence of Contemporary Critical Theory & Technology. 05 Oct. 2002.
http://www.cyberartsweb.org/cpace/ht/jhup/history.html

Brief page defining "hypertext" conceptually, through lens of Barthes and Nelson.
Mishra, Punyashloke; Nguyen-Jahiel, Kim. Presentation @ AERA, April 1998. "Reading print and hypertext fiction: Reader stance and its impact on meaning making." 16 May 2002.
http://punya.educ.msu.edu/PunyaWeb/pubs/print/hypertext/hypertext.html
Results of a study on the process of meaning making by six readers as they read printed and hypertext fictions.

                     Embedded Link

Back to top

FIGURE 4.10   Detailed, annotated text links, with embedded link "Back to top." Full bibliographic information about each site includes complete URLs and summary-abstracts. An embedded link sends visitor to a different section of the same Web page.

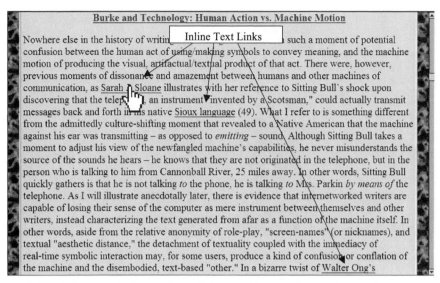

FIGURE 4.11   Inline text links are hyperlinks used in text-heavy electronic pages.

Image or Graphic Links

The image link (Figure 4.12) is becoming almost as common as the text link. Although using media other than text to create a link might seem more complicated, it actually is quite simple for the hypertext code writer. Web designers often prefer graphical button links over text links for artistic and design reasons, but also because text that appears as part of an image file is technically just a part of the picture and cannot be altered when the visitor changes the browser text size or font settings on her own machine. Figure 4.13 shows several types of image links.

Although images make Web pages come alive, they do present challenges for Web managers and writers. How much visual variety is too much? Remember, when visitors call up a page, every image on that page must be downloaded, thus increasing the amount of time it takes to see the page. Every time changes are made to the site, writers have to integrate the images and layout in order to make visual as well as textual sense for their readers: visitors, designers, and other writers who may inherit the task of making updates and revisions of an evolving Web site.

The **image map** link is created by writing extra tags and code that accompany the image. Hyperlinks are embedded into different areas on the image. Clicking on each part of the image connects visitors to different destinations. An example is shown in Figure 4.14.

```
<a href="http://www.drugstore.com"><img src="clickhereforsavings .jpg"></a>
```

FIGURE 4.12   HTML code for image link.

FIGURE 4.13 Types of image links. (a) Advertisement image link. Text in this kind of image is not hypertext: It is actually part of a static image. (b) Picture-style image link. Most images on Web pages have been formatted as .gif or .jpg files. Any image can be used as a link simply by using hyperlink tags in the same fashion as linking a section of text to a destination on the Web. (c) Button-style image link. Often, the "buttons" on Web sites are actually two images: one that looks convex, and one that is concave. When we click on the link, the image changes to look as though we have "pushed" the button.

Linking Destinations

A URL (uniform resource locator) or Web address of a site contains all the information needed by a Web browser to get a specific document from a server. When creating a hyperlink, make sure the URL is correct or the correct file will not be found. The information required is as follows (also see Figure 1.4 in Chapter 1):

- *The type of service* that should be used to get the data and, consequently, the port number of the service (HTTP, **FTP**, etc.)
- *The name and location* of the host computer (server) storing the document the user is attempting to locate and download—the domain name
- *The location of the file* on the host computer, including directory names, path names, and filenames (note that in most browsers, a page whose filename is "index.html" will be called up as the default page when a particular directory is accessed)
- *The location on the same page* or on another page within the same Web site— an embedded location within a page

Most links target one of the following five sources:

1. *A remote Web site.* These links can connect to any page on the World Wide Web, whether it is stored on a server in Honolulu, Tokyo, Moscow, or Taos.
2. *A page within the same site (local or **internal links**).* Frequently, coding shortcuts tell a browser just to look for a page title within the same directory as

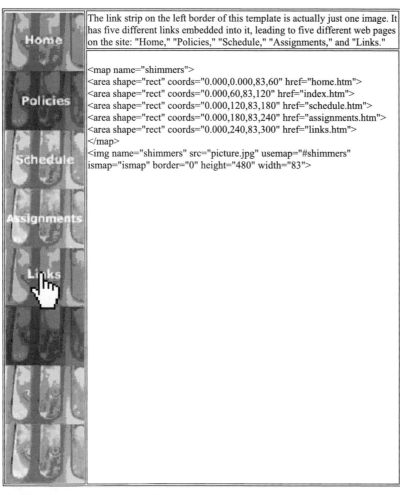

The link strip on the left border of this template is actually just one image. It has five different links embedded into it, leading to five different web pages on the site: "Home," "Policies," "Schedule," "Assignments," and "Links."

```
<map name="shimmers">
<area shape="rect" coords="0.000,0.000,83,60" href="home.htm">
<area shape="rect" coords="0.000,60,83,120" href="index.htm">
<area shape="rect" coords="0.000,120,83,180" href="schedule.htm">
<area shape="rect" coords="0.000,180,83,240" href="assignments.htm">
<area shape="rect" coords="0.000,240,83,300" href="links.htm">
</map>
<img name="shimmers" src="picture.jpg" usemap="#shimmers"
ismap="ismap" border="0" height="480" width="83">
```

FIGURE 4.14 Image map coding. The link strip on the left border of this template is actually just one image. It has five different links embedded into it, leading to five different Web pages on the site: Home, Policies, Schedule, Assignments, and Links.

the one it is already displaying. This may seem a simple convenience, but it becomes crucial when an entire Web site, with all of its hypertext files, images, and media files, must be lifted and moved to a new domain.

3. *A "mailto" or e-mail link.* When users click on a mailto link, the e-mail composing program (such as Netscape Messenger, Eudora, MS Outlook Express, Pegasus Mail, Mozilla Thunderbird, etc.) is launched and automatically shows the e-mail address in the "To" field. These links should be used judiciously. They usually don't work correctly when users are logged into a lab or Internet café computer.

4. *An embedded link.* Embedded links allow users to jump to a specific part of a Web page. They are usually seen in a long document (same page) or can cross-reference to a specific location on a different page. It is usually smart to include

a "Back to Top" embedded link that will bring the reader back to the top of a long page. In text-heavy Web articles that use inline links connected to a footnote, it's a good idea to add another link so that after reading the footnote, the reader can click back up to where she left off.

5. *A link to media stored on the same site, or another site, other than Web pages.* Image files, Word documents, sound archives, video files, and streaming video are common forms of multimedia that need clearly identified links. (The National Public Radio Web site is a good example of well-managed media file links, as are the sites of many NPR affiliates.)

Linking Display Targets

Of increasing importance to Web writers is the need to disrupt the reader's experience as little as possible. Because interruptions and confusing off-links initially caused Web users to refer to their experience as "surfing," writers quickly began to adapt by insisting that many hyperlinks be targeted to call up the new destination materials in a separate window, or in a different "tab" of the browser window. Thus, the reader does not have to trace a tangled path back to where he left off when he clicked on a link. Although savvy Web users right-click to open new links in separate windows, thoughtful Web writers code their links so that new materials automatically display in a separate window.

EXERCISE 4.4

Alone or with a partner, examine a link-heavy home page or portal site such as the Farm Service Agency page shown in Figure 4.15. Other examples might include the main sites operated by the U.S. government, the Library of Congress, the national Republican or Democratic party Web sites, or sites of nonprofit organizations such as the National Rifle Association, Greenpeace, or Habitat for Humanity. Try to identify every link on the page, classifying and naming its features and attributes. Mouse over (run your cursor over) the entire page. Determine the style, destination, and target of each link. Capture the page so that you can display it for the class and systematically identify the following for each link on the home page (don't forget advertisements and those tiny navigation bars at the bottom of the page!):

1. Styles: Is it a text link (and is it in list format, or inline format within paragraphs)? Is the link an image link? Or is it part of an image map? If it is part of an image map, can you tell how many links are embedded (or mapped) within the same image? Use your mouse to find the links; the destination URL should display in a bar at the bottom of your browser window.

2. Destinations: Does the link connect to a destination that is remote, local/internal (within the same Web site/domain), mailto (an e-mail link), embedded (linked to a spot on the same page or a particular location on another page within the site), or a media file?

3. Targets: Does the link open in the same window, a new window, or a new tab in the browser?

FIGURE 4.15   Link-heavy portal page: U.S. Department of Agriculture Farm Service Agency Web page. *http://www.fsa.usda.gov/pas/default.asp.*

INTERACTIVE PAGES: FORMS, BUTTONS, DIALOG BOXES

Ad campaigns and public service announcements frequently exhort us to "Come visit our interactive Web site!"—but just what do they mean by *interactive?* From a Web programming standpoint, *interactivity* refers to the ability of a site to accept visitor input and deliver corresponding output. Although the programming behind the scenes is often so slick it appears seamless when we want to shop, play games, download software, or pay bills online, there are quite a few steps in the path to completing these actions online:

1. The visitor enters input (by typing text into fields or mouse-clicking on page elements).
2. Her computer sends input to a server.
3. A program on the server interprets and responds to her input.
4. If everything is working correctly, the visitor receives output on her computer screen.

Interactivity can refer to something as common as clicking on a simple hypertext link, or it can refer to something more complex, such as scheduling a flight on a travel site. Web writers, designers, and programmers work hard to make sure that

FIGURE 4.16 "Is that the new Dead Metaphors album?" "Oh yeah. And it only cost me $90 plus the download subscription fee!"

elements on their pages clearly indicate how visitors can input the proper information and select the right choices on the screen. When visitors can easily navigate these sites and accomplish tasks, programmers say the site has "high usability." If the labels on buttons, choosers, and information fields are confusing or hard to find, the site is said to have "low usability." Good writing—and especially good labeling— can often increase usability on Web sites that feature a large number of text fields, chooser elements, and dialog boxes.

Forms: Collecting Visitor Information

When a Web site provides forms for visitors to fill out, it is very important that each field be labeled clearly and that visitors can understand exactly what information they need to provide. Of course, when asking visitors to provide personal information, be sure to tell them exactly how their information will be used and how their privacy will be protected. Asking for sensitive information such as credit card numbers, account numbers, and passwords always requires heavily encrypting the interface between the Web site and the information system.

Whenever possible, forms should include fields that have the added forcing feature of a finite number of spaces and characters. In the field shown in Figure 4.17, the product key code referred to has been provided in the materials that accompany a software package or other item that the user has bought. The form boxes precisely delimit the number of characters that can be typed into each box. The instructions explain that it will not matter if the user types in capital or lowercase letters.

Because the kinds of targets or destinations to which the information can be pointed will vary in type and purpose, it is important for writers to think about just how confusing these online forms can be and to use language that is clear and

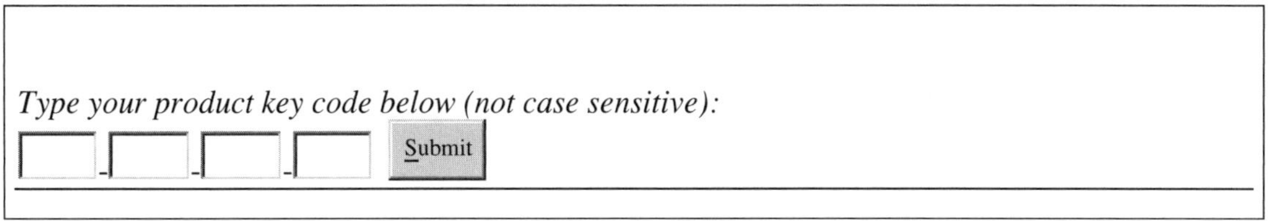

Type your product key code below (not case sensitive):

[ ] - [ ] - [ ] - [ ] [Submit]

FIGURE 4.17 Forms should provide easy-to-follow instructions and fields.

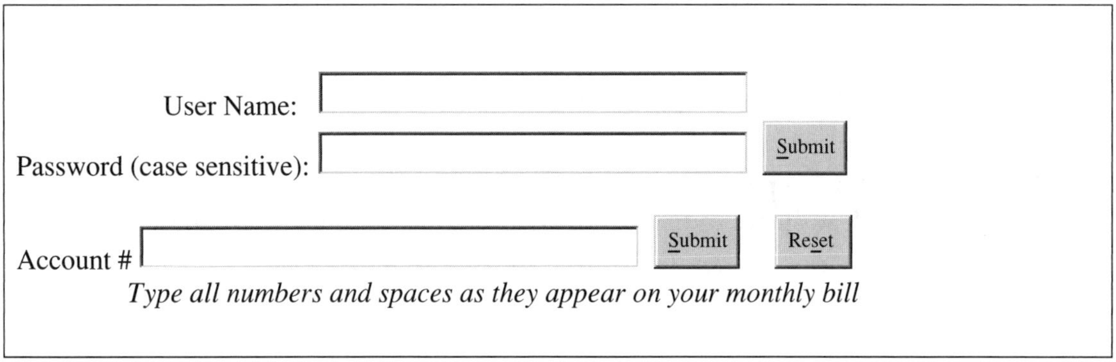

User Name: [ ]

Password (case sensitive): [ ] [Submit]

Account # [ ] [Submit] [Reset]

Type all numbers and spaces as they appear on your monthly bill

FIGURE 4.18 Fields provided for returning visitors are not always helpful to newcomers.

precise. The fields shown in Figure 4.18 are clearly labeled for regular visitors to a site. People who know their user names, passwords, and account numbers will have no trouble filling out the form. But further labeling and instructions will be necessary before newcomers understand exactly what they should type in the field boxes. New visitors should also be told what the results of their actions will be. For example, the text should tell them whether clicking the Reset button will erase all of the information they have typed, or simply permit them to edit elements they have previously submitted.

Radio Buttons and Check Boxes

As most document designers know, it can be easier for everyone involved if an interactive online form simply provides preformulated options to be selected or deselected. When information needed at the destination is already "prepackaged" (delimited), it can be run directly through the computer software. Some examples of delimited choices are shown in Figure 4.19 and Figure 4.20.

The writer's job is to make sure that each choice is clear and that users know what it is they are turning "on" or "off" when they click on a radio button or check box. To understand the difficulties posed by even this seemingly easy job, study the next sample ballot you receive in the mail prior to a local or regional election! An example is shown in Figure 4.21.

What age group do you belong to?
18—25
26—35
36—50
50 +
Submit
Reset

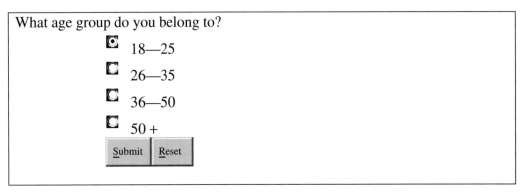

FIGURE 4.19 Radio buttons work like toggles. Visitors choose among items on a page.

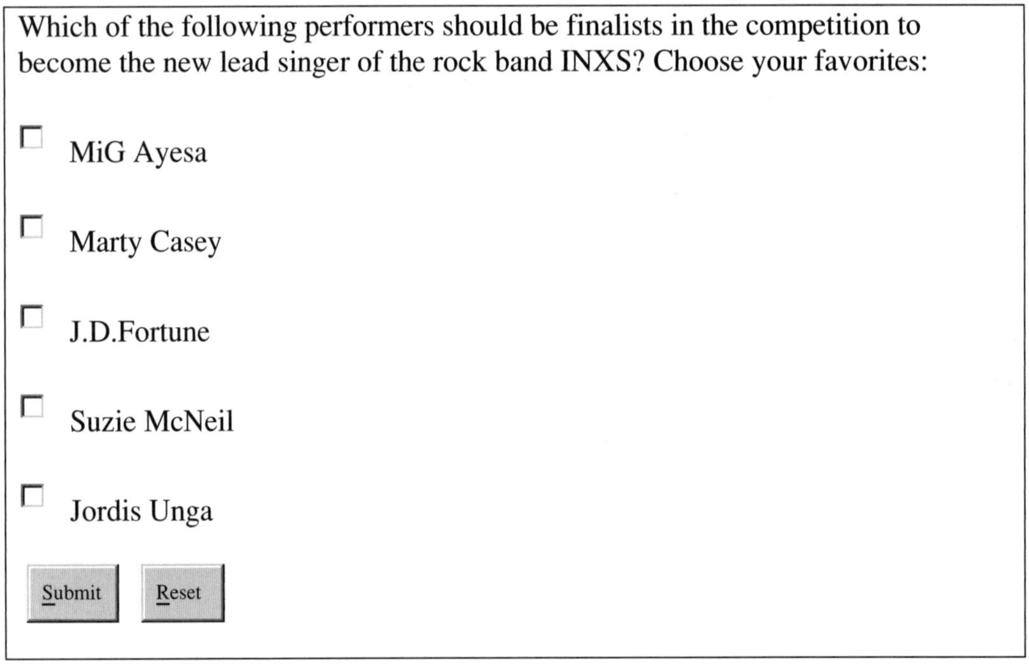

Which of the following performers should be finalists in the competition to become the new lead singer of the rock band INXS? Choose your favorites:
MiG Ayesa
Marty Casey
J.D.Fortune
Suzie McNeil
Jordis Unga
Submit
Reset

FIGURE 4.20 Check boxes work as choosers that let visitors select (or deselect) some function or option.

Dialog Boxes

A *dialog box* is a small window that appears on the computer screen requesting you to perform an action or select an option before moving on. It may simply provide information the site feels obligated to tell you and require you to acknowledge that you have read it. For example, a dialog box may ask you questions such as, "Do you want to save this document?" or "Are you sure that you want to exit this program?"

PROPOSITIONS

PROPOSITION NO. 1

(Economic Development/Boeing)

SHALL THE COUNTY OF TULSA, OKLAHOMA, BY ITS BOARD OF COUNTY COMMISSIONERS, LEVY AND COLLECT A FORTY PERCENT (40%) OF ONE PERCENT (1.0%) SALES TAX FOR THE PURPOSE OF PROMOTING ECONOMIC DEVELOPMENT WITHIN TULSA COUNTY, OKLAHOMA, AND/OR TO BE APPLIED OR PLEDGED TOWARD THE PAYMENT OF PRINCIPAL AND INTEREST ON ANY INDEBTEDNESS, INCLUDING REFUNDING INDEBTEDNESS, INCURRED BY OR ON BEHALF OF TULSA COUNTY FOR SUCH PURPOSE, SUCH SALES TAX TO COMMENCE ON THE FIRST DAY OF THE CALENDAR QUARTER FOLLOWING EXECUTION OF AN AGREEMENT BY THE BOARD OF COUNTY COMMISSIONERS WITH BOEING OR AN AFFILIATE TO LOCATE A NEW 7E7 AIRCRAFT MANUFACTURING/ ASSEMBLY FACILITY IN TULSA COUNTY, OKLAHOMA, AND CONTINUING THEREAFTER FOR THIRTEEN (13) YEARS FROM THE DATE OF COMMENCEMENT OF SUCH TAX?

FOR THE PROPOSITION - YES   ☐

AGAINST THE PROPOSITION - NO   ☐

FIGURE 4.21 Visitors can understand the choices are "Yes" and "No," but does the text of the proposition explain clearly what each choice will mean in terms of public policy? Official County Ballot, Special County Election, September 9, 2003; Tulsa County, Oklahoma, *http://www.vote2025.com/documents/ballot.pdf*

FIGURE 4.22 Dialog boxes usually force the computer user to stop and take some action before continuing.

Or it may simply tell you that "You are about to view an encrypted page" (see Figure 4.22).

When a dialog box appears on-screen, usually it provides a field for the user to enter information or respond to a query (often with choices such as "OK" and "Cancel"). Web programmers use dialog boxes when they want to force visitors to stop and carefully consider the requested action or information. Usually, the dialog box prevents users from accessing buttons and toolbars on the main application (such as a browser or graphics editor) until the action requested is taken (or the box is simply closed via the "X" button).

Dialog boxes have to be programmed and written for ease of usability. Although many kinds of informational and procedural dialog boxes are written in

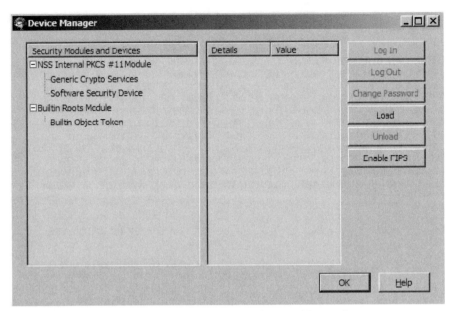

FIGURE 4.23   Some dialog boxes aren't easily understood by novice users.

standard boilerplate, some require unique instructions or messages. Web writers need to ensure that dialog boxes are clear and contain enough information for the average site visitor. Warnings, errors, and instructions that make sense to experienced Web programmers may not be helpful to others (see Figure 4.23).

The example in Figure 4.23 illustrates what happens when dialog boxes do not include information that the average computer user can understand. Usability often depends as much on good writing as on good programming. Writers who keep usability issues in mind can help visitors get the most out of a Web site by following these guidelines:

- Test your instructions to make sure that users can easily understand what they are being asked to do.
- Bridge the gulf of execution: Make sure that users receive feedback messages that let them know their actions have set in motion the desired result. This can be as simple as displaying a visual indicator that the system is responding. A written message is also reassuring. Visitors appreciate courteous messages such as "This could take a while—thank you for your patience," or "Please wait while we access that information for you."
- Bridge the gulf of evaluation: Make sure that users receive feedback messages that show how much of the process has been completed when they have entered information and clicked a button to initiate a desired process. The gulf of evaluation can be bridged with status bars and "Download complete!" messages.
- Compose specific, clear messages that tell users exactly what transaction has transpired. If they have made a purchase, make sure that upon completion the

purchase amount and shipping information are clearly displayed in a printable form; if they have subscribed to a site or publication, make sure their log-in information is provided clearly. Ideally, completion messages should also be e-mailed by the system to the visitor so that he receives a record in a form that arrives in his own account (for example, if he has been executing the transaction from an Internet café, office computer, or campus computer lab, printing or saving capabilities may not be available).

COMMUNITY-BUILDING PAGES

Sometimes visitors to a Web site are motivated by a desire to interact with a community (see Figure 4.24). Webbed discussion boards enable visitors to participate by posting messages that will be saved and displayed to all members who log on. Such community sites provide a terrific way to facilitate community bonding around themes, topics, hobbies, interests, issues, and even educational subjects or courses. Name it, and there is probably a discussion board for it:

- Motley Fool stock market investment discussion boards, *http://boards.fool.com/boards.asp?fid=10100*

FIGURE 4.24 Somewhere on the planet, people are chatting, e-mailing, posting messages—connecting—and we can make it work!

- Canadian Actors Online Discussion Board, *http://www.canadianactor.com/info/moderators.html*
- The United Methodist Online Community, *http://www.umc.org/*
- Buffistas: Buffy the Vampire Slayer Discussion Board, *http://www.buffistas.org/index.php*

Web-enabled discussion forums are easy and inexpensive to host, so if we can't find a ready-made discussion forum for our chosen topic, we can just hop over to a message board service and start one. Message boards are easy to use. They are often "threaded," or sorted by topic. Messages (usually called *posts*) can sometimes be sorted by subject headings, by date, or by the username of the sender. Many of these boards include chat programs, a private message center for each member, and e-mail forwarding capabilities. Some have closed, exclusive memberships; others are open to the public. Message boards can also be used, in a more formal way, by organizations, schools, and corporations for online collaborative work and team building. A writer who must compose the greetings and introductory materials for a discussion or chat forum may find important differences between a space that has grown organically by attracting interested visitors from all over, and one that has been supplied to employees or students who are required to log in and submit their work.

When users are posting messages to a discussion because they have been attracted by the topic or the community hosting the site, they tend to be more invested in the content and interactions there because they are *intrinsically motivated*. Often they have arrived at the site by searching for discussions of specific subject matter, or they may have learned about the community by word of mouth from other members. When intrinsically motivated visitors consult materials provided by the forum Web site, they are usually seeking community-based information, topic-related resources, technical assistance, or community rules and conventions. They are interested enough to work at getting the information they need, and they may help by contributing suggestions, information, and relevant materials.

Visitors who are *extrinsically motivated* to participate in a community-based Web site are required to do so by outside (extrinsic) forces such as a teacher or employer. They are not always as indulgent and patient as those who are intrinsically motivated. Visitors who have been required to contribute to an information or idea-sharing online community do not want to spend extra time clicking and searching for topics, threads, or conference areas on the site. They may even resent having to use Internet technologies for collaborative projects or for online meetings, so the instructions and guidelines provided for them need to be crisp, direct, and time-saving.

Internet community expert Clay Shirky[2] has pointed out that as much as most online communities want to be open and democratic, it is their forum administrators' very wish for openness and tolerance that often makes these groups vulnerable

---

[2]Clay Shirky is author of *Planning for Web Services: Obstacles and Opportunities,* and numerous online articles tackling topics and issues in Web-based business and technical communication. The extract that follows is from "A Group Is Its Own Worst Enemy." Keynote address, O'Reilly Emerging Technology Conference, Santa Clara, CA. 24 April, 2003.

to trouble from without and from within. Sometimes groups gain an impressive number of participants, enough to merit some kind of attention, including mention in the popular press. Internet communities that attract attention also tend to attract hackers (whose form of disruption is usually technological) and "trolls" (who attack social structures). Online groups can also be disrupted internally when disagreements or even **flame** wars (nasty, inflammatory exchanges) erupt.

Writing for the Web means more than simply getting information and ideas across to a mass audience. It also means listening, responding, and adapting to communities of people who connect with each other online. If the purpose of a Web site includes facilitating community, writers should spend some time learning about how these online communities form, grow, maintain themselves, and, unfortunately, how they fail. Online communities tend to form fast, grow quickly, reach peak intensity, and then cool off as the initial novelty wears off. Writing for a Web site that accompanies an e-mail community, Web discussion board, or chat community starts with respect for community members, a knowledgeable focus on the common purpose or topic of the community, and a sense of the community's "personality." In addition, it does not hurt to have a powerful command of rhetorical strategies that can draw out the best behavior from community members:

> And the worst crisis is the first crisis, because it's not just "We need to have some rules." It's also "We need to have some rules for making some rules." And this is what we see over and over again in large and long-lived social software systems. Constitutions are a necessary component of large, long-lived, heterogeneous groups. . . . As a group commits to its existence as a group, and begins to think that the group is good or important, the chance that they will begin to call for additional structure, in order to defend themselves from themselves, gets very, very high.

> *(http://www.shirky.com/writings/group_enemy.html)*

When we're called upon to write for an interactive community or collaborative Web site, it's extremely important to understand who will be using the forum and how they will expect to be treated. Some groups are familiar with technological issues and computer systems. Usually, technology-oriented communities will not mind blunt, terse messages about the expected protocol and use of a forum's features.

Other groups may not be accustomed either to computer technologies or to interacting online and should be given more guidance and gentle handling as they get accustomed to the Internet environment. The rules and guidelines provided on a site usually change over time, as the group itself grows and evolves. Therefore, when writing for a community Web site, you should not think twice about making changes, additions, and amendments to previously drafted guidelines when asked to do so.

Online forums provided for groups who also meet face to face, such as in a classroom or a work setting, often have fewer written guidelines posted to the site, since materials and discussion about forum protocols can be distributed or discussed in person.

EXERCISE 4.5

On your own or in a group, use an online search engine to locate 5–10 discussion boards on the Web. Look for sites that openly display the discussion threads (so that you do not have to subscribe or join the discussion forum just to see its topics). Look at the various welcome and forum guidelines sections of the online discussion board site. Choose a discussion board that you are interested in studying closely, either because it seems typical or because it is unusual or strange in some critical way.

1. What is the name of the forum?
2. What is the purpose of the forum? Do the discussion board's technological components fit the level of user-knowledge the members will be comfortable with (i.e., is it easy enough to use)? In what ways? Do the discussion thread subject headings match up with the purpose? Are there digressions? What kind? If full messages are available for display, do the messages themselves tend to match up with the stated purpose of the forum? Can you add further statements about the forum's purposes to your initial impression?
3. Identify and describe the group(s) of people expected to participate in the forum. What marks them as potential members of this online community? An interest? Geographical location? Culture? Race? Other feature? Do the members seem to fit the expected profile? In what ways?
4. How would you characterize the style and tone of the rules and guidelines for group interaction? Use qualitative words like "friendly," "harsh," "stentorian," "controlling," "relaxed and cheerful," and so on. Why do you think this particular tone is used? Is it appropriate? Why?
5. If you belong to a classroom or work forum that supplements an off-line, school, or work group that regularly meets in person, what comparisons can you make between the kinds of interactions and language used in the school or work forum, as opposed to the online-only community forum you were looking at for questions 1–4?

HELP PAGES

Many Web sites become large and complex enough to call for a special help section. It is important not to confuse the help page with the frequently asked questions page. Even when help pages are organized in a question-and-answer format, they should be organized around specific, logical topics—including how to contact the site host for further help. Unlike a FAQ page, help pages are expected to be comprehensive and organized by logical topics. Help links may activate subprograms that include indexing, search tabs, and alphabetized contents. Many help topics may be needed only on rare occasions, but including them can save visitors great amounts of time and inconvenience (Figure 4.25).

It is no secret that writing help files and help pages can be extremely difficult. One way to get organized and avoid feeling overwhelmed is to break your help page(s) down into separate tasks.

FIGURE 4.25   "No, really . . . has anyone seen my spare isotopes?"

1. Understand who most of the readers will be. Gather enough details about their level of expertise so that you are not over- or underexplaining. Although formal, clear, courteous language is always a safe choice, the site may be specialized to a specific "discourse community" and call for certain types of technical jargon or at least some specialized vocabulary that will be appropriate for its scope and contexts. The first passage that follows is for users of a UNIX-based e-mail list distribution program called Majordomo. Obviously, the help page writer assumes that the reader will be more concerned about using correct command lines than about any personal or social connection:

> When Unsubscribing: Majordomo has no use for your human name, only your email name. Mis spell [sic] your human name, & it won't care, misspell your email address, & Majordomo will certainly fail to work as you want.

> Julian H. Stacey (2004), *http://berklix.com/~jhs/robot/majordomo/#index*

The next passage was written for a Web discussion board help page. Compare the tone and "attitude" in this passage with the Majordomo help.

> Setting up Email Notification: If you like, WebBoard will notify you by email when new messages are posted in specific conferences. The message is sent once a day when new messages are present. The time the email is sent is determined by the WebBoard administrator.

> Help File: *WebBoard* Software

Whereas the first passage is blunt, and to an outside audience might seem almost unfriendly ("Majordomo has no use for your human name"), the second uses warm, even conciliatory language ("If you like, WebBoard will notify you").

2. Gather enough information about the site and its scope to have a good idea how extensive (and intensive) the help page or pages should be. If the size is substantial, you may want to consider using *help file–generating software* to create your topics and instructions, or at least creating a subdirectory of pages to organize help links in a usable fashion.

3. When writing step-by-step instructions, walk yourself through the same steps you are describing. After you have completed a draft, hand your instructions to someone willing to test them. Most of the time, describing a task we're familiar with is harder than describing an unfamiliar one. When we are used to doing a task often, we unconsciously complete subtasks that must not be omitted, so be prepared for a humbling experience! Consider it a game. "How many steps did I forget to describe?" Shoot for zero, but smile if a list comes back from your tester (and buy a gourmet coffee and a donut for the tester who makes thorough and helpful suggestions about your instructions!).

4. Write each help topic so that it can stand alone as much as possible without the need to reference instructions found elsewhere. Visitors do not read help files unless they need assistance, and they can't be expected to read around or beyond the topic that they need help with. If we force them to refer back to other instruction sets or different subdirectories, they will get lost or frustrated and leave. If we try to tell them more than they need to know, they will become exhausted with information overload and leave. If the help categories are organized properly, visitors should be able to find out just enough to correct the problem they have encountered.

5. Make sure that visitors can contact someone for assistance when they encounter an unexpected or highly complex problem that they can't solve on their own. In fact, if the help pages and topics are organized efficiently enough, visitors should be able to tell very quickly if their problem is beyond the scope of a help page.

6. Finally, the team that manages a substantial corporate or institutional Web site should make sure that those who receive e-mail, phone calls, and other customer input about problems can forward these questions and problems to the Web writer in charge of the help pages. If the site's growth and development is functioning properly, these customer queries should be considered for inclusion in the help pages, and if changes in the Web site or the organization create a particular question or problem that will arise often enough, it should be copied on the FAQ page, as well. The key, of course, is communication. Help page writers make it their business to know what kinds of problems are happening so they can make periodic adjustments or additions.

EXERCISE 4.6

Gather information about an organization or service at your school and write the text for a "Help Page" that could be added to its Web site.

Assignment 4.3

Working alone or with a partner, create a plan (or mock-up) for a small multiple-page Web site. Your instructor may give you a theme or topic, or you may wish to choose a hobby, a local nonprofit organization, or a local business upon which to base your Web site. Organize the site in a logical fashion and include one each of the following page types:

- Home page: the main portal, or "anchor" page. Write the main greetings and any information or messages that appropriately greet and orient visitors to the site.
- "About" page: tells about the site host(s). Provide text that gives information you believe visitors and peripheral site-surfers would find most useful.
- FAQ page: frequently asked questions (and answers!). Provide at least five questions and their answers.
- Links page: properly labeled and titled hyperlinks to off-site resources. Provide at least 15 links that you think site visitors will find useful.
- Interactive page(s): retail transactions, discussion board, e-mail list subscription, chat portal, database portal, and so on, or any combination of these. Write text that introduces the interactive elements and provide instructions that visitors can use to get started.
- Help page: Important troubleshooting information for visitors (include contact information). Determine the kinds of help your visitors will need and organize a list of important help topics and subtopics.

You (or your instructor) may wish to include other kinds of pages such as a contact information page, advice pages, controversy/editorial essay pages, letters, blog (Web log) entries, and so on.

5 Style for Web Writing

- Style: Strike a Pose
- Style and Writing for Effect
- General Constraints: Subject, Timeliness, Audience, Purpose
- Style Goes Beyond "Correctness"
- Common Writing Problems
- Style and Technical Jargon
- Some Helpful Rules for Developing Style

Glossary Terms

Archives
Java
Platform

A scrupulous writer, in every sentence that he writes, will ask himself at least four questions, thus:

1. What am I trying to say?
2. What words will express it?
3. What image or idiom will make it clearer?
4. Is this image fresh enough to have an effect?

And he will probably ask himself two more:

1. Could I put it more shortly?
2. Have I said anything that is avoidably ugly?

George Orwell, "Politics and the English Language"

STYLE: STRIKE A POSE

When writers talk about the style they use for creating Web site content, they often use terms such as "tight," "compact," "sparse," "punched-up," "straightforward," and "technical." But these terms are descriptive and intuitive without necessarily being very helpful to Web developers. To many Web programmers, writing for the Web can mean writing the actual lines of computer-language code that make up the underlying functional structures of a Web site. The methods and patterns that govern that kind

FIGURE 5.1 Style results from an array of choices: flamboyant, plain, formal, casual, or technical language—all have their place. All have different effects on readers. All create individual impressions.

of "writing" are very precise and structured, with rules that create tangible constraints upon the designer. Writing in English (or any other human language, for that matter) requires a vast amount of language ability and complex, internalized networks of meaning, the bulk of which we acquire as children. In school we learn to refine our usage from the free-form and repetitive patterns of speech to the more formal patterns of written English.

Many people see writing as a very personal, individual activity. But the writing we do in the workplace or in a public forum takes on the exciting (and sometimes nerve-wracking) dimension of serving a larger purpose. The written word becomes a medium for accomplishing some purpose that involves others. Web writing is a public activity, whether we treat it as such or not. By definition, writing for the World Wide Web is writing for the world. Uploading our words to a server and assigning them a URL is nothing if not a demand for an audience.

STYLE AND WRITING FOR EFFECT

If writers have a specific purpose in mind, whether for print, Web, or other media, they can focus on specific writing elements that work together to get the job done. There is really no mystery about how writers develop and execute certain styles of writing, but putting all of the elements together with confidence and consistency takes study and practice. Writing for the Web adds particular problems to be solved. There are unusual constraints of space and visual arrangement, pixilated typefaces, variable refresh rates, attention fluctuations, gender-based Web user habits, hypertext architectures, and click-and-print options, to name only a few. The trick is to list the specific demands of a site or even of its separate sections ahead of time and write for them, rather than ignoring or resisting them. At each stage of content development, it is important to review rhetorical, technical, grammatical, and professional demands that are being made on the work we are doing.

GENERAL CONSTRAINTS: SUBJECT, TIMELINESS, AUDIENCE, PURPOSE

Constraints are the limitations and parameters that define the scope of available options when we write professionally. Writing for a corporate, organizational, or institutional Web site involves identifying and following the parameters of technical, aesthetic, physical, political, economic, and even legal limitations set forth by the managers and owners of the site. The first step to identifying, developing, or adopting a style for each site is to understand the parameters within which we will need to work, and then focusing our beginning content drafts around the constraints we are certain of.

Here are some useful, rhetoric-based questions that we can use to focus and evaluate our choice of writing style. Not all questions will be relevant to *every* site, but they can be applied in a general sense to evaluate the soundness of our written Web content:

Subject
- Have I double-checked and verified factual information?
- Have I represented the subject matter fairly, in a way that reflects the purpose of the site?
- Is the information historically accurate?
- Is information couched within the proper context(s)?
- Does the amount of information satisfy the requirements of the site (i.e., not too much or too little)?
- Has it come from the most reliable sources (properly cited and credited, of course)?
- Does it comply with intellectual property (copyright, trademark) laws? Has it been vetted by the corporate legal department (if applicable)?

Timeliness
- Is the information up-to-date and relevant?
- Is the content perishable? How often will it require updating?
- Does the content make sense to a contemporary site visitor, or would it need explanation/contextualization?
- How will events in the world affect the way the site and its content are received?
- Is the content affected by seasonal and fiscal events or considerations?
- How long is this site likely to remain in existence?

Audience

- Who is the primary audience for the Web site—the targeted readers?
- Who is the supervisory audience for the site—who is paying for the site's construction, and who is the chief Web manager for the site and its content? That is, who supervises the writers and the written content of the site?
- Who is the secondary audience for the site—those who deal with site-related issues? Who will be responsible for customer service, help desk, e-mail inquiries, site architecture, programming upgrades, and so on?
- What are the age demographics of the site's targeted visitors?
- What are the ethnic demographics of visitors likely to use the site?
- What are the socioeconomic demographics of visitors likely to use the site?
- What are the gender-based demographics of visitors likely to use the site?
- What are the computer-literacy demographics of visitors likely to use the site?
- What are the education-based demographics of visitors likely to use the site?
- What are the special interests of visitors likely to use the site?
- How would you describe the most targeted group of Web users for whom the site is designed?

Purpose

- What are the site owner's reasons for creating and launching a Web site in the first place?
- What primary purpose will the site serve for its owner(s)?
- What additional purposes will the site serve?
- What primary purpose will users have for visiting the site?
- What additional purposes might users have for visiting the site?
- How can the site realistically serve the purposes its owners hope that it will satisfy?
- How can the site realistically serve the purposes users will have for visiting it?
- What is your own purpose for working on this site as a writer?

STYLE GOES BEYOND "CORRECTNESS"

We've all heard the old saying that for every grammar rule in English there is an exception. And generally that is true. The English language has a checkered past. Originating from Old West Saxon, German, and Celtic dialects almost two thousand years ago, it somehow survived the invasions, batterings, conquests, and infusions of Latin, Old Norse, and multiple dialects of Old and Middle French. Each wave of change brought with it new grammars, syntaxes, and vocabularies. Thus English has become a psychedelic stew of regulars, irregulars, cognates, and idiomatic structures that is almost impossible to untangle.[1] But this very complexity created by its

---

[1]I say "almost impossible" because anthropological studies of the history of the ·English language are fascinating and quite good. Modern studies in linguistics encompass many of the thousands of social, political, historical, structural, and even psychosexual influences that create change in human languages.

cumulative past makes English the largest and one of the richest languages in the world. Each wave of influence brought subtle shifts in definitional and connotative meaning to hundreds of words. For example, as the French influence in the Middle Ages pushed the word *fruit* into common generic usage, the old Anglo-Saxon term *apple* shifted away from its generic definition (any kind of fruit) and came to denote a specific *kind* of fruit, and so on. Rather than complaining about the complexities and difficulties of writing clean, correct English, we should be excited about the many options available to us when we are planning and composing our written content.

Web supervisors must be as choosy and perfectionist as their print-editor counterparts when written work is submitted. For like it or not, readers can make very harsh judgments about a company's professionalism, personnel, and products based *solely* on the preciseness or sloppiness of the text on a corporate Web site. Would we schedule medical treatment at a clinic whose front-door sign reads "Open-Heart Surgeree & Nose Jobs R Us"? We can think of a company's Web site as its online storefront. If we walk into a store or factory where materials, tools, and equipment are dirty, sloppy, disorganized, and in ill repair, our impression of that business and its management is not going to be favorable. On the contrary, if the front office, retail space, and warehouse are clean, well ordered, and easy to navigate safely, we have a good impression of that company. We might even be impressed enough to invest in them. *That* is what the professional Web manager is aiming for: the impression of efficiency and professionalism above all else.

COMMON WRITING PROBLEMS

Web writers have to be vigilant about correctness not only because they are trying to make an impression of efficiency and professionalism, but because they are writing for a vast audience. For even though a Web site may be designed to appeal to a specific audience, its very availability to the online world has created a large *peripheral audience*—readers whose interests in the main content of the site are cursory or only tentatively related to the site's theme. There are some very common ways for technical writers to get their sentences into awkward and confusing situations:

- Pronoun confusion:

    "The lawyer hugged the doctor, even though she didn't like her very much." (Who didn't like whom?)

- Idiom confusion:

    "It's a doggy-dog world." (It's a *dog eat dog* world.)
    "All the sudden he fell into the lake." (*All of a sudden* . . .)
    "You should of turned left." (You should *have* turned left.)

- Misused terminology:

    "Red-hot molten dogma poured from the volcano." (*Magma* pours from volcanoes.)
    "Mr. Jones is presently in a meeting." (*Presently* means *soon*; *at present* means now.)

- Punctuation problems:

  "He thanked his parents, the Pope and the First Lady." (Without a second comma after "Pope" it appears he is the son of the Pope and the First Lady!)

- Colloquialisms (sometimes called *low* or *base register*):

  "The early monorail system sucked because of maintenance problems."

- Garbled sentence structure:

  "Talking to the judge, your dog was not to blame for the neighbor's garden." (The dog was talking to the judge?)

  "As far as sick leave, see Mrs. Tanner by the last Tuesday each time." (This sentence has some meaning, but readers will not work to get it!)

- Wordiness:

Common (often confusing) puffed-up phrase:	Concise phrase:
She was cognizant of the fact	She knew
Our understanding of the situation was that	We understood that
We examined various aspects of	We analyzed

- Words that sound (or look) alike:

accept	except	
conscience	conscious	
woman	women	
advise	advice	
prejudice	prejudiced	
its	it's	
lead	led	
than	then	
were	we're	
where	wear	
all ready	already	
all right	alright	
may be	maybe	
compliment	complement	
principle	principal	
affect	effect (n.)	effect (v.)
to	too	two
there	their	they're

STYLE AND TECHNICAL JARGON

Sometimes we hear the term *jargon* applied to confusing or arcane language, but for professional and technical writers the word actually refers to phrases and terms that are specific to a particular trade, profession, or group. *Jargon* in a broad sense refers to terminology and colorful language that group experts and insiders use.

Often the meaning of the jargon is not understood outside the group or occupation. The problem with Web sites that make heavy use of jargon is that the Web is not specific to those groups or professions.

Once documents are posted to a site, readers will come from all kinds of backgrounds. Even though Web designers can use structures and meta tags designed to attract searches of particular terms and subjects, people arrive at open Web sites in many different ways, including from references made in e-mail lists that have open **archives** on the Web. If a site's owners and managers would prefer to restrict the readership of a site, there are ways to password protect and limit membership. But many organizations and companies would rather open their sites to as many visitors as possible rather than "closing off" their online presence. Good organization and design can make a site as "friendly" for peripheral readers as it is for primary, secondary, and supervisory audiences.

Even highly technical Web sites can try to prepare peripheral readers for the level of topic-specific technical language they will find as they venture deeper into the site. Most good computer programming sites, for example, open with general descriptions of the materials available and then give visitors the option of clicking deeper into the site for further technical discussion or assistance. Sun Microsystems has a very popular and highly developed site that opens with a generic explanation of what they are developing and selling:

The Java programming language is robust and versatile, enabling developers to:

- Write software on one platform and run it on another.
- Create programs to run within a web browser.
- Develop server-side applications for online forums, stores, polls, processing HTML forms, and more.
- Write applications for cell phones, two-way pagers, and other consumer devices.

Sun Developer Network
(*http://java.sun.com/developer/onlineTraining/new2java/index.html*)

Clicking a couple of menus into the site, we can easily find introductory pages to Java programming tutorials. These pages carry some technical terminology, at first intentionally avoiding heavy saturation:

"Hello World" for Microsoft Windows
It's time to write your first application! These detailed instructions are for users of Microsoft Windows platforms, which include Windows XP, 2000, ME, and 98. Instructions for other platforms are in "Hello World" for UNIX . . . and "Hello World" for Mac OS X . . .
A Checklist
To write your first program, you need:

   1. The J2SE TM Development Kit 5.0 (JDK TM 5.0). You can download the Windows version now. . . . (Make sure you download the JDK, not the JRE.) Consult the installation instructions. . . .

2. A text editor. In this example, we'll use NotePad, a simple editor included with the Windows platforms. You can easily adapt these instructions if you use a different text editor.

These two items are all you need to write your first application.

Sun Developer Network *(http://java.sun.com/docs/books/tutorial/getStarted/*
cupojava/win32.html#win32-1)

The language of this paragraph refers to operating systems that most people have installed on their computers, and then it adds terms that visitors interested in tutorials may already be familiar with: "application" (another word for "software program"), "text editor" (a program that displays text when we type it, without adding formatting code such as that used by common word processing programs), and "download" (copying a file from another computer system to our own). The deeper we click into Sun's Java tutorial Web site, the more technical the language becomes. Even then, the tutorials are written methodically and clearly so that even relative newcomers to programming and to programming languages can follow the lessons and patterns established:

In the Java programming language, all source code is first written in plain text files ending with the .java extension. Those source files are then compiled into .class files by the Java compiler (javac). A .class file does not contain code that is native to your processor; it instead contains bytecodes—the machine language of the Java Virtual Machine. The Java launcher tool (java) then runs your application with an instance of the Java Virtual Machine.

Sun Developer Network *(http://java.sun.com/docs/books/tutorial/*
getStarted/intro/definition.html)

At this point, the reader is expected to be someone who has already invested some time, interest, and effort into the complex activity of programming in Java. Every sentence contains at least one term that is not considered common knowledge outside the community of computer programmers. The writer at this point can assume a fairly high level of engagement between the tutorial text and the site visitor: Programmers understand that the specialized language has been created so that objects and concepts with technical names can be precisely identified and manipulated properly.

EXERCISE 5.1

Visit a site that is designed for visitors who have some expertise in a sport, hobby, or pastime that you are interested in. Find and list every term that is specific to the site's technical subject matter. Include all terms that are unusual or unknown to the average reader who does not share this professional or recreational interest. Using a 5-point scale, evaluate and then describe and explain your evaluation of the level of technical expertise required to understand:

- The home page
- Pages with instructional articles

- Opinion pages
- Discussion boards or other interactive posts
- News and events pages

SCALE:

1 Not technical
2 Introduces technical language
3 Some technical ability required
4 Very technical
5 Experts only

Note: For best results, steer away from widely generic/familiar topics such as football, basketball, NASCAR, cooking, shopping sites, major portal sites, and news-center sites. Best results come from sites that are aimed at specialized knowledge: agriculture, astronomy, meteorology, law, environmental science, chemical testing, geological survey, and the like—interests that require a fairly high degree of technical expertise.

Assignment 5.1

Use search engines, Web glossaries, online dictionaries, and/or CD-ROM resources to locate and write definitions of the following terms *in your own words*. Create a glossary Web page, making sure your definitions are precise, correct, and complete—if appropriate, use examples and descriptive language to make your definitions clear to people who are not familiar with the terms.

cyberspace	IRC	multimedia
e-commerce	Listserv	online trolling
filesharing	MUD, MOO, MUSH	virtual reality

SOME HELPFUL RULES FOR DEVELOPING STYLE

Style in writing tends to refer to "how you say it" rather than "what you said." Obviously, style and content cannot be so easily separated—"what we say" is directly contained in the words that make up "how we say it." But when writers choose a style for conveying ideas or information, they draw from patterns of diction (word choices), syntax (word order), and usage (rules and principles) they have become accustomed to seeing in various categories of written texts. Writing for Web sites is challenging not because writers are given a limited amount of space to write in, but because they are often expected to convey a large amount of clearly expressed, crucial information within that limited space. Although many styles of writing can be said to have certain *conventions*—generally agreed-upon principles and forms— "Web writing" is not actually one style.

Creating the textual content for an effective Web site is often more about adapting to many different kinds of styles, and it is also about being able to adapt the written information to the multimedia environments unique to the computer screen. Web writers can be called upon to write in a "business" style for their interoffice local area network (LAN) sites and for Web sites that company employees and managers are expected to use as resources. The same writers may need to understand what has come to be called "database" style as well—a form of writing that has become crucial to object-oriented sites that call up various elements from different databanks and assemble them together on a page (such as shopping Web sites and information-heavy search engine sites). Companies also tend to call upon their technical writers to put together online news releases, trade publications, and in-house newsletters that are expected to conform to the conventions of journalism, possibly even the strict requirements of the Associated Press style manuals.

Web writers can be called upon to use specific approaches to many different kinds of textual content, but these styles can be learned and applied, even though the stylistic conventions tend to gather into groupings that appear to be arbitrary and artificial. It is therefore important to follow several rules of style:

Style Rule 1: Read everything you can get your hands on.

Expose yourself to many different styles of written expression—business transactions, memoranda, legal documents, news reports, poetry, fiction, nonfiction, political treatises, scientific articles, art criticism, academic essays, technical manuals—the more styles you are exposed to, the more models you have to work from.

It may seem irrelevant to the project of constructing good Web sites to say that it is important to read widely and read well, but this is, in the end, the most effective and intensive way to expose ourselves to the possibilities of style. It is not enough to simply read other Web sites and imitate them, although it is a good idea to do so. Style is something that emerges from a deep and extensive knowledge of the best works a language and culture have to offer. If we only expose ourselves to Web site writing, we quickly exhaust the range of possibilities from which to draw when we construct a new site. Many Web sites are poorly written, simply because they have not gone through an extensive editing and reviewing process before their "publication."

Strong writers are people who read voraciously, always with an eye cocked to catch unusual and powerful strategies that other writers have incorporated into their works. It is easy to dismiss this vital element of a writer's development and to assume that reading works of history, philosophy, literature, and science are a waste of valuable time. But writing for the Web is not one isolated style. Good Web writers and developers are eager to draw from every possible resource they can find to create something new, exciting, and compelling. Success for Internet developers is based upon the ability to capture and hold the attention of an increasingly attention-deficient audience. Web surfers become impatient within a few seconds, unless they are given either (a) exactly what they want and expect or (b) something intriguing and worthy of their reading and viewing time. They want something that entertains and delights them enough to keep them reading and to make them come back for more. If they don't get it, they simply move on.

Writers, then, must know how to employ at least two kinds of general writing abilities: (a) how to write cleanly and accurately in expected, user-satisfying styles and (b) how to develop exciting and stimulating new kinds of writing that will attract the attention and hold the interest of those fickle, click-happy Internet surfers. We acquire the ability to satisfy expectations simply by learning the established formatting and styles that have been developed and standardized in different industrial and professional fields, and we can learn them by looking at examples of various kinds of writing in the workplace.

The second ability, the ability to develop new and innovative styles, is something writers often describe in vague terms, partly because most of the grammatical, mechanical, and figurative bits and pieces that go together to make up any one writer's style have been assimilated and internalized by those who read a great deal. Many writers and critics are hard pressed to explain exactly what it is that makes the work of Amy Tan or of Sarah Vowell so unusual or distinctive. But we do have a sense of each writer's uniqueness. We can chatter all night about the "clean" style of Hemingway, or the "evocative" nature of Eavan Boland's poetry, or the "warm humor" of Erma Bombeck. But until we actually read what they wrote, we haven't seen them in action, and we can't dissect or analyze what they have done. Until we actually experience the work itself—until we read insatiably and read widely—we really can't claim to have much of a "toolbox" available for our own Web writing.

> *Style Rule 2: Learn about the parts of speech, the basic elements of sentences, and sentence structures so that you understand the kinds of choices other writers have made.*

At the very least, as a writing professional you should be able to identify the eight basic parts of speech: the verb, the noun, the pronoun, the adjective, the adverb, the preposition, the conjunction, and the interjection. Writers also need to know about simple, complex, and compound sentences. They need to know about branching and cumulative types of sentences. It is *crucial* to know the materials and the tools we're working with if we are going to make any confident or consistently successful choices in our work. Writers who are in the dark about how phrases and clauses combine to inform, describe, persuade, and narrate are basically uninformed about their own basic tools. They are cabinet makers who don't understand hinges and joints. They are plumbers without wrenches. If we lack understanding of the patterns of logic and thought within English sentences, we perpetuate error and confusion. If we take some time to strengthen our analytical skills with language, then we not only gain an entire workshop full of tools to use, but we also become more closely attuned to the nuances and persuasive strategies of other communicators in the commercial, political, and private sectors of our lives.

> *Style Rule 3: Learn about genres, movements, trends, major influences, famous writers, crossover influences, and historical periods.*

Many technical writers feel that it is somehow wrong to draw upon artistic influences, but technical communication is as much an art as it is a skill. Artists spend a great deal of time and energy informing themselves about the history and major movements and trends in their fields. The best painters, musicians, sculptors, architects, photographers, and authors always learn as much as they can about many different forms and styles. The early works of the great abstract painter Pablo Picasso and of surrealist Salvador Dalí include quite "traditional" landscapes and figure studies. Rock singer Linda Rondstadt surprised and delighted her fans when she crossed over to record torch songs, and then put together an album of Spanish tunes. Rocket scientist David Brin is an award-winning science fiction writer who also publishes scientific journal articles. Each of these artists unabashedly studied and learned from others who had previously mastered various techniques. Because they are professionals, expected to produce results, they know that style is not an accident: It is the result of persistent practice and intensive study. The more genres and styles you expose yourself to, the more options you'll have when tackling your writing projects.

Writers should know about traditional forms and also about the many nonconformist approaches to style. Some of the great authors establish some kind of a "trademark" device. Emily Dickinson's poems exploit slant-rhyme and are heavily decorated with dashes. F. Scott Fitzgerald's novels are as piercingly visual and dramatically constructed as any play or movie script, because he works hard to find accurate language to describe settings and actions in direct, active sentences. Erma Bombeck's anecdotes are funny because she sets up the reader's expectations with a predictable-sounding clause or sentence, then twists the content at the end with fresh comparisons. Each writer will exploit and craft the language around particular features and preferences used in others' writings. Stylistic devices were developed from already-existing features of spoken and written English; very few writers invent their own style from scratch. Most expose themselves to a huge number of novels, poetry, and documentation in the workplace, so that they have a huge repertoire of devices from which to choose. Even memoranda (usually called memos) in the workplace can have historical impact. Imagine the kinds of writerly decisions that U.S. presidents must make when composing history-making memoranda such as the one Harry Truman wrote when he "fired" General Douglas MacArthur from the job of leading troops in the Pacific:

> With deep regret I have concluded that General of the Army Douglas MacArthur is unable to give his wholehearted support to the policies of the United States Government and of the United Nations in matters pertaining to his official duties. In view of the specific responsibilities imposed upon me by the Constitution of the United States and the added responsibility which has been entrusted to me by the United Nations, I have decided that I must make a change of command in the Far East. I have, therefore, relieved General MacArthur of his commands and have designated Lt. Gen. Matthew B. Ridgway as his successor.[2]

The style used in this statement is in no way inflammatory or abusive, even though the two high-profile men had a notoriously stormy professional relationship. Writers who know a bit about historical documents will understand that such carefully chosen phrases as "unable to give his wholehearted support" is a euphemism for "this

---

[2]Truman, Harry S. "Statement and Order by the President on Relieving General MacArthur of His Commands." 11 April, 1951.

person is an uncooperative prima donna" (Truman called MacArthur a few other, more colorful names, as well).

Style Rule 4: Imitate different styles.

Learning to use styles expected in scientific, medical, legal, and other specialized settings means that a writer must become meticulous and precise in ways that will pay off in the real world. It is not an exaggeration to say that one comma misplaced in a legal document can have dire consequences in the settlement of a criminal or civil case. Drug and chemical companies usually employ in-house technical writers who have extensive knowledge and understand the scientific and industrial applications of the information they organize and transmit. Imagine the level of technical, scientific, medical, legal, and editorial expertise required to assemble a drug company Web site featuring databases that describe the effects, dosages, and known side effects of various prescription and over-the-counter drugs.

Style guides and resources are available for constructing print and online documents that conform to conventions of different fields and subjects. It is important for technical writers of all kinds to know where they can find these resources. When faced with the task of constructing a Web site that must conform to the conventions and style manuals of a specific field or discipline, nothing can substitute for actual samples of the kind of writing we're being asked to do. Technical writers often ask content experts to provide them with a variety of documents and correspondences that already conform to the styles they want the written content of their Web sites to use.

EXERCISE 5.2

Voltaire said: "All styles are good except the tiresome kind." What features in some Web writing do you think are "tiresome"? Why? Give examples.

Assignment 5.2

"Translate" the following doctoral dissertation–style paragraph into language that might best be suited for a different audience. You might, for example, paraphrase the text so that it is suited for (a) a sixth-grade social studies Web site, (b) a science fiction hypertext story, (c) a college freshman history studies Web site, (d) a 'zine (online magazine or periodical) such as *Slate* or *Salon*.

> Technologies arrive often as a result of military or industrial development. Advances in civil engineering, manufacturing, information technology, food production, and product distribution technologies result from economic and political prioritization, which is to say, that is where the money is. Technologies developed in one sector of a society often benefit others through adaptation and extension of principles, infrastructure,

and production resources. Word processing technology, for example, was developed originally not for literary or educational purposes, but for the purpose of "information exchange" in military and scientific projects. If we allow a broad definition of "word processing" to mean the general storage and display of alphanumeric characters on printout or video display, then we might even allow that the word storage and display technology proceeds from a set of scientific and military-industrial assumptions about the nature and uses of written language.

6

Important Styles for Commercial Web Sites

- Commercial Styles
- Business Style
- Database Style
- Marketing Style

Glossary Terms

Adware
Document
Spyware
Table

COMMERCIAL STYLES

Within the context of each Web site, a writer must adjust his or her approach—word choices, sentence types, paragraph length, level of formality—to the purpose of each page. Writers adjust to the purpose of each unit of writing within these pages as well, and to the purpose behind text that appears within small pop-up windows that may be linked to the main pages. In Chapter 5 we looked at general constraints that affect Web writing: subject, timeliness, audience, and purpose. This chapter discusses the most common styles used for commercial Web sites and describes their specific features.

Writers often consider style to be a very personal, individual set of choices and techniques that do not lend themselves to formulaic reproduction or imitation. Style is frequently described in vague, intuitive language that may evoke feelings about the way a text is written, but it does nothing to further our understanding of the actual mechanics involved. Critics (in the arts) and managers (in the workplace) often use terms such as "friendly," "harsh," "clean," or "convoluted" to describe the writing of others. Terms such as these seem descriptive but actually only describe the feeling invoked in the reader. These descriptions do not explain the nuts and bolts elements that the writer used to achieve the desired (or in many cases, accidental or even undesired) effects. In this chapter we look at some of the specific, reproducible forms and techniques used to produce various Web writing styles.

This chapter discusses and demonstrates three of the most common styles of writing that corporate and commercial Web developers will ask for:

1. Business style—writing strategies used for corporate Web sites, local area network (LAN) webbed environments, and online business documents
2. Database style—writing strategies for Web-based information management systems
3. Marketing style—writing strategies for online retail marketing and sales

BUSINESS STYLE

Businesses use the Web and local area networks to store and provide access to a great deal of information that is necessary for their day-to-day operations. As Web browser software has become capable of finding more kinds of files online—such as Microsoft Word documents and Adobe Acrobat .pdf documents stored on remote servers—they have been set up to launch the associated software so that many of these commonly used **documents** have ported over to the Web in a way that appears seamless to the average user. For workers who must locate, download, modify, and make use of these documents, this is good news. But for Web managers in the workplace, the management of different kinds of document formatting can be a challenge. Each time a regulation or policy changes, many different documents can be affected, and a clear, businesslike style of writing will be required and expected by readers at all levels in the corporate chain of command.

Workplace writers can be lulled into a false sense of security about the level of formality required when their writing is put online. Many workers tend to use habits they have developed through home use of the Internet in e-mail, instant messaging, and special-interest message boards. But these styles are casual and unfiltered. They often foster misunderstandings and even flame wars (argumentative exchanges featuring abusive language and personal, verbal attacks). This level of informality and lack of editorial oversight within the context of the workplace often leads to a great deal of confusion and miscommunication.

Writing that is placed online, whether it is on a local area network or a public Internet server, often is not password protected and can be downloaded and read by anyone who has a network connection and access to the file server. This wider spectrum of audiences complicates the writer's job, for it multiplies the risk of misinterpretation. Workers can easily lift chunks of text from one document and paste them into another, sometimes not bothering to completely proofread and clarify the information they are dropping into a new context. The availability of online business documents supports a cut-and-paste culture in which any number of people can move discrete units of data around so quickly and easily that the possible ways of combining information become almost infinite. Therefore managers and administrators must think seriously about the manner in which they wish their electronic business documents to be created, formatted, and distributed in the first place.

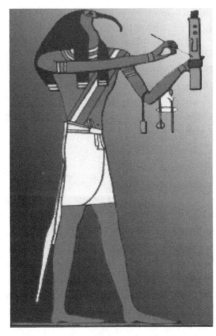

FIGURE 6.1   "Take a memo? Hmm . . . Dog-head, dog-head, squiggly lines, ibis, ibis, huge eye-of-Ra . . . Yours truly, Amen-Hotep."

As an example, consider an e-mail message that an office manager sends to everyone in his department. Attached to the message is a table of data for the department's monthly report. One recipient takes the data and enters it into a spreadsheet program to make further calculations. Another office worker asks for a copy of the spreadsheet so that she can upload it to a LAN Web forum later in the week. A third worker pastes the table of data into an early draft of the annual report. A fourth person copies one column of figures from the spreadsheet because they apply to her own team's project; she pastes the figures into a memo to be printed before a team meeting that afternoon.

An added complication for technical Web writers comes from well-meaning clients who, new to the world of Internet resources and capabilities, are susceptible to "Internet mania." In their zeal to "take it live online," these clients may ask writers to create hyperlinks and multimedia versions of a wide variety of standard documents. Some of these innovations are exciting and can increase usability for many workers. Others, when handled with little overall planning or design, can create more problems than solutions, frequently in the name of "coolness."

It is best to be wary of clients and supervisors who become excited about cool Web sites. Being cool is a relative perception, and for business writers the coolest kind of writing is the kind that moves information in clear, understandable, and usable ways. In the workplace, it is not unusual for technical writers to spend as much time talking with workers and executives about their specific needs and procedures as they spend actually writing, revising, and editing. Web writing in a business environment entails all of these things *plus* a responsibility to explain to zealous clients and managers the advantages and drawbacks of placing various kinds of documentation online. A powerful local area network can provide a terrific means for online collaboration and documentation. But displaying documents on large networks also means paying attention to security issues. Before uploading business documents to any LAN, WAN, or Internet server, make sure that its availability online will not breach any privacy or security policies.

EXERCISE 6.1

Following is a short list of the most common types of business writing formats that will appear in hypertext environments. Working as a class or in groups, find some examples of each document online. List and then discuss (or write about) the ways each document could be "complicated" by the use of hyperlinks and online Web site technologies, including graphics and sound.

Memorandum	Performance review	Press release
Résumé	Interoffice e-mail	Newsletter
Executive summary	Timesheet	Pricing policy
Proposal	Annual report	Procedures manual
Job description	Business letter	Insurance forms
Invoice	Balance sheet	Inventory

Some Features of Business Style

Business writing emphasizes discipline and conformity rather than creative expression. At first this may seem a stifling principle, but learning to craft powerful, efficient sentences within the constraints required by business can be exciting! Good writing can get things going, win contracts, attract investors, sell products, and solve communication problems that might otherwise cripple a company.

Business Writing Is Precise and Correct

There is no room for error when profits, contracts, delivery schedules, and the company's reputation are all on the line. In the business world, writing that has not been corrected for error and content is judged as hasty, careless, uncaring, and uninformed. Furthermore, professionals report that when they are given materials containing faulty sentences, they feel that the writer may be a person who does not think things through and perhaps is altogether unable to think logically. Writing researcher Larry Beason found that writers who do not catch and correct errors in their own work can be seen as people who do not handle details well and who "might overlook other (and often more important) details connected with their jobs." For Web writers, the message about correctness and precision should be loud and clear. Business owners and professionals consider sentence-level errors to be "junior high stuff," and some professionals may even harshly judge the writer to be a sloppy or lazy business person.

Business Writing Is Blunt and to the Point

Executives need to access information as quickly and easily as possible, which is one reason they often migrate important charts, flowsheets, and documents to corporate computer networks. They need to be able to locate information resources and files, scan the pages quickly, and be able to make sense of what is represented on the page. Text-filled screens unbroken by markers, pointers, or subheadings look like a sea of gray when the regional manager on the phone needs data *now*. Long, flowing sentences with multiple clauses and modifiers tend to impede clarity when people want facts quickly. When adapting writing style for business environments, remember these tips:

- Shorter, active-voice sentences help readers get to the information faster.

  Too long: For all intents and purposes, fiscal responsibility generally depends on certain factors that are really more psychological and ethical in kind than on any given budgetary aspect of management.

  Better: Fiscal responsibility depends more on psychology and ethics than on budgetary factors.

- Cut out fluffy explanatory phrases and use direct connectors to help readers see cause-and-effect relationships more quickly.

  Too indirect: It is possible that the implementation of last quarter's new payroll policy resulted in the occasional unfortunate delay in disbursement of employee salary payments.

  Better: Payroll checks arrived late three times last quarter because of the new policy.

- Break up long and rambling descriptive phrases and clauses.

  Too rambling: It goes without saying that we are acquainted with your procedures for filing shipping orders, and we have every intention of complying with the ISO standards that you have asked us to look at.

  Better: We plan to comply with your procedures and the required ISO standards.

- Condense passages by replacing long-winded sections with precise terminologies and bulleted lists.

  Imprecise: We plan to attract business by advertising sale items in the spring such as harness and bridle equipment used for training horses, outdoor-ready horse blankets, and various kinds of enriched dietary products for horses.

Better:

In our spring sale we plan to feature

- running martingales
- turnout blankets
- feed supplements

In addition to these writing strategies, be sure to use visual strategies to make important units of information easy to find, interpret, and transmit:

- "Chunk" information (see the discussion in Chapter 3) into sections that can be easily moved around. Stand-alone chunks can port into meeting presentations and related documents such as contract proposals, standard forms, and annual reports with minimal editing.
- Create charts, graphs, and diagrams to make numerical data easier to study.
- Use hypertext and multimedia enhancements sparingly and only when they improve the usability (and usefulness) of an online document.
- Consider using **tables** to ensure text and graphic placement and alignment on the screen. Whether sites are constructed using templates, frames, or individual HTML pages, browser and monitor settings will affect the way written data are displayed. In the example in Figure 6.2, a one-cell table was used to place the graphical chart in the upper-left-hand corner of another one-cell table, to ensure placement within a frame or browser window.

Business Writing Does Appeal to Emotions

Business research and reports often contain both good and bad news. Reporting on statistics and budgets may seem a dry and thankless job, but expert business writers know that even grim facts and projections should be framed in ways that are useful and encouraging. Rather than simply dumping the raw numbers on the company network, the Web writer's task is to dig further and deeper into the market, the economy, and the company's internal structures to create resources and links that will lead to workable solutions. Obviously it is important to follow standards of ethics and report only the realistic, truthful picture at all times. But there are ways to handle information that may be disheartening or even frightening without hiding the facts:

- First, prepare the reader for shocking or disappointing news. If executives are likely to react with disbelief or denial, writers can affect how the information is received. Present the information in firm and realistic terms: A problem can't be solved until it is acknowledged. "The report we requested has arrived, and some serious issues are facing the company this quarter. According to Arbitron, the station's ratings have dipped significantly since the new format was introduced."
- Next, point toward action that can solve the problem. Provide reliable research into available solutions and options. Readers will be more calm and ready to act

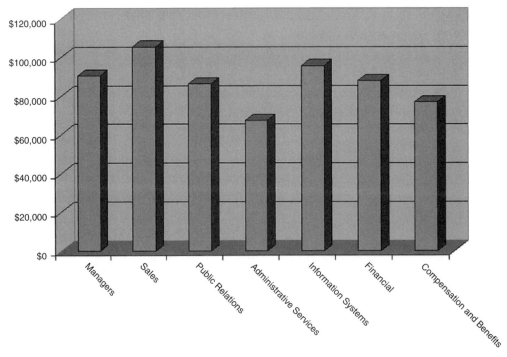

FIGURE 6.2   Tables force alignment of graphics and text. Web link URLs should always be visible, because statistical data are often printed out for reference (meetings, presentations, bound reports, etc.) in the workplace. United States Bureau of Labor Statistics, *http://www.bls.gov*.

upon information if they are told, "The current marketing approach does not have a high success rate industry-wide. However, following is a summary gleaned from recent studies that show how ratings can be improved by adding some standard features to morning and evening drive times."

- Finally, maintain a professional, respectful tone whether the news is good or bad. Rough, sarcastic, sexist, or insensitive language will certainly reflect back upon the writer. It will mark him or her as unsophisticated or even hostile.
- In addition, be keenly aware of your readership within the company and its subsidiaries. An announcement that may cheer one group or team within the company may broadcast bad news for another. For example, chirpily announcing, "Great news! We're outsourcing 300 jobs!" could be a notification of shut-downs and massive layoffs for a large sector of the corporation.

Business Writing Is Task-Driven

When writing for business and corporate sites, the first question writers need to ask themselves and their managers is, "What am I trying to *accomplish*?" The best way to assess the success or failure of a business Web site is to discover whether it has done the job everyone was hoping for. Because of its task-oriented nature, this kind of site tends to require that the writer develop specific constraints for accomplishing a goal.

A *constraint* is a factor that creates limits or boundaries around a task. If writers think of business documents as instruments that get things done, then it is easy to see how constraints on workplace writing are helpful. The accompanying table is an example of ways that writers can chart the goals or purposes of a business Web site and define writing strategies that may work best. Writers should focus Web materials so that they get the job done for visitors.

Content	Goal	Strategy
Employee benefits information	Help employees manage and understand their benefits.	Provide help files, organized categories, definitions, contact information; use helpful tone.
Annual report	Inform management, investors, governing boards, and workers of corporate gains, losses, achievements, goals, assets, and obligations of the company.	Use powerful editing tools to organize and display a variety of text and graphics; maintain professional and precise language; satisfy different audiences by soliciting feedback from as many different departments and divisions as possible before releasing the report.
Résumé	Display employment record and qualifications; supplement print document; gain employment; provide a reference bank of worker skills for various corporate proposals and reports.	Employ appealing graphical and textual elements; demonstrate ability to use professional language; use hyperlinks to online samples of your work.
Recall announcement	Disclosure and information for the public and government regulating bodies; satisfy legal department; encourage consumers to take advantage of replacement/refund opportunities.	Write in strong, clear, honest language; make sure company legal advisors have vetted the announcement text; reassure consumers that all efforts are being made to remedy the error; apologize for inconvenience to investors and consumers.
Office procedures manual	Provide easy access to standard operating procedures for office managers and workers.	Create usable navigation tools, bulleted lists, links to important information and office resources; use smart indexing/organizing; employ feedback-oriented information management.

EXERCISE 6.2

Evaluate a dozen or so résumés that have been posted online by people who have qualifications and experience similar to yours. Create an online résumé for yourself or someone you know. Experiment with standard and nonstandard layout techniques. When you have finished, write a short cover letter to your instructor (or to the person for whom you created the résumé) explaining your use of various Web elements to enhance your résumé materials and information, such as links to online portfolio items, digital graphics, or multimedia elements.

Assignment 6.1

In a group or as a class, create a plan for a small business Web site (if possible, consider using an actual local business or organization rather than a fictitious one). Consider the types of documentation you should put online (see the following list). You may wish to make a diagram of the structure of the site. Remember to talk about the kinds of constraints that will affect the content, organization, and design of each document.

Office procedures manual	Executive summary	Business letter
Sick leave policies	Employment policies	Insurance forms
Company benefits	Proposal	Inventory
Employee drug testing policy	Marketing survey report	Invoice
Sexual harassment policy	Procedures manual	Balance sheet
Sales and promotion	Job description	Newsletter
Antidiscrimination policy	Customer satisfaction	Press release
Application for employment	survey	safety policy
	Overtime policy	

If the course includes a Web design component, consider creating a small business Web site as a course project. The site may include some or all of these documents.

DATABASE STYLE

Database style refers to methods writers use for content management, especially when they are working with object-oriented sites that assemble and display Web pages from units of information stored in online databases. Writers who work with such sites are operating within specific constraints that govern sets of discrete units of text. Web programmers sometimes ask writers to think in terms of *objects* that contain consistently formatted textual or graphical information. Even traditional documents, when placed online, often have been disassembled into objects. Content elements are then cobbled together or "assembled on-the-fly" by programming scripts that run in the background of the Web server. Users should be unaware of the amount of programming and organization that make the elements come together on their computer screens. They can be easily confused or put off by poorly planned database-driven Web sites. Web browsing programs merely assemble separate, discrete elements on the screen, plugging text and images into assigned (coded) spaces. The assembled "Frankenstein" documents, if not handled carefully, can result in misinformation and inconvenience for workers and customers who are left to make sense of them.

One way to identify database sites is to look in the "Address" window of your browser. The browser will display URLs with long, coded strings of commands, such as shown in Figure 6.3.

Search engines, commercial retail sites, library online catalogs, and news sites all use powerful database systems to store and retrieve information. Online electronic data transfer systems that connect manufacturers, wholesalers, and retail suppliers all depend on databases and the on-screen textual (and graphical) displays that help workers to manage them. Even very small businesses keep their payroll and customer billing information organized in computer databases.

Database elements often comprise one term or a discrete, separate unit of meaning, such as a name, address, zip code, or catalog number. But writing in database style can also mean composing short passages of text that can be called up as objects on preformatted screen pages. To accomplish this, written elements have to follow structured patterns. In addition to ordering types of information in a parallel manner, database writers sometimes deliberately use fragments and phrases in place of full sentences to save space and time. Where possible, database managers try to break information into as many logical units as possible so that users can access what they need by means of as many terms as seem reasonable.

For example, to manage a tropical tree database, we might enter information into specific fields important to landscapers and homeowners. A first pass at organizing information about palm trees might lead us to plan for a lively, descriptive style. But as we work with the database in mind, we might decide to provide specific details in a structured, predictable order so that visitors to the site can easily scan the page for trees that satisfy their needs.

---

http://www.google.com/search?hl=en&lr=&q=%22database+style%22&btnG=Search

http://www.amazon.com/exec/obidos/search-handle-form/002-8931342-2928042

FIGURE 6.3 Database call-up URLs. Lines of code make these Web addresses all but impossible to type out by hand, much less remember. When pointing to these sites, sometimes it's best to include only the domain or home site address and instruct readers to use a keyword in the Web site's database search form.

EXAMPLE: DESCRIPTIVE STYLE VS. DATABASE STYLE

DESCRIPTIVE STYLE

There are many ways to write general information about palm tree varieties. Materials here have been supplied in an unstructured, inconsistent style. The information is useful and interesting, but different features and qualities are given for each variety listed. For a magazine or specialized customer catalog, this format could work fine. But for a database, the style is too loose and could produce frustrating results. Readers might find information only if they know the specific scientific names for the trees:

1. *Arecastrum romanzoffianum*—Queen Palm: This large palm can grow to 50 feet. The leaves are graceful and arch, where the king palm leaves are rather rigid.
2. *Butia capitata*—The grace of the hourglass figure in the head of this palm does it all by itself. This tree has a slow to moderate rate of growth. I think that rather nice when looking at these upwardly mobile telephone poles.
3. *Phoenix reclinata*—Senegal Date Palm: The slender trunks of the Senegal date palm are magnificent. *Phoenix reclinata* can reach up to 12 meters but is most often between 3 and 6 meters. These trees are a true menace when the fronds are left low enough that they could be run into.
4. *Sabal palmetto*—Cabbage Palm, Blue Palm: The saw palmetto palms are noted for their medicinal properties as well as their tropical beauty. They can get to seventy feet tall, though that would be unlikely here on the West Coast. They have small $\frac{1}{2}$" black fruit.

DATABASE STYLE

Information has been shaped into a consistent structure for each entry so that each tree will be displayed with the same categories of information: (1) common name, (2) scientific name, (3) height, (4) style and shape of leaves, and (5) rate of growth.

1. Queen Palm (*Arecastrum romanzoffianum*):

    Height: Can grow to 50 feet.
    Large; leaves are graceful and arching.
    Can grow 2–3 feet per year.

2. Pindo Palm (*Butia capitata*):

    Height: Normally reaches 12–15 feet.
    Graceful; gray swirled and feathery leaves.
    Grows slowly, less than 1 foot per year.

3. Senegal Date Palm (*Phoenix reclinata*):

    Height: Reaches average height of 25 to 30 feet.
    Security-thick palm; fronds are thick and sharp.
    Grows slowly, less than 1 foot per year.

4. Cabbage Palm (*Sabal palmetto*):

> Height: This ornamental palm can reach 50 to 70 feet.
> Ornamental; leaves are fan-shaped, with some feathery shaping.
> Grows slowly, less than 1 foot per year.

What kinds of grammatical choices have been made in these entries?

For information managers, the structured, consistent format—information written in database style—is easier to handle, especially when a huge amount of information is stored. Each tree can be entered into the database for fast reference and call-up, as shown in the search form in Figure 6.4.

Database style is used when every element called up on the screen must be phrased and organized in a consistent format. Chunks of written information have to add up to readable, logical information no matter how the different items are combined. Consistent formatting and style are even more important when searches and call-ups can consist of several different values that are combined. For example, retail Web sites frequently handle hundreds, even thousands of bits of information that assemble on their product catalog pages: Item names, images, model numbers, catalog numbers, prices, colors, styles, shipping costs, sales tax, and service charges are called up when customers or sales representatives look for product information. Government and institutional Web sites must likewise be capable of handling vast amounts of digitized data. An example of a government data retrieval page is shown in Figure 6.5.

Writers may think that composing entries for database call-up can be boring and repetitious. But repetition and consistency of terms, phrases, category names, and numerical values create pages that are scannable. Readers appreciate the ease with which they can run their eyes over well-organized and consistent screens of data and information.

Common Name:	Submit	Reset
Scientific Name:	Submit	Reset
Height:	Submit	Reset
Style of Leaves:	Submit	Reset
Rate of Growth:	Submit	Reset

FIGURE 6.4 Database search forms should be clearly labeled and structured so that data can be structured according to different visitors' needs and priorities.

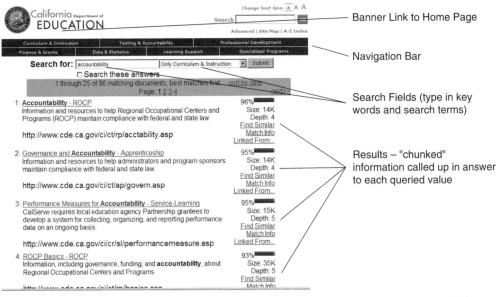

FIGURE 6.5   Database styles: Writers need to work with database administrators (known as *DBAs*) to ensure that information retrieval is easy and effective. *http://www.cde.ca.gov/scripts/texis.exe/webinator/ search?pr=default&prox=page&rorder=750&rprox=750&rdfreq=250&rwfreq=0&rlead=750&sufs=1& order=r&query=accountability&cq=1&submit=Submit*

Assignment 6.2 Writing in Database Style

Work alone or with a classmate, using the information bank in the accompanying, "Palm Tree Varieties."

1. Use an Internet search engine to find and write out the specific kinds of details researchers and purchasers will want to know about each variety of palm tree. (Note: In a previous example, height, leaf type, and growth rate were used, but there are other features that customers and researchers might be interested in, as well).

2. Enter information into the "Description" field for each tree, rewriting and editing as you go, so that each one is uniformly phrased. For example, if you decide that active voice is best for describing the tree, use active voice for *all* tree descriptions. Keep the following in mind:

   ■ Who is the audience for a Web site containing this information?
   ■ What are they going to do with the information?
   ■ How much description will they need?

3. Next, using paper and pencil or a computer application with which you are comfortable, work out various page layouts that would make sense

for displaying the information. In what order should information in each entry be displayed?

4. Finally, make a list of appropriate keywords that can go into a database index so that visitors to the site can easily call up the trees and pricing information they need. For example, customers might be more interested in keywords such as price, size, color, and sunlight/water requirements. Researchers might be more interested in each variety's resistance to disease and region of origin.

Optional: If there is time and the appropriate software tools are available, create a small database with your palm tree information and discuss or write about the challenges and advantages of writing, organizing, and revising your information ahead of time.

Palm Tree Varieties   To order call toll free 1-800-555-PALM

Formal Name	Common Name	Available	Price	Description
Archontophoenix cunninghamiana	King Palm	3 feet to 15 feet, single and multi-trunked trees	$50/foot	
Arecastrum romanzoffianum	Queen Palm	10 feet to 30 feet	$50/foot	
Brahea armata	Mexican Blue Palm, Blue Hesper Palm	24" box 36" box	$95.00 $145.00	
Butia capitata	Pindo Palm, Jelly Palm	24" box 36" box	$125.00 $175.00	
Chamaerops humilis	Mediterranean Fan Palm	1 foot to 12 feet	$45/foot	
Howea forsteriana	Kentia Palm, Paradise Palm, Sentry Palm	1 foot to 12 feet	$250/foot	
Livistona australis	Australian Fan Palm	15 gallon box 24" box 1 foot to 15 feet	$75.00 $100.00 $95/foot	
Livistona decipians	Ribbon Fan Palm	1 foot to 15 feet	$95/foot	
Phoenix canariensis	Canary Island Date Palm	24" box Field grown to 15 feet	$95.00 $65/foot	
Phoenix roebelenii	Pygmy Date Palm	1 foot to 12 feet	$95/foot	
Washingtonia filifera	California Native Fan Palm	1 foot to 12 feet	$50/foot	

MARKETING STYLE

Most of us associate marketing language with its worst, most obnoxious exemplars:

- Exaggerated claims:

    "Lose 30 pounds in 2 weeks!"
    "Draw this cartoon and enjoy a lucrative graphic arts career!"
    "Guaranteed to find your perfect mate!"

- Over-the-top adjectives and adverbs:

    "Zestiest sauce you've ever found in a jar!"
    "Most powerful V-8 engine in the world!"
    "Newer, better, faster than ever before."

- Sweeping generalizations:

    "No other bank cares as much as we do."
    "Everyone you know will want one."
    "All other suppliers envy us."

- High-pressure language:

    "Act now—limited offer!"
    "Only 3 days left to buy!"
    "Buy now or pay more!"

- Impressive but unlikely credentialing:

    "Top recording artists" (but . . . you've never heard of them—)
    "Our trained investment advisers" (who took a mail-order class—)
    "Experienced pilots!" (big deal; it takes flight experience to get a pilot's
        license—)

- Superlatives:

    "Greatest new & used car deals in the nation."
    "You've never felt this good."
    "The best-tasting ice cream ever!"

Advertisers and marketing executives frequently employ *push* Web technologies. A push technology is one that electronically displays unrequested—and often unexpected—advertising materials onto the computer screen. Many people are irritated by pop-up windows that appear when they are searching or browsing the Web; these windows often are programmed to "pop" onto the screen in multiple, cascading groups that are sometimes difficult to get rid of. Such programming practices can make anyone's Web surfing miserable. Internet marketers have continued to use these pop-up advertisements even though most Internet users have a negative reaction to them, and a number of Internet service providers have worked to create software that can block them. The problem, according to many who study the Internet as a marketing and communication phenomenon, is that the Internet has created an "economy of attention." Advertisers claim that the busy, multimedia-crowded screens of Internet portals and high-traffic news sites have placed people's attention at a premium, and that they need to take bolder, ever more extreme technological measures to grab attention.

Although marketing experts point out that such annoying practices must be working (or why else would advertisers risk so much negative reaction?), most Web analysts have begun to advise smarter approaches to using Internet sites and software to advertise products. Pop-up windows, automatic redirect scripting (Web pages that automatically send users to a commercial product Web site), and unsolicited e-mail advertising messages (known as *spam*) are all ways to push products and services into the faces of thousands of users each day. But the more annoying and nerve-wracking these practices become, the more likely consumers may be to support legislation that restricts and controls Web marketing practices.

What *does* stand between consumers and the worst snake-oil abuses of advertising claims and offers is the federal Truth in Advertising Act. Because Section 5 of the Act declares "unfair or deceptive acts or practices" to be unlawful, most marketing and advertising executives have a healthy respect for the power of words to get them into legal trouble and to keep them out of it. Therefore the wording of special claims and offers in advertising can be tricky to master. Writers must be extra careful that they aren't promising the impossible or offering undeliverable products and services. These truth in advertising laws are the reason we see advertisements for weight-loss products that claim "Use our supplement *together with a recommended program of diet and exercise* and we guarantee results!" These ads often sell the product quite successfully, even though it seems likely that diet and exercise alone would have the same results. Their on-screen spokespersons wear lab coats and speak sympathetically about the difficulties of losing weight through diet and exercise alone. Marketing experts know that the lab coat and sympathetic tone are more powerful selling instruments than the carefully worded copy. When an authoritative-looking scientific "expert" speaks so sympathetically to us, we may not be listening too carefully to what he is saying.

On the Web, messages do not just go one-way from the advertiser to the viewer, as they do in other media such as network television and broadcast radio. The Web is interactive, and if visitors are annoyed by flashing, obnoxious messages they simply ignore them or find ways to block them. All the more reason to use sharp, clean, appealing text. Marketing is selling, and selling means persuading visitors that what we're offering is worth their hard-earned cash. In fact, modern psychology can show writers how to choose strategies that make sense and work persuasively. In *Influence: The Psychology of Persuasion,* Robert Cialdini describes seven major categories of persuasion used by professionals: value, reciprocation, commitment and consistency, social proof, liking, authority, and scarcity.

Value

To psychologists, this particular persuasive strategy is obvious and can be taken as a given. Who would not be inclined to want a good thing at a terrific price (or even free) with no strings? On the Internet, however, visitors and online shoppers tend to be leery of "something-for-nothing" offers. The "click here for free stuff" download link can result in the unintentional installation of **spyware** or **adware**—small, hidden programs that send out browser data, download advertising scripts, and work other kinds of hacking mischief—on a personal computer. For this reason, it is important to ease the concerns of (understandably) cautious visitors to a Web site by explaining the privacy policies of your company in clear language. If the site you are writing for is owned by programmers who do plan to engage in such "stealth download" practices, you should rethink your decision to work for them. As their Web copy writer/editor, you could be liable for any legal action that may be brought against them.

Reciprocation

One of the most powerful psychological principles of social interaction and persuasion is the urge to return favors and gifts in kind. A number of cost-free Internet sites ask that for the privilege of access to their pages we "subscribe" by providing personal information. Such personal information can be bought and sold to advertisers and mass-marketers for substantial sums of money, so smart Web users tend to look carefully at these sites' privacy policies before providing their personal data. Often, users simply fill in false data to prevent Web site owners from making use of their information. Many "subscriber access only" news sites offer news that is otherwise available; news services such as the Associated Press and Knight-Ridder often sell the same stories to dozens of publications. Subscribers are told that access to online materials is being offered *in return for* users' demographic information, and people sign up because it seems fair *to give something in return* for reader privileges. But good Web marketers avoid resorting to empty offers or bait-and-switch tactics. When a good product is offered at a good price, it is our job to say so. As writers we can make this happen by:

- Letting buyers know exactly what they are getting by describing the products or services in crisp, straightforward language
- Making sure customers understand how the offered value stands up to comparison shopping
- Explaining to shoppers and casual visitors all of the reasons it is a good idea to buy from our company, including any extra amenities such as easy shipping terms and toll-free telephone support services

Writing from a forthright model of reciprocity based upon good value for the customer's money builds good customer relations. From a buyer's perspective, this kind of "value-for-the-money" marketing is satisfying because customers not only feel they have been treated fairly, they also receive an equitable exchange, a fundamental social interaction we psychologically crave.

Commitment and Consistency

Marketing strategists understand that people tend to build psychological supports and frameworks to hold up their decisions and commitments. The principle of commitment and consistency is in place when we observe people buying their favorite music group's latest CD (even when they admit they don't like it very much); it is at work when we observe couples remaining together long after the relationship has become irreparably broken; and it is in place when your best friend is still buying that awful, cheap brand of beer the two of you drank in college. Once these beliefs and assumptions are in place, they become more solid and difficult to jar loose over time. When advertisers tap into these tendencies, they can help buyers, subscribers, and investors to make decisions. It helps if writers can construct persuasive ad copy that is consistent with the personal, community, and professional identities people have constructed for themselves. Writers can employ specific approaches to align their products with the common types of self-image and commitments their customers envision. A few of these strategies are quite familiar:

- Definition—to clarify, to complicate, to compare/contrast, and to assign parts/duties/roles to the reader: "You've always been an *original* thinker, ahead of your time—and our *original* line of skiwear is designed to keep up with you!"
- Repetition—to emphasize familiar values and identification markers: "American workmanship, American quality, and American style."
- Familiar sayings, conventional phrases, and "feel good" aphorisms that reassure buyers about their world view: "Holiday meals delivered, just like Mom used to make!" "A day without orange juice is like a day without sunshine."
- Praising the qualities of regular customers and subsidiaries: "Choosy mothers choose Jif®."

Social Proof

Another strong behavioral influence that marketers tap into is the principle that, when in doubt, people tend to do what those around them are doing. In most civilized societies, this serves to create smooth social events and peaceful coexistence. Although most of us would agree that intelligent, money-wise customers would smirk at "monkey-see, monkey-do" sales pitches, the principle of social proof should not be ignored. It can work in a company's favor to show that visitors to the Web site belong to a special and worthwhile social group. It helps to use language that reinforces the feeling of social belonging. Several techniques can accomplish in a brief space the heavy lifting necessary to emphasize feelings of community and belonging. These strategies include some common slogan types:

- Appositives—descriptive phrases that reinforce identity: "The few, the proud, the Marines."
- Playful celebration of the "in" group of customers and clients: "I'm a Pepper. He's a Pepper. She's a Pepper. We're a Pepper. Wouldn't you like to be a Pepper too?"
- Reinforcement of positive attributes of the "in" group: "Aren't you glad you use Dial? Don't you wish everybody did?"
- Testimonials—"I'd walk a mile for a Camel." "All my men wear English Leather . . . or they wear nothing at all."
- Appeals to common sense or common experience: "Coke—There's nothing like it when you're thirsty." "Jockey underwear: What the well-dressed man is wearing this year."

A writer's purpose in fostering social identity should be to respond to the natural tendencies in the typical customer, not to force people uncomfortably into a mold or self-image they will want to cast off as soon as the glow of postshopping satisfaction has worn off. Graphics and Web design can only go so far in recreating the kind of environment customers would find if they were in a real-world retail store or dealership.

Web writers may want to remind customers of the social subculture that surrounds a company's products or services. Language can describe the sounds, textures, and smells of the merchandise they like to shop for—smooth leather goods, shiny new cars, tinkling wind chimes, aromatic garden herbs—all of these things have distinctive sounds and smells in the real world. Using words and phrases that simulate environments they enjoy will help readers to recreate the experience and feel good about what you are selling. A sprinkling of "insider" terms and phrases works further to create a group-identity atmosphere, and if used moderately (to avoid alienating newcomers to the group), they can reinforce social identity and encourage customers to frequent a Web site.

Liking

The persuasive principle of liking works because human beings are more likely to be persuaded by people they know (or seem to know) and like (or find generally likable) than by strangers or those they feel uncomfortable about. Advertisers can take advantage of this rule simply because it is not too difficult to create the illusion of familiarity and camaraderie. When an insurance company reassures us that "You're in good hands," it seems touching (well, for a moment at least) that those good people at Allstate cared enough about our feelings to reassure us. There are hundreds of factors that can make us like an individual or group of individuals. One of the most important factors is our overall willingness, as social animals, to like and be liked. According to Cialdini and his researchers, most of the factors that influence liking can be placed into one of several common categories of likeability and familiarity:

- Physical attractiveness is an almost frighteningly powerful element that influences our willingness to be won over. Nobody was surprised when model/actor Kelly LeBrock sold tanker-loads of shampoo simply by pleading in a sultry voice, "Don't hate me because I'm beautiful."
- Similarity is also an important contributor to likeability. Simply put, we all tend to like people who are similar to ourselves, and we like to be reminded of shared likes, dislikes, and desires: "Bet you can't eat just one!" "Everybody doesn't like something, but nobody doesn't like Sara Lee." "I can't believe I ate the whole thing!"
- Compliments also engender liking—we like people who like us and who tell us good things about ourselves: "We believe you're the best parent for your child."
- Contact and cooperation strategies work by creating a context in which the Web visitor sees herself as having worked alongside us toward a common goal

(nonprofit organizations such as Planned Parenthood, Greenpeace, and the National Rifle Association use messages and informative news-style writing on their Web sites to create a sense of camaraderie and "working together"): "Together we can make a difference."

- Social conditioning and association tend to create a positive (liking) or negative (disliking) image of others. Cialdini explains social conditioning and association by pointing out that otherwise reasonable people can often irrationally blame the television weather forecaster for thunderstorm conditions and credit him with sunny skies. Although the individual has no control over meteorological conditions, he is so closely associated with the weather in our minds, and our minds have for so long been conditioned to associate him thus, we can get confused about the relationship he really has to the local weather. In other words, we shouldn't blame the innocent messenger for the message he brings, but by simple association, we want to. So strong is this principle that one daring manufacturer of pain relief medicine centered a half-serious ad campaign around the slogan, "I'm not a doctor, but I play one on TV."

It is important to experiment and test these kinds of "liking" strategies. The Web browser window provides precious little space and time for a writer to make a connection with shoppers and Web surfers. Humor can play a positive role when we want people to like us, but it also signals a lack of formality and can leave the site open to ridicule and scorn. Emotional connection can be great, but sometimes people instinctively back off when they sense we want their affection and loyalty too quickly, before they've had a chance to shop around.

Authority

Some advertisers have astutely increased sales by taking advantage of the deep-seated sense of duty to authority within us all. Titles, clothing, and other trappings of professional power can easily win people over, especially if they are lower-ranking members of the same profession. Studies show, for example, that within our main culture, there is a "hospital subculture" in which nurses tend to follow the orders of doctors with little or no question, even when experimenters posed as MDs and asked for treatments and dosages that were obviously dangerous or inappropriate. Workers in dangerous areas of manufacturing plants sometimes take unnecessary risks simply because they are instructed to by their superiors. The 1986 nuclear disaster in Chernobyl stands as a bleak example of the dangers we can face when authority goes unquestioned, even in the face of overwhelming evidence (workers were asked to trust faulty and falsified operating records rather than their own observations and training). Military personnel will follow orders they know to be questionable. One lone law enforcement officer can contain a crowd and prevent mayhem on the strength of a blue uniform and a badge. College professors sometimes complain that after discovering their title and profession, people defer to them and become dull and acquiescent conversation partners.

Used responsibly, this tendency for people to trust scientific, medical, and political authority can be an important tool to save lives and prevent harm—such authority figures often endorse public service announcements about health and safety recommendations. Used in deceptive or irresponsible ways, the appeal to authority has a huge potential to backfire. When people feel abused or exploited, their trust vanishes. However, when credible evidence and authority can provide valid backing for our claims, the appeal is almost irresistible: "Four out of five dentists surveyed recommend Trident sugarless gum for their patients who chew gum." If we look closely at this well-known, carefully worded claim, we can catch its slant—the Trident company wants to represent its survey information in a favorable light without misrepresenting the common attitude of most dentists, which is that patients really should not chew gum at all. Thus they include the qualifier "for their patients who chew gum," indicating the limitations or parameters within which the dental experts were willing to give their endorsement of the product. Writing from authority can be a tricky business, sometimes even including the resistance or challenge to authoritative sources. Writers should consider a number of concerns when making appeals to authority:

- Identifying the nature of the authority: "Tim Berners-Lee is the director of the World Wide Web Consortium, senior researcher at MIT's Computer Science and Artificial Intelligence Laboratory, and professor of computer science at the University of Southampton Department of Electronics and Computer Science."
- Comparing one kind of authority to another: "Whether your guide is Emily Post, Miss Manners, or the Fab Five, our designers can make your home and office get-togethers as classy as you are."
- Matching the authority with the message and its context: "Doctors recommend Bayer aspirin" is a valid appeal to authority, matching the product with the kind of experts who know its qualities and uses.

One of the most famous examples of the ethical use of celebrity endorsement was basketball player Charles Barkley's statement: "These are my new shoes. They're good shoes. They won't make you rich like me, they won't make you rebound like me, they definitely won't make you handsome like me. They'll only make you have shoes like me. That's it."

Scarcity

Opportunities, products, events, and services seem more valuable to us when their availability is limited. The thought of losing out on a potentially good deal can be more powerfully motivating than the idea of gaining something of equal value. This is the principle upon which online auction Web sites achieve success: People hurry to outbid each other because they *perceive* that an opportunity to acquire some object will be limited—even if that is not necessarily the case. Advertisers spend a great deal of time worrying about meeting ad campaign deadlines in order to set limitations on sales, specials, and free gift offers because of the power of this principle to produce results. Web marketers look for effective ways to create a strong sense of urgency to attract online customers. Some of their strategies are common to retail and auction Web sites:

- Make sure visitors to the site can see that the Web pages are up-to-date. Even if pages on the site are not changed daily, regular visitors should be able to tell that the pages have been updated regularly.
- Announce limited offers clearly on the home page, on merchandise pages, and on some spot at the top of every page, since visitors may come through deep links that bypass the site's home page. Customers should react well to a tasteful yet eye-catching link or button that simply says, "Click Here for Limited Offers!"
- Give sensible reasons for pushing buyers to act quickly. Consumers tend to understand laws of supply and demand, and they will be more likely to buy if they know that supplies and resources are limited. They also understand that some sale items are "loss lead" merchandise for which the retailer is willing to take a loss in order to drum up business. However, it is not fair to abuse this principle: If consumers find that they've been deceived, your Web sales support staff may face disgruntled demands for refunds and, worse, a bad rating in consumer Web site reviews.
- Consider letting customers know how many units are available when supplies are limited—they just may decide to buy more, stocking up now, rather than gamble that the supply will be replenished later.
- Be clear about the opening and closing dates of a limited offer; be sure to include the time and the time zone, as well. If the offer ends at midnight, Internet users from around the country (or from around the world) will need to know *which* midnight (and remember, 12:00 AM is midnight, 12:00 PM is noon).

Working from a psychological framework presents options at every decision-making turn. Some companies frequently participate in bait-and-switch tactics and other devices designed to make the sale at any cost. If you have worked with a retail Web site, be sure to visit that site periodically to see if the sales and service practices offered there are being honored by the company. Product information links—including price—should be posted up front (i.e., shoppers should not have to click on the "Buy now!" link and provide several screens of information before the price is displayed). Most shoppers are happy to be persuaded to buy merchandise— but they will turn ugly if they feel tricked or cheated. Be certain that you understand all of the restrictions and limitations when writing about special offers and deals. According to most ad copy writers, it's not as easy as you might think!

EXERCISE 6.3

Research a specific, expensive sporting goods item (choose one from the following list) available for purchase on 10 or 15 Web sites (look at the same or similar manufacturer/make/model). Note the amount and kinds of information the sellers provide.

Skis	Motocross bike
English jumping saddle	Set of golf clubs
Surfboard	Sailboard
Pool table	Racing bicycle
Hang glider	Ultralight aircraft
Hunting rifle	Kayak
Scuba diving computer	Paintball gun

1. Which sellers use language that assumes a knowledgeable/experienced buyer? What kind of language choices indicate this?
2. Which sellers use language that is accessible to novices?
3. What kinds of writing strategies do sellers use to communicate with less knowledgeable potential buyers?
4. Which ads include the kinds of details buyers will look for if they are in a retail store?
5. Which ads include contact information for interested buyers?
6. What specific product information do you find missing in most Web ads?
7. What information do you think is excessive or unnecessary?
8. How many sites have set limited sale deadlines or announce limited supplies?
9. Are there limits on "specials" and "sale prices"? What kinds of limits and restrictions have been placed on special offers?
10. What kinds of celebrity endorsements, if any, are used?
11. How many online retailers offer rebates or other types of "reciprocation"?

EXERCISE 6.4

As a class or in groups, go on a "scavenger hunt" for the principles of persuasion. Try to find at least one Web site whose main selling strategy strongly emphasizes one of the principles discussed in this chapter. Answer the following questions:

1. Value: What value is offered? Is it "real" or just hype? Would you recommend the offered value to customers? Why or why not?
2. Reciprocation: What does the site claim to have given visitors? What does it expect in return?
3. Commitment and consistency: How does the site illustrate or describe its commitment to customers? What has the brand or organization been "consistent" about? How and why are customers supposed to be "committed" to their product or service? Explain.
4. Social proof: How does the site demonstrate that its product or service has won popularity among people we identify with or look up to? Explain.

5. Liking: How does the site's writing create a warm feeling in visitors? How do images and text make the company likable? Explain.
6. Authority: What authority figure or figures have been employed to instill confidence in customers/visitors? Are they genuine authorities or contrived? How effective is the authority strategy? Why?
7. Scarcity: How does the site create a feeling of scarcity? What is scarce? Why is it important to "act now"? Does the site's use of the scarcity principle work? Explain.

Assignment 6.3

Create copy (and possibly some layout and design graphics) for a Web page designed to sell a specific high-end sporting goods item. Display your page to the class and explain the specific kinds of language and appeals you have used.

Important Styles for Informative Web Sites

- Style for Academic and Scientific Web Sites
- Style for Instructions and Help Files on the Web
- Journalism Style in the Age of the Internet
- Tips for Success

Glossary Terms

Banner
Deep linking
Inverted pyramid

STYLE FOR ACADEMIC AND SCIENTIFIC WEB SITES

Academic and scientific Web sites tend to be constructed on the model of print periodicals. Many are actually Web versions of print journals. However, in growing numbers, academic and professional organizations are replacing their former print publications with Web publications. These sites archive long textual articles and essays, which visitors expect to download and print easily. Diagram-heavy technical and scientific articles written by expert researchers are expected to be properly laid out and captioned both on-screen and on paper. (See Figure 7.1.) Statistical charts and graphs should print properly, without losing captions and labels. Documentation, citation, and usage generally conform to common standards of the disciplines, which can be found in manuals of style for academic, technical, and scientific writing, such as:

- *MLA Style Manual and Guide to Scholarly Publishing* (Modern Language Association)
- *APA Publication Manual* (American Psychological Association)
- *The Chicago Manual of Style* (University of Chicago Press)
- *Scientific Style and Format: The CBE Manual for Authors, Editors, and Publishers* (The Style Manual Committee of the Council of Biology Editors)

Rather than assume or guess at grammar, citation, and documentation conventions, if you are building or maintaining a Web site for such a publication, simply ask the

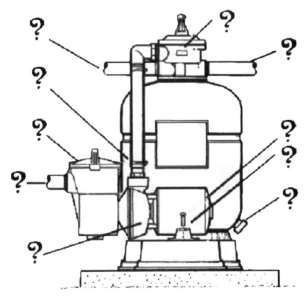

FIGURE 7.1 Scholarship, science, and journalism Web sites are "text-heavy." The images provided on these publication sites must be accompanied with correct information and documention.

site hosts which style guide they are using. (Note: If they express no preference or have no clue, you are probably not dealing with a recognized or accredited organization.)

Usually these Web sites are managed and edited by professional content experts, but these experts are not necessarily experienced at managing Web sites. Designing and building Web sites for specialized groups can be challenging. The editors and sponsors of specialized sites take the content seriously. Academic site owners usually manage most of the editing and indexing themselves, hiring technical assistance that will facilitate the online storage and delivery of their work. Sometimes university interns or graduate research assistants maintain these sites. Often (but not always) academic and scientific sites are stored on university Web servers. An academic Web site will take advantage of a Web writer's skills in organizing files, archiving previously published documents and articles, creating navigation links, and in some cases providing technical instructions for site visitors. But the bulk of the site will be occupied by writing that is much different from the usual "Web styles" we develop for site navigation and content.

Style in Academic Writing

Scientific, technical, and academic writing is not usually subjected to the same kinds of simplifying and cleaning-up strategies that we can use on business and advertising materials. When the subject matter gets complicated, the ways experts write about it (and discuss it) tend to get complicated as well. The reading audience for these specialized articles is often limited to researchers and highly educated specialists. The writers and editors of scientific and technical reports assume that their primary readers expect a certain level of complexity and technical vocabulary.

Academic readers and researchers are hungry for something meaty; they do not need or want an interpreter to "translate" complex language for them. They operate on the assumption that scientists are responsible for reporting every detail of their experimentation and investigation. Sociologists are responsible for explaining their approaches and observations in specific and precise language that conforms to the standards of their field. Philosophers are held accountable for every logical step in their reasoning—including the foundations laid by earlier theorists and the basis of any worldview or belief system upon which they are grounding any arguments or syllogisms.

Academic and professional researchers in most fields are responsible for providing an overview or "survey of the literature" that summarizes previous research relevant to their studies. They need to lay the groundwork for their own investigations and show their peers that they know what kind of investigations have preceded theirs. Researchers are responsible for reporting with excruciating accuracy the data they have collected. In short, they must prove to their peers' and their own satisfaction that the research they are doing will not be an exercise in reinventing the wheel, but instead adds new information or ideas to the body of knowledge in that discipline. The academic journals in which they publish tend to be organized in structured, standardized ways, usually incorporating commonly recognized kinds of *front matter, body text,* and *back matter.*

Technical articles, reports, and even institutional "white papers" (reports on industry innovations and theories, or research-based statements of policy) include several typical components that we, as tech writers, can recognize and suggest as linking-off points should they wish to create a Web-friendly version of a report or research article.

The typical organization of academic articles, technical papers, and scientific reports is shown in Figure 7.2. Compare it with the common structure of news media items—who, what, where, when, how/why (plus as many details as a few columns of space will allow). You might compare this difference to the difference between the student in algebra who intuitively "gets" the answer to a complex algebra problem, and the student who actually "shows the work." Usually, the algebra professor is less interested in the "right answer" than in the student's ability to work through the problem algebraically.

In print form, these documents are organized in fairly straightforward ways by writers and editors. On the Web, however, visitors might expect management of these intense, text-heavy sections of information to be handled differently. In the case of many corporate and government-sponsored studies, some of the reports can exceed 300 pages. The Columbia Space Shuttle Accident Investigation Report, for example, went online at just over 400 pages. The average Web visitor will not appreciate having to download an item of that size in one big lump. A file that large might cause slower Internet connections to time out or shut down. Following is a

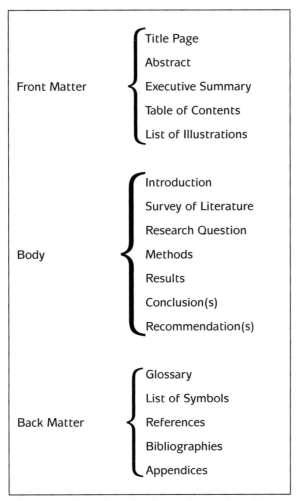

FIGURE 7.2 Typical organization of academic articles, technical papers, and scientific reports.

list of some of the typical kinds of industrial, institutional, and academic text-intensive reports:

- Lab reports
- Site studies
- Progress reports
- Fact-finding reports
- White papers
- Environmental impact statements
- Analytical reports
- Completion reports

- Annual reports
- Informational reports
- Status reports
- Interim reports
- Quality control reports
- Ethnographic studies
- Academic theory
- Feasibility studies

Because many computer users prefer to print longer articles and read them away from the computer, most sites that publish and archive academic articles and industrial reports offer different versions of each item—one for reading on-screen, the other for printing. (See Figure 7.3.)

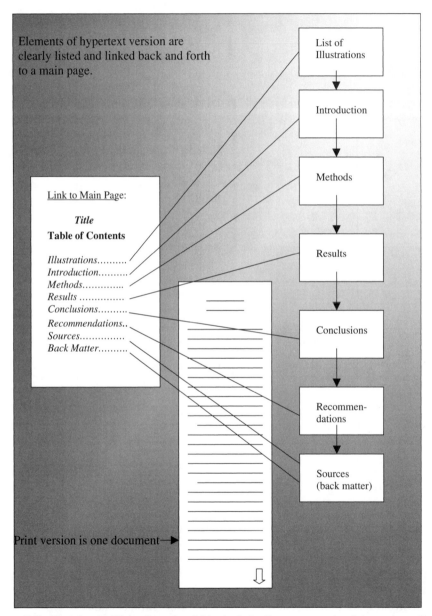

FIGURE 7.3 Text-heavy Web sites should include both screen and print versions for reader convenience.

Preparing a Printable Version of Documents

Printable versions of longer documents should be saved as one complete file. Many site managers prefer to use .pdf files for printable documents, because they save all elements on the page as one entire image. Browser and screen settings do not affect the printable area of the page. If your report or article includes charts that are formatted in hypertext tables, these can easily end up split between printed pages. Other kinds of graphical and layout elements can also end up looking strange when print-layout documents are converted to HTML, no matter what kind of editing software is used. It is good to be familiar with desktop publishing software and to employ special features when creating .pdf documents (such as bookmarking features). Visitors to the site should be able to grab all or part of the printable version of a document without having to click around to several nodes and links just to get the section or article they want, along with its publication information.

All publication and copyright information—including the URL of the Web site—should be included in the document so that readers to whom a printed page has been passed along can find it easily online. Pagination should be correct, especially if researchers will be citing the online version of a print journal.

Organizing the Web Version of Documents

When organizing documents for online readers, it is important to make sure that information is organized in intuitive, practical ways. Articles, sections, chapters, front matter, and back matter should have clear and helpful links to and from navigation pages and tables of contents. Essays, articles, and chapters should not be treated as "dead ends." Make sure the online reader always has some easy option for linking back to navigation aids in the site. For example, if the editors of the online site insist upon offering reports or articles in .pdf form, make sure the documents open in a separate browser window so that visitors still have the navigation window to go back to when they wish to locate other resources on the site.

A main home page should be the central node or portal for the Web site. This creates a conceptual anchor for users to go back to when they are exploring the resources and documents in the site. A typical online academic journal might have the file structure shown in Figure 7.4.

Remember to include a site map or other navigation page, no matter what kind of organizational method or file management system you decide to use. On text-heavy Web sites, visitors need to navigate easily among the documents, articles, abstracts, and/or executive summaries. The whole point is to make information easy to access—even if the information is highly complicated, scientific, philosophical, or technical.

Technical, Academic, and Scientific Style

When writing for an academic or specialized audience, writers not only comply with mechanics and usage as prescribed in style manuals. Scholarly and scientific

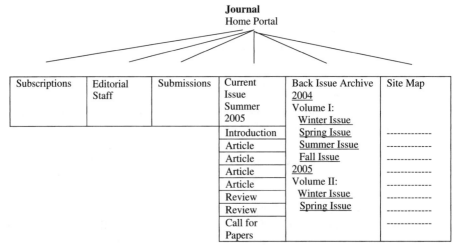

FIGURE 7.4 The site organization usually is mapped out before the online journal launches onto the Web. Typically, academic sites employ both shallow and deep Web organization strategies.

journal writers employ specific subject- and audience-driven techniques:

- ■ ***Jargon:*** Sentences may be densely packed with technical terminology. They are written for experts who are comfortable with the vocabulary and syntax of their field. Example:

  Rupture of the papillary muscle is most often associated with an inferior-posterior infarct due to right coronary artery occlusion. It produces acute, severe mitral regurgitation and is characterized by the sudden appearance of a loud apical systolic murmur and thrill, usually with pulmonary edema.

  > *The Merck Manual of Diagnosis and Therapy,*
  > Section 16. Cardiovascular Disorders; Chapter 202. Coronary Artery Disease.
  > *http://www.merck.com/mrkshared/mmanual/section16/chapter202/202d.jsp*

- ■ ***Complex syntax:*** The text features a substantial number of complex, compound, and complex-compound sentence structures. Note also the indulgent, strained syntax in the following example—the "not un-" double negative construction is sometimes called *litotes*. Example:

  The trance-susceptible shaman and the initiated antelope-priest are not unsophisticated in the wisdom of the world, nor unskilled in the principles of communication by analogy. The metaphors by which they live, and through which they operate, have been brooded upon, searched, and discussed for centuries—even millenniums; they have served whole societies, furthermore, as the mainstays of thought and life.

  > Joseph Campbell, *The Hero with a Thousand Faces*
  > (Princeton: Princeton University Press, 1949)

■ *Symbols and equations:* Scientific and technical articles incorporate advanced symbol systems. When we must reproduce such articles, it is critically important to proofread all symbols and technical terms for even the slightest error. The audience for these scientific reports is expected to know what the symbols mean, and they in turn expect to find precise and detailed usage of these symbols in their publications. Example:

By measuring the intensities (photon number per second) of the output beams, one can recover the phase difference φ between the two internal optical paths A' and B'. Formally, the input-output relation of the apparatus is completely characterized by assigning the transformations of the annihilation operators a, b, c, and d associated with the fields at A, B, C, and D, respectively. These are $c \equiv (a' + ie^{i\varphi b'})/\sqrt{2}$ and $d \equiv (ia' + e^{i\varphi b'})/\sqrt{2}$ with $a' = (a + ib)/\sqrt{2}$ and $b' \equiv (ia + b)/\sqrt{2}$ the annihilation operators associated to the internal paths A' and B', respectively.

> Giovannetti, Vittorio, Lloyd, Seth, Maccone, Lorenzo. "Quantum-Enhanced Measurements: Beating the Standard Quantum Limit." Review. *Science,* 00368075, 11/19/2004, Vol. 306, Issue 5700.

■ *Words, phrases, or entire passages in other languages:* Some academic discourse adopts the convention of assuming that well-educated scholars in literature and the humanities should have a reading familiarity with Latin, German, French, and possibly ancient Greek. This conceit has begun to fade in some disciplines, although scholars in comparative literature can be expected to assume their own readers and peers are multilingual, since their specialty *is* the comparison of texts in multiple languages. Still, it helps to include translations, if editorial supervisors allow it. Example:

> . . . In all such cases, *caeteris paribus,* we might expect an entelechial pressure in the direction of the more drastic version, as regards the motives of a "perfect paradigm." (393)

> Kenneth Burke, *Language as Symbolic Action* (Berkeley: University of California Press, 1966)

■ *Extensive explanatory footnotes/endnotes:* Many scholarly works provide footnotes and/or endnotes to help clarify and explain historical, scientific, arcane, or archaic materials. Depending upon the overall length of the main text, these notes can be handled as links to the bottom of the hypertext page or as links to separate frames or pages. Some Web sites format explanatory notes as pop-up links and as *hover text* (i.e., the note appears when the cursor passes over the main text or image).

This example is an endnote from Allen Mandelbaum's 1980 verse translation of Dante's *Inferno.* Here Mandelbaum offers historical and canonical expansion upon references made by Dante in the fourth canto of the poem, and even wraps up this note with a reference to *another* note:

> CANTO IV. 52–61 Virgil died in the year 19 B.C.; Christ descended into Limbo after His death in 33 A.D., when Virgil had been in Limbo about 50 years. Christ's descent into Limbo, from which he removed the Old Testament worthies, is known as the Harrowing of Hell. It has its source in the Apocrypha, in a portion of the Gospel of Nicodemus, and was proclaimed as dogma at the Fourth Lateran Council in 1215 and at the Council of Lyon in 1274. (Together with the Old Testament worthies, the Roman Cato of Utica may also, according to Dante, have been delivered from Limbo at that time. Cato will serve as the guardian of Purgatory. For his wife, Marcia, see 127–129, note.)

> *The Divine Comedy of Dante Alighieri: Inferno.* Trans. Allen Mandelbaum
> (New York: Bantam, 1980)

Sometimes commercial and technical writers become impatient or frustrated with academic writing. They may see it as "cluttered" or "convoluted" and even overly repetitive. But there are reasons for this kind of discourse. For one thing, academic writing does not assume that primary readers will take the ideas, data, information, and arguments on face value. On the contrary, academics are trained for years to *question* the research, evidence, and theories of other scholars, not simply as an argumentative exercise, but from the standpoint of education, experience, and expertise. Although a casual novice reader may think that a philosophical or linguistic treatise is somewhat belabored and filled with extraneous citations or references, the philosopher and the linguist are carefully studying the piece, looking for errors in logic, statistical inconsistencies, and even for missing data. They are questioning the authority of the text not simply as an exercise in asserting their individuality, but rather they question, test, make notes, and check references because they are the *peers*—members of the same academic community as the author (biologists, astrophysicists, social psychologists, etc.). Technical and commercial Web writers who may not have expertise in the content subject matter of an academic site are still needed, however, to organize and provide support such as help files, instructions, submission guidelines, archives, and publication policies.

EXERCISE 7.1

Working alone, with a partner, or in a small team, go to your college or university library. Select an academic or scientific journal that does not provide an electronic archive of its current and past published issues on the World Wide Web. (Note: You may wish to ask your library periodicals staff to help you determine which journal would be a good candidate.) Find the library's collection of bound issues of the journal and work with its finding aids—indexes, tables of contents, and so on—to develop a plan for creating a Web version of the journal. Write a brief report and proposal in which you:

1. Create a mock-up home page for the journal. (Optional: Add digital graphical elements to simulate the proposed "look and feel" of the online journal.)
2. Create a mock-up site plan for the journal that shows the organizational plan of the site, using a diagram or flowchart.
3. Create a mock-up site map for the online journal, showing all of the major sections, links, and sublinks on the site.
4. Write a brief (250–400 words) description of the site, explaining the types of file management strategies you would use to organize the current articles, reports, reviews, and/or essays. Also explain the basic structure and organization of archived back issues.
5. Describe the hypertext tools (buttons, navigation bars, in-text links, etc.) the site will use to help readers navigate the site.

STYLE FOR INSTRUCTIONS AND HELP FILES ON THE WEB

FAR/AIM 91.207 (b)

Each emergency locator transmitter required by paragraph (a) of this section must be attached to the airplane in such a manner that the probability of damage to the transmitter in the event of crash impact is minimized. Fixed and deployable automatic type transmitters must be attached to the airplane as far aft as practicable.

Federal Aviation Administration, *Federal Aviation Regulations/Aeronautical Information Manual* (2003)

Instructions and help files should always be audience driven. Before beginning to construct online help files or instructions, writers have to understand as much as possible about their primary audience—the readers who will visit their Web sites for help. Ironically, technical experts are among those who often have the most trouble creating a useful set of instructions or advice, at least without a good deal of revision and thought. For example, the preceding excerpt from the Federal Aviation Administration's aviation regulations may seem overly fussy or convoluted to the average outsider, but for pilots and workers in the aviation industry it answers important questions about the type of emergency locator transmitter required by law, and where it should be installed (note, for instance, that in aviation the term *aft* is actually more precise and clear than the terms *rear* or *back* of the plane).

One reason experts have trouble writing instructions and hire technical writers for this job is that they are so thoroughly familiar with the subject that they must work very hard to "forget" the massive depth and breadth of their own knowledge and place themselves in a novice's shoes. Processes that seem simple to experts may in fact be quite complicated and daunting to the average consumer. Social critic Thorstein Veblen (1857–1929) called this phenomenon *trained incapacity*. Workers who specialize in managing and understanding industrial or technological systems may focus so heavily upon their specific areas of expertise that adjusting their vision backwards, to view their work from the angle of the uninitiated, is nearly incomprehensible to them.

Technical writers sometimes comment that some engineers, scientists, and scholars adopt a kind of attitude that makes them seem impatient with co-workers and consumers who have not taken the time and effort to familiarize themselves with the technical intricacies of their inventions and ideas. Their ability (and perhaps in some cases their willingness) to see through the novice's eyes is for all practical purposes "incapacitated." Even when technical experts are clearly capable of writing lucid, helpful instructions and guidelines, they are often too busy (and too expensive!) to spare the amount of time from their workday that it takes to develop online manuals or full sets of general support documents.

Technical communicators are then hired to step in and translate technical jargon into everyday language. Their job is to create easy to follow, step-by-step explanations and instructions that anyone can understand. When we move these instructions, manuals, and help files onto the Web, it is important that they be formatted and linked so that visitors to our Web sites can find the information they need. In order to get a clear understanding of the likely strategies people will use to get help from Web sites, writers first have to understand whom they are writing for.

Understanding Your Audience

Writing online help documents demands that we understand specific things about our readers. Rather than trying to attract visitors for commercial purposes, help writers operate from the assumption that visitors have sought out the site on purpose and that our job is to keep them there until they are satisfied and their problems are solved. Answering some or all of the following questions *in complete, thoughtful sentences and paragraphs* can be a good starting place when we are trying to organize and articulate helpful online support pages.

- What level of knowledge do my primary readers have?
- What level of reading ability do my readers have?
- What level of experience do my readers have?
- Does gender matter? If so, how will I handle any possible gender issues or bias?
- What age group(s) do my primary readers belong to?

- What percentage of my instructions will readers be required to learn or memorize for later use?
- What kinds of information and help will most readers be looking for?
- Who are my supervisory readers (i.e., your immediate supervisors)?
- Who are my peripheral readers (i.e., legal department, sales associates, help desk personnel, competitors)?
- Do my primary readers speak and write English as a second language?
- Will readers primarily remain online while using the instructions, or will they want to print (or even buy) a hard copy?
- What other information is important to know about my readers?

You can probably think of even more questions a good help site writer should ask about the audience, including, "How much technical terminology can my readers understand?" "What kinds of tools and materials are they likely to have on hand?" "How much explanation and functional description do they want to know?" or even, "At what stage should they be advised to phone the support line for one-on-one help?"

EXERCISE 7.2

To the best of your ability, consider the audience for which the following instructions were written and try to answer all the preceding questions about audience as completely as possible. Add any additional questions you deem important. Then develop a brief but comprehensive (250–300 words) description of the primary readership. (Writers sometimes call this guided process of question-and-answer planning an *invention heuristic*.)

6-3-5 FUEL DUMPING

a. Should it become necessary to dump fuel, the pilot should immediately advise ATC. Upon receipt of information that an aircraft will dump fuel, ATC will broadcast or cause to be broadcast immediately and every 3 minutes thereafter the following on appropriate ATC and FSS radio frequencies.

EXAMPLE: ATTENTION ALL AIRCRAFT—FUEL DUMPING IN PROGRESS OVER (location) AT (altitude) BY (type of aircraft) (flight direction).

b. Upon receipt of such a broadcast, pilots of aircraft affected, which are not on IFR flight plans or special VFR clearances will be provided specific separation by ATC. At the termination of the fuel dumping operation, pilots should advise ATC. Upon receipt of such information, ATC will issue, on the appropriate frequencies, the following:

EXAMPLE: ATTENTION ALL AIRCRAFT—FUEL DUMPING BY—(type of aircraft)—TERMINATED.

FAA Aeronautical Information Manual (2004)

Writing Instructions for the Web

When writing instructions, remember that you are describing a step-by-step process. Instructions should always be tested before the pages go online. It is a good idea to find others to follow the instructions and evaluate their usability so that you can be sure nothing has been left out. Instructions often are best when the standard model for describing and analyzing a process is incorporated and adapted to your Web site. The accompanying table gives guidelines.

Guidelines for Writing Instructions

Introduction and Preparation	• State the overall goal, purpose, and desired result.
	• Make online instructions easy to save on a personal computer.
	• Make online instructions printer-friendly.
	• List and describe all parts and materials needed.
	• List and describe all tools and supplies needed.
	• Provide clear, accurate diagrams, maps, or drawings, if possible.
	• Describe *all* preparation that must be done before the process can begin. This may entail describing preparatory subprocesses.
	• Provide a preparatory checklist of all materials, tools, preparations, ingredients, etc., so that readers can begin the process without stopping sporadically to root around for tools and supplies or take a trip to the store. For example, recipes usually start with a description of preparation materials and a list of ingredients.
	• Create links to pages, documents, or Web sites that can provide further assistance.
Steps to Follow	• Describe step 1 in detail, making sure to use clear, direct language (using illustrations or photos where appropriate).
	• Describe step 2 in detail, making sure to use clear, direct language (using illustrations or photos where appropriate).
	• Describe step 3 in detail, making sure to use clear, direct language (using illustrations or photos where appropriate).
	• . . . and so on, until the process is completed.
Results	• Describe and, if possible, provide illustrations or diagrams of the finished, desired result.

EXERCISE 7.3

Use the table of guidelines for writing instructions to create a set of brief, step-by-step instructions for one of the following:

1. Retrieve and listen to a message on your cell phone.
2. Download and play a song on your iPod (or other music storage/listening device).
3. Transfer a call from your phone to someone else's extension in your workplace.
4. Set the time on your automobile dashboard clock.
5. Order a new AC adapter for your computer.
6. Use the Web to find the titles and showtimes of movies playing in your local theaters this weekend.
7. Brainstorm in groups or as a class to suggest other operations or processes for which a set of online instructions would be useful.

TIPS FOR SUCCESS

1. Walk yourself through the process: Perform the task yourself at least twice. First go through the entire process and make some notes about the overall operation. Then start over, moving slowly and methodically, stopping and starting as you perform each step or suboperation, jotting down notes and descriptions as you go.
2. When creating instructions, make sure you write about a *process,* which means steps must be taken in the exact order you explain them (otherwise, you're just listing bits of advice—and a list is not the same thing as a step-by-step process).
3. If it's not clear *why* each step should be performed before the next one, then make a case: Explain to your reader why specific steps must be performed in the order you've created.

Constructing Online Help Files and Manuals

Online manuals and help file Web sites are usually more ambitious than the average set of instructions. They are often created as separate small programs (subapplications) that can be accessed from the toolbars on powerful games and software commonly in use. These subapplications tend to incorporate detailed contents, indexes, hyperlinks, multimedia files, and search functions. Online manuals and help files are created for various purposes:

- Product ownership, use, and care
- Product repair and maintenance
- Policies and procedures
- System administration and management

Many of the same principles that apply to smaller sets of online instructions can be applied to more ambitious sites, especially where audience is concerned. It is important to know as much as possible about primary, secondary, supervisory, and peripheral readers. Above all, when constructing online help files and manuals, Web writers need to create sites that are scannable and searchable so that visitors can easily find the specific information they need as quickly and easily as possible. Although visitors to a help site may have a variety of reasons for stopping by, most have specific needs. They probably have no intention of spending one minute more than it will take to solve the immediate problem or question. Adolescents and teens are even less likely to have patience enough to search and click through confusing menus or indexes than older visitors.

Unlike print manuals, which provide tables of contents, introductory cautions, and indexes that readers flip through as they search for answers, online help site writers must anticipate readers who will "deep link." **Deep linking** refers to arriving at the single page that references the problem—without visiting any of the introductory or explanatory pages. Web users, when possible, would rather skip any introductory or cautionary pages you may have painstakingly provided.

Subject Indexing and File Organization

An index is simply an alphabetical list of important terms, concepts, people, places, and things covered in the Web site. Indexing is crucially important to most online manuals and help file projects. Visitors to these sites often use the index to locate specific pieces of information. Any online help site of substantial size should include a good index that is accurately hyperlinked, comprehensive, effectively subindexed, and user-friendly. Ideally, terms in the index should be linked not only to the relevant documents and Web pages, but should also, if possible, link visitors to the relevant section of that page. Visitors should not have to use the scroll bar or the "find" function of their browser to locate a term they want to read about once they arrive on the page.

Accurate Hyperlinks

Whether in print or online, it is crucial for index reference locations to be accurate. Consider the inconvenience that would be caused if a new edition of a book contained the index from the old edition. Readers would quickly discover that the pagination of some or all of the sections within the book had changed. An index with the wrong page numbers is essentially useless. The same is true of an online index with broken links. This can happen when sites are moved from one service provider to another, when domain names are changed, or when file structures on a server are rearranged by system managers. One way to avoid problems when files are moved is to use clean, simple internal links and to organize the site's documents within a simple file structure that has as few subdirectories as possible. With a little planning, your Web folders, files, images, and documents can be saved within one closed file directory and moved as a unit to any new location without losing internal linking structures. When help files are named, organized, and stored together in a logically structured way, visitors to your site will want to return and will trust that they can find assistance without wasting time.

Comprehensive Listings

Collecting and listing all of the subjects and terms likely to be sought by visitors to your Web site is more of an art than a science. There are software applications that can help in the creation of online help and reference files, and these programs frequently include indexing tools. But it takes a human eye to determine the proper depth and breadth of an index. Book indexes tend to list approximately two or three terms per page of main text, although this is just a rough guide. Web site manuals and help pages vary in length and depth, so indexing becomes tricky and—for want of a better term—*intuitive*. Soliciting feedback from site visitors can be a healthy and productive way of developing and launching improved versions of online user manuals and help file sites. An important issue to remember is that, unlike books, whose pages and sections are visible, linear, and easy to skim one by one, Web site elements and documents are often *opaque* in organization and structure, at least to the average online visitor. When a term or concept is covered on a number of different Web pages (or in a number of database files), visitors cannot always simply "flip to the next page" to see if the discussion or explanation continues. They will need an index that includes logical, alphabetical entries and subentry headings linked to all of the major and minor references that apply to each term. The trick, of course, is not to overwhelm visitors with too many entries and main headings. Larger reference sites tend to provide alternate indexes with topics separated into manageable categories.

Effective Subindexing and Cross-Referencing

Lists of entries and subentries should not be so detailed that they confuse visitors or bog them down with too many decisions and downloads. On the other hand, providing too few choices can force visitors to sort through pages of materials that do not answer their specific questions. Even sites with search engine capabilities should employ some smart indexing and organizing so that visitors are not required to read through pages filled with searching instructions. Good indexing can also prevent ineffective searches that result in a screen full of random, unsorted, and ultimately unhelpful listings.

Cross-referencing can help visitors who may not know exactly which terms will help them the most. In print documents, indexed entries use *see* and *see also* (in italics) to help with navigation. These navigational helpers can be employed on Web sites as well. *See* ordinarily points to a main or standard entry. For example, "USB

Drive; *see* <u>Storage Devices</u>." *See also* is used when pointing to related entries. For example, "<u>Peripherals</u>; *see also* <u>printers</u>; <u>external drives</u>; <u>scanners</u>."

User-Friendly Design

Probably the paramount rule for all help sites is: *Don't make visitors work too hard.* (See Figure 7.5.). They were working hard before they arrived at the help site, and they will probably have to work hard after they leave. Meanwhile, as they sort through the online files or manuals we have provided, visitors should feel as though

FIGURE 7.5 Products and services often are accompanied by owner's manuals and instructions that leave customers' heads reeling. Companies make friends and keep clients when they provide well-written, helpful sites (complete with "help desk" staff and contact information).

the purpose of the site is to meet their needs, not the other way around. Consider the following guidelines when working as a writer for these kinds of Web sites:

- *Welcome visitors to the site.* Their trust in our ability to provide help is not to be taken lightly. It is a privilege to have readers who are confident in us and in our knowledge base.
- *Maintain a respectful tone.* Manuals and help files are necessary because products, systems, and policies have reached historic levels of complexity. Workers seeking online help files often must answer to investors, constituents, taxpayers, government agencies, clients, and hosts of other concerned parties. They deserve to be treated with dignity.
- *Do the work.* Making things easy for others means putting some thought and planning into the resources we put online.

  > Page elements should have a consistent look and feel.
  > Navigation bars and buttons should be uniform and easy to scan.
  > Site architecture should be sturdy and well organized.

- *Simplify.* Use bulleted lists, alphabetical indexing, logical categories, and easy-to-follow headings and subheadings on all pages. Avoid burying links within text-heavy passages. Provide diagrams and other graphical aids where possible.
- *Provide printable versions* of instructions, illustrations, directions, maps, and diagrams when possible.
- *Keep distractions to a minimum.* Branding, advertising, and sponsor-identification are common necessary evils on most Web sites but should be used ethically. Don't allow sleaze-filled **banner** ads or spyware links to populate your help site.

JOURNALISM STYLE IN THE AGE OF THE INTERNET

The satellite phone is the only piece of [technology] I had with me. . . . I strapped it to my belly, which was very uncomfortable. But this satellite phone was my only link to the outside world, and I remember the very first time I happened to be under heavy bombardment . . . I was talking to my editor right before the plane appeared in the sky. I had to abandon the satellite phone, but . . . I ran back. The very idea of losing this satellite phone, this link to the outside world was terrifying to me.

Journalist Anne Nivat, author of *Chienne De Guerre: A Woman Reporter Behind the Lines of the War in Chechnya* (from an April 9, 2001, broadcast interview on National Public Radio)

Reporting news on the Web can become an exercise in racing to keep up with the latest scoop. For over 100 years, print periodicals were expected to release news on a daily or weekly basis. Today, news sites feature updates throughout the day as hot news unfolds. Web surfers tend to expect fast turnover and immediate reporting. They are accustomed to the responsiveness of huge, corporate news organizations such as CNN. Full-blown news sites often contain huge, searchable archives and multimedia resources (featuring images, video, and sound). The level of complexity and difficulty of reporting news online usually depends upon the corporate expectations and mission statement of the news organization that owns and operates the site. News site editors and managers should have a clear understanding of the purpose, scope, and readership of their online publications before jumping into the wired world of news reporting.

Ideally, online journalism would adhere to media practices and ethics generally considered to be standard in the free world. In reality, the Internet has created a kind of publishing free-for-all environment that is both exciting and perplexing.

Some general categories of online journalism include these types of Web sites:

1. News sites that reproduce an already-established print publication (such as the *Washington Post, Chicago Tribune, Wall Street Journal*)
2. News sites affiliated with established broadcast media news services (CNN, National Public Radio)
3. Professionally run online news sites that are Web-generated only (*Slate, Salon*)
4. Trade journals—periodicals that publish news, product reviews, and other items of interest for a particular trade or industry (*Tea & Coffee Trade Journal, Tattoo Artist Magazine, PRW: Plastics and Rubber Weekly*)
5. Online magazines, also called e-zines or 'zines (*Salon, The Onion*)
6. Nonprofit organization and special-interest news (*NRA Publications, Greenpeace, Amnesty International, Doctors Without Borders*)
7. Newsletters—news bulletins produced for specific readers, such as employees, organization members, or interest groups. Usually these are linked and archived on the company or organization Web site. Newsletters tend to be brief (four to eight pages), are produced in-house, and ordinarily do not sell advertising space on their pages. Some of these are even distributed via e-mail rather than on the Web.

Writers who wish to work for an online news organization may find that their job is similar to that of the traditional news reporter. Articles need to be submitted in the format designated by the news organization and completed on deadline. Usually this means learning to use the correct file extensions and electronic data transfer protocols. Reporters working in war zones or other sensitive investigative fields also need to understand how to improvise where communications resources can be interrupted or cut off, and they will even need some basic understanding of encryption and security where electronic report filing is concerned.

Writers who wish to start their own news Web sites need to organize a long-term plan for publication deadlines and schedules, and for archiving past issues.

This is generally true of both small, independent "fanzines" as well as for full-blown news site startups. Planning and organization are crucial. Two of the most important questions these entrepreneurs will ask are:

1. Five years from now, who will be maintaining this site?
2. Who will be visiting the site regularly?

Like small print publications, modest online news sites can be run on a shoestring. All it takes is a budget and a bit of server space. Print periodicals tend to go under because subscription sales are too low and because they fail to sell enough advertising to pay for the presses, office space, and reporters' salaries. Online periodicals fail for those reasons too. But usually smaller online 'zines fizzle and die simply due to boredom and exhaustion on the part of their owners. Gathering and disseminating information is extremely labor intensive and requires a rather large commitment—along with a realistic plan—from the start.

Large organizations with substantial fund-raising or profit-making budgets usually want to include news and updated information on their Web sites. Unlike conventional, independent journalism, these sites are the online equivalent of print-based organizational newsletters. Even when ethical and accurate, their reports are "news with a slant." They should never be represented as unbiased or free from the Web owners' agenda. When citing news reports from these Web sites, it is important to highlight the source of the information.

Journalistic Style

Good reporters tend to write in a style that adapts very well to the Web. Because they are accustomed to writing stories that can be cut from the bottom up, they pack the most important information into the opening sentences of the piece. The **inverted pyramid** may be a news-writing cliché, but it works very well for transmitting quickly as much information as possible. (See Figure 7.6.) This format was developed because, once upon a time, typeset articles were literally "pasted" to layout sheets, and when a late-breaking scoop came in, stories were cut—literally, with an X-acto™ knife—to make room for the new story. Since these last-minute changes could happen after writers had gone home for the day, editors needed to know that they could work their way up from the bottom/end of the story, cutting at any point, even up to the beginning of the story where the bare essentials—who, what, where, when, how, and why—were given.

EXERCISE 7.4 WEB NEWS ANALYSIS

Work alone or with a partner. Open your word or text editing program. Then open the Web browser and call up each of the Web sites listed below. Copy and paste the headlines of the top four or five stories on each news site's front page ("top story" means the stories "at the top of the page").

1. Quickly skim over the first few paragraphs of the top news stories and note the level of replication—that is, how many of these sites are using the same news services and publishing the *exact same stories* as other sites?
2. How many of the news sites are publishing the *exact same photos* as the other sites? Are the same one or two photos featured on almost every site? What is the subject matter? Do these photos seem important enough to be replicated world-wide on several news services?
3. Rank the stories in order of their newsworthiness (i.e., the number of people whom you believe would be interested in the story).
4. Rank the stories in the order of what you believe to be their real importance, in terms of their effect on the world today. Is the story you believe to be most important the same story that is replicated (repeated) the most? If so, why do you think that is? If not, why?
5. What can we say about the diversity (or lack of it) among news sites on the Web?

http://www.cnn.com   *http://www.reuters.com*
http://www.foxnews.com   *http://www.usatoday.com*
http://abcnews.go.com   *http://news.com.com*
http://news.google.com   *http://news.bbc.co.uk*
http://www.cbsnews.com   *http://www.washingtonpost.com*
http://news.yahoo.com   *http://www.npr.org*
http://www.msnbc.msn.com

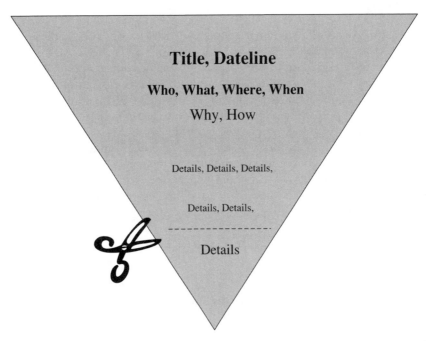

Title, Dateline

Who, What, Where, When

Why, How

Details, Details, Details,

Details, Details,

- - - - - - - - - - - - - - - -

Details

FIGURE 7.6 Journalistic style. The inverted pyramid format allows extra details to be cut from a story.

Assignment 7.1

Choose a campus organization or a local small company or nonprofit organization. Design a newsletter Web site for it.

Planning

1. First, create a list of purposes and goals for the site based upon discussions and interviews (either in person or via e-mail) with the organization managers and staff. Do they already have a print newsletter? If so, how closely should the Web site resemble the print newsletter?
2. Next, create a publication schedule based upon the amount of relevant news and announcements staff members are willing to generate.
3. Third, sketch out a typical weekly, monthly, and annual schedule of events the organization would like to report to their patrons, customers, benefactors, friends, and employees. Decide how many issues should be generated annually and be ready to explain why.
4. Finally, plan the "look and feel"—the visual design of the Web site (unless there is a heavy design component to your class, you might want to keep it "clean and simple"). Suggest background colors, logo images, page placement of text, and banner design.

Production

Create a mock-up site for the organization's first online newsletter. Your instructor may ask you to work in a group or team to provide actual articles, banners, digital graphics, and photographs for the site.

8

Entertainment Web Sites

- Web Writing—For Art's Sake
- Blogs
- Satire
- Facilitating Feedback Interactivity
- Humor
- Literary Sites
- Cartoon Sites
- Multimedia and Interactive Multimedia
- Community Sites

Glossary Terms

Blog
MUD
Multimedia

> We can now see that a writer must disguise his art and give the impression of speaking naturally and not artificially. Naturalness is persuasive, artificiality is the contrary; for our hearers are prejudiced and think we have some design against them, as if we were mixing their wines for them.
>
> Aristotle

WEB WRITING—FOR ART'S SAKE

Writing for the Web isn't all work and no play. Many Web sites are constructed simply for the pleasure and expression of writers and multimedia artists. Web site visitors sometimes like to read and enjoy Web-based media for entertainment. For technical communicators, these sites present an opportunity to provide interactive gaming texts and scenarios, video and audio scripts, instructions, terms of use, help files, captions, FAQs, and information updates for site visitors.

FIGURE 8.1 "And then, according to the script, you rise from the ashes of your own funeral pyre! What a spectacle! Oh, don't worry, we've hired a stunt phoenix."

BLOGS

The term **blog** is an abbreviation of "Web log." Originally meant to be a sort of ironic, online personalized diary or journal, a growing number of blogs are posted by high-profile figures hoping to get exposure for their favorite issues, causes, and candidates. The term has become so popular that many organizations and companies have taken to posting press releases and corporate announcements on their Web sites and labeling them "blogs." Thus, even though the blogging craze began with writers who use blogs as something cool, creative, ultra-personal, and *avant-garde,* the word *blog* seems destined to become a sort of generic term for "Web site journal-keeping" in a large and vague sense.

Some might argue that quality is not an issue in blogging, since a blog site is more or less just the personal thought-space of an individual. But there is some evidence that the best writers attract more attention than mediocre or poor writers, and some of these talented bloggers even achieve "crossover" publication in other media. The blog called *Where Is Raed?* belongs to a blogger known as "Salam Pax," the "Baghdad Blogger." He is a young resident of Baghdad who kept his identity secret and continued to update his powerfully written blogs as American troops entered the city. Salam blogged about his life and experiences as an Iraqi citizen throughout the United States' military incursion into Iraq. The site became popular among journalists worldwide, whose movements in Iraq were understandably limited (or even prohibited) during the U.S. occupation. Eventually, excerpts from the blog were published in a book titled *Salam Pax: The Clandestine Diary of an Ordinary Iraqi* (New York: Grove Press, 2003). Following is an excerpt from *Where Is Raed?*

Saturday, March 06, 2004

Karbala was one of these things I will never ever forget in my whole life. . . . I, my mother and my cousin were out of the center of the city, running, by the third mortar. It was the last two that did the damage and it happened near the shrine of Abbas not al-Hussein where we were staying. I am not sure I am more phased out by the rituals I saw and witnessed there or by the attacks and their consequences. . . . I frikkin' met an Ayatollah! a real life Ayatollah, I watched him eat a banana and then he put his hands on my shoulder and prayed that I get married soon, my mom was beside herself with joy and I just couldn't stop laughing.

Salam Pax. "Saturday, March 06, 2004." *Where Is Raed?*
http://dear_raed.blogspot.com/.

SATIRE

Satire is a literary form that uses humor and ridicule to highlight flaws and malfeasances in human society. (Probably the most famous satirical Web site is *The Onion.*) In the strictest sense, satire's purpose is to scrutinize some social problem—to point out injustices and inequities—and not simply to heap scorn upon "innocent" bystanders. The great news about satire is that mocking things that our audience finds ridiculous can garner great adulation and leave site visitors asking for more. The bad news about satire is that those who find themselves on the receiving end will be alienated quickly. Before embarking on satirical Web projects, it is always a good idea to make informed decisions about the goals of the site.

- What kinds of topics and issues will the site be covering? What will its size and scope be? Will it need writers, editors, cartoonists, and multimedia specialists?
- Who will the main audience of this project be? That is, who can be expected to return to the site repeatedly? Can you name or describe your target audience?
- To what level of harshness or gentleness will the satire rise (or stoop)? Are the site's writers good enough to mock the "bad guys," get a clear message of some kind across, and still be entertaining enough to keep readers coming back for more?
- How will the site will be financed? Will advertisers, endorsements, and other financial considerations compromise the satirical goals of the site (that is, will the site owners fear to make fun of some aspect of society because they are afraid paying advertisers will be offended)?
- What kinds of reactions and responses are expected and desired? Will contributions be solicited? Will the site be interactive?

Remember, satire is a form of social criticism, so the site's managers and contributors should be ready (and willing) to accept scrutiny and criticism from outside sources. The old adage, "If you dish it out, you have to be able to take it" is doubly true for satirists. Web sites that feature satire and political criticism usually provide technical writers with the opportunity to create open spaces for dialogue and discussion. However, without sufficient preparation and guidelines, such spaces can quickly devolve into shouting matches and mudslinging wars.

FACILITATING FEEDBACK INTERACTIVITY

Many creative and entertaining sites invite visitors to respond or participate in discussion about the site topic. Technical writers are often called upon to provide pages that introduce interactive spaces such as discussion boards, newsgroups, MOO spaces, chat rooms, blog spaces, and e-mail forms. (See Figure 8.2.) Each type of forum has different capabilities. Web writers are often asked to provide pages that help visitors get the most out of the site's interactivity:

- Welcoming new and regular visitors
- Introducing the community
- Assisting users (logging in, passwords, posting, etc.)
- Explaining purposes of the interactive forum
- Providing rules of conduct
- Linking to FAQs, help files, and further information
- Gatekeeping (discouraging disruptive users)
- Providing guidelines for managing and administering
- Providing contact information

Interactive sites tend to take on the character and flavor of the interest group hosting them. Depending upon the level of interactivity, writers who work on the site may even be called upon to moderate disputes, answer queries, squelch "flame

You agree to release, indemnify, and hold us, our contractors, agents, employees, officers, directors and affiliates harmless from all liabilities, claims and expenses, including attorney's fees, of third parties relating to or arising under this Agreement, the Services provided hereunder or your use of the Services, including without limitation infringement by you, or someone else using the E-mail Service with your computer, of any intellectual property or other proprietary right of any person or entity, or from the violation of any of our operating rules or policy relating to the service(s) provided. When we are threatened with suit by a third party, we may seek written assurances from you concerning your promise to indemnify us; your failure to provide those assurances may be considered by us to be a breach of your Agreement and may result in termination of our Services to you.

"Terms of Service" at MyBlogSite.com, http://myblogsite.com

FIGURE 8.2 Web sites that offer interactive services use legal language in their "terms of service" statements to protect themselves from liability. By clicking on a button that says "I Agree," the visitor is assumed to have entered into a legally binding agreement with the stated terms.

wars" (verbally abusive exchanges), or deal with "trolls" (interlopers whose posts are designed to disrupt or even disband the community). Before taking on the task of creating interactive spaces for a Web site, make sure the site owners understand the labor-intensive nature of hosting interactive sites.

HUMOR

Humorous Web sites abound for almost every interest or subject. Many offer to e-mail you (or a friend) their "daily humor" updates (complete, of course, with embedded advertising). Most of the time, the humor on these sites consists of recycled jokes heard in comedy clubs, read in books, or performed on television. When creating a humor Web site, it is important to review copyright issues and ethics so that you aren't just stealing other people's jokes and passing them along.

LITERARY SITES

There are some very good poetry and fiction Web sites online, as well as valuable searchable online libraries that have archived license-free translations of ancient texts—the Gutenberg Project at MIT houses works from ancient Greek and Roman authors as well as many more classic works. Managing these sites is much the same as managing archives for scientific and scholarly online publications. While e-books and other technology-enhanced formats for literature are being developed and introduced into some markets, typical online poetry and fiction sites can vary widely in quality and content-type. Pornographic poetry and fiction are fairly popular, as are "fan-fic" sites, where fans of particular films, television shows, or books will write (and extensively critique) stories based upon already established and well-known characters. Poets and serious fiction writers have not been convinced that Web publication is the way to make their mark (or a living!) as writers. Perhaps justifiably, they feel that nobody will buy their books if their work is distributed electronically. Although most experts agree that literary works that have not gone through a professional editorial process tend to be of inferior quality, in the long run, readers will likely determine the success or failure of such sites.

Hypertext Fiction

Already a fast-disappearing art form on the Web, hypertext fiction is an experimental and exciting storytelling environment. Fiction writers in the late 1990s became interested in the possibilities of allowing readers to follow their tales in nonlinear ways. Instead of turning (or clicking) pages in a preset order, hypertext fiction holds the possibility of linking story elements in interesting and creative ways that give *readers* the choice of elements to follow within the text of the work. Unfortunately, authors of avant-garde and interesting hypertext fiction have become reluctant to post their fiction on the open Web for fear of intellectual property theft. Some works are available on CD-ROM, but few survive as open sites on the World Wide Web. This is sad news. Writers who are brave enough to experiment with hypertext fiction should be encouraged.

CARTOON SITES

Creating a cartoon Web site can be exciting and fun, but unless your 'toons are copyrighted and carefully protected, you might want to think twice before uploading them for the whole world to view and copy. Likewise, if you wish to feature other artists' cartoons on your site, it is necessary to get *written permission* from the artist and from any publisher or company that may own the cartoons.

MULTIMEDIA AND INTERACTIVE MULTIMEDIA

Sites that feature video, sound, and animation—**multimedia**—are also popular. "Interactive multimedia" is often defined as any site that interacts with users by allowing them to control what elements will be presented on screen and in what order. Visitors to interactive multimedia sites can, to a certain degree, control the flow of information and perform tasks, usually by means of a mouse, joystick, or keyboard.

Not every site is for everyone, although some are difficult for most of us to resist. Almost any person with a sense of humor can appreciate Angry Alien Productions' "30-Second Bunnies Theatre" Web site (famous films, each encapsulated humorously in 30 seconds by animated bunnies: *www.angryalien.com*; see Figure 8.3).

"Jaws"

"The Rocky Horror
Picture Show"

"Scream"

FIGURE 8.3 30-Second Bunnies Theatre, "in which a troupe of bunnies parodies a collection of movies by re-enacting them in 30 seconds, more or less." Copyright Jennifer Shiman and Angry Alien Productions, used by permission. *http://www.angryalien.com*.

From a writer's perspective, the responsible multimedia Web site will include cautionary pages, including warnings about any adult content or other possibly offensive material. Visitors should also be given specific information about software, plug-ins, or operating system requirements needed to view media elements.

Writing for interactive multimedia can involve many different writing styles, formats, and skills. Interactive online gaming, for example, is a huge industry, and many games are becoming Web based. The skills writers use in writing for game sites are usually accumulated through experience with games and gaming and through trial-and-error scripting. Not only do game writers need to develop a great sense of linear storytelling and dramatic suspense, they also have to be patient and creative with the written and visual choices offered to game players along the various stages and levels of the game. Writers for such sites must prepare text elements that are used both in-house (behind the scenes) and on-screen:

- *Proposals:* Games and multimedia projects can require expensive high-end design and programming to get off the ground. A well-written proposal can make or break the backing a project receives at the start.
- *Treatments:* When seeking financial backing for new games and multimedia projects, writers usually provide a treatment—a compact, prose version of the main story elements of a game or video production. A good treatment details a blow-by-blow summary of the story, including important details of setting, action, and character. Usually told in present tense and generally with no dialogue, the treatment's main purpose is to capture the attention and interest of potential backers.
- *Scripts:* Multimedia Web sites—even those that appear spontaneous and "reality based"—tend to be carefully scripted. Video and audio media scripts provide visual descriptions and actions of characters and their dialogue.
- *Walk-throughs:* Developers are often required to explain step-by-step the capabilities and procedures within the multimedia project or the interactive game. Often such walk-throughs are designed for customers or usability testers who provide immediate feedback.

- *Document designs:*   Manuals, help files, and other materials included with multimedia projects are often provided online as well as in print format.
- *On-screen text:*   Pop-ups, directions, menus, links, and other textual elements within a game should be stylistically consistent. They should match the dramatic purposes of the story or game.
- *Stories:*   Writers for multimedia—film, audio, video, gaming projects—are storytellers who know how to create characters, develop conflict and tension, craft scenes, and drive the action forward. Interactive storytelling is especially complex (and often intense!) for both writers and site visitors. Those interested in developing these exciting projects should spend time and effort learning the craft of creative storytelling. They need to be willing to take constructive critique from usability testers and from more experienced writers.
- *Dialogue:*   Putting words into characters' mouths is more than an ability to write down natural, conversational language. Good dialogue should be realistic *within the world of the game or story* and should match the characters speaking it.
- *Characters:*   Even instructional videos are expected to present personalities who have interesting and attractive features and styles of communication. Whether the dialogue is for action-adventure heroes or personal hygiene instructors, readers and listeners expect to be engaged and swept along, not bored or repelled by the personalities on the screen (except, of course, in the case of monsters, villains, and other antagonists).
- *Narratives:*   Frequently, interactive sites provide text-based narratives that help visitors to understand the background and context of the experience they've logged into.
- *Voice-over narrations:*   Whether watching a video or maneuvering through the levels of a complicated game, visitors often enjoy a "host" or narrator who guides, teases, encourages, or simply informs them.
- *Interface design:*   Sometimes writers work with designers and media artists to develop interface elements, and other times writers are asked to work within the interface already created by others.
- *Visual metaphors and icons:*   Graphical and textual elements rely on carefully selected metaphors to help users make sense of on-screen content. Desktop metaphors usually guide users through everyday computer systems such as Microsoft Windows or Macintosh operating systems. But creative directors often look for new and exciting ways to move users and players through the scenes and actions of a multimedia site.
- *Linking:*   Direct links are labeled clearly and connect visitors to specific materials they choose to download. Indirect links (sometimes called "if-then" links) are used by games and creative sites to connect users to surprising elements that result from their actions. Intelligent links (or "smart links") are programmed to "remember" the choices a visitor has made along the way as he or she navigates through the site.

Each of these writing tasks has its own conventions of style and usage. The best way for writers to enter the world of interactive multimedia is through studying, experiencing, and learning as much as possible about the various media and game-building arts for themselves. It is especially helpful for Web writers to have one or more specialty areas of interest or expertise.

EXERCISE 8.1

Visit the "Angry Alien" Web site (*http://www.angryalien.com*) and view the "30-Second Bunnies Theatre" films. Discuss the strategies needed for compacting and condensing these famous movies into 30 seconds. (Optional: You may want to write out the 30-second script and compare it to the entire screenplay, if your library has a copy.)

Next, working alone or with a partner, choose a famous film not performed by the Bunnies Theatre and write a 30-second script that tells the essentials of the story. Instead of bunnies, choose another animal for your star performers. It is probably safe to assume that you are writing for an audience that has already seen the film and will appreciate the elements of the film you have chosen to include. Having viewed the entire story at least once before, they should be able to mentally fill in the blanks if your encapsulation includes the key lines and plot elements of the story that really stand out in viewers' minds. To get you started, some suggested film titles are:

Thelma and Louise (1991)	*Footloose* (1984)	*The Day the Earth Stood Still* (1951)
Norma Rae (1979)	*Kill Bill* (2003)	*King Arthur* (2004)
Fight Club (1999)	*Top Gun* (1986)	*Braveheart* (1995)
Million Dollar Baby (2004)	*Gladiator* (2000)	*Triple X* (2002)

When you are through writing, revising, and editing the 30-second condensed script of your film, select classmates to read the parts aloud for the class.

1. How did you make decisions about selecting characters to include and characters to eliminate?
2. How did you access the original film/screenplay for reference (i.e., DVD/VHS, "movie quotes" Web sites, word-for-word from memory, approximate quotes from memory, a library copy of the screenplay, etc.)?
3. Discuss the script with the class. Did classmates who had seen the original film react differently from those who hadn't? If so, in what ways?

COMMUNITY SITES

Name a topic, hobby, interest, movie, television show, art form, celebrity, sport, lifestyle, or medical condition, and there just might be dozens, perhaps hundreds of Web-based online communities that focus on it. Chat communities, newsgroups, special Web archive "bulletin board"–style sites, **MUDs** (Multi User Dungeons), and online gaming sites all have their own personality, tone, and conventions. Many blog sites advertise their "community" or "blogosphere" nature, although the level of interactivity among bloggers varies from service to service and interest to interest. Often it helps if a technical writer gathers together some of the agreed-upon rules of etiquette and puts them online for everyone to access.

Caution: Respect Intellectual Property Rights

When creating sites where writers and other artists can show off their work, be certain that both the site owners and the artists are as aware as possible of the risks and hazards of posting their own—or anyone else's—intellectual property on a public online Web service. It is also a good idea to explain clearly to site visitors the nature of the site. Official gallery sites and author-hosted sites are not the same thing as casual, personal pages where artists or amateur writers simply "self-publish" their own work online.

EXERCISE 8.2

Search the Web for sites that encourage creativity (or visit sites your instructor recommends). These might include some of the following:

- Fan fiction sites
- Poetry sites
- Mainstream fiction writing sites
- Science fiction sites
- Literature sites
- The Gutenberg Project
- Shakespeare on the Web
- Cartoon sites (original cartoons, not copied and pasted syndicated 'toons)
- Other multimedia sites

1. What kinds of materials or interactive elements are on the sites?
2. Whose work is it? One author/artist/designer/programmer? Several? Many?
3. Is the site edited and peer reviewed?
4. Is it a community site with discussion groups provided?
5. What kinds of materials do these sites solicit, if any?
6. How would you evaluate the literary work published on the site?
7. How would you evaluate the site's *technical writing*—instructions, help files, contact information, and so on?

Assignment 8.1

Using this book's appendices or other books and materials on writing that you like, create some online helpful tips or instructions for writers that provide good advice for writing poetry, fiction, blogs, satire, humor, or gaming tips for an Internet publication or readership. Your helpful messages might be in the form of pop-up windows, linked frames, flash animations, or any other creative presentation format in which you would like to experiment. Show your work to the class and invite discussion about the options and possibilities for creating helpful Web elements that are not simply lists of rules, FAQs, and help indexes. For example, your helpful suggestions might be written in the form of haiku or mouseover messages.

Case Studies for Writing and Discussion

CASE 1: DATABASE STYLE, INFORMATION MANAGEMENT, AND BUILDING COMMUNITY

Jamie Sommers was hired by Alligator Rescue, Inc. (AR-Inc.) to manage the company's public relations and advertising desktop publications. One of her first tasks was to create a database of information and vital statistics on all of the company's employees. This way, she reasoned, she would be able to call up key information about the background and qualifications of company personnel as she worked on press releases and advertising copy. Other employees eagerly jumped on board with the idea, suggesting important fields (chunks of information common to each record) that should be included in each record (the complete set of data fields for one main item—in this case, each employee job title comprises a record in the database). Some of the positions currently filled at Alligator Rescue include:

Head alligator rescuer	Alligator enclosure designer
Press agent	Alligator wildlife preserve manager
Manager, business office	Alligator wildlife preserve maintenance
Attorney	Staff zoologist
Alligator rescuer	Research assistant
Alligator rescue assistant	Veterinarian
Alligator wrangler	Animal caretaker

After setting up a simple database on the company's server, Jamie sent e-mail to the entire employee list, asking people to fill out the form on the company Web site (Figure A.1.1). The instructions on the Web form simply said:

Make sure your information is correct and up-to-date. Please write clearly and professionally; please use full sentences in the "bio" section. Thanks!—Jamie.

Several problems ensued:

- Jim Dugan, the staff zoologist, had his research assistant fill out the form. She forgot to add "M.A., Ph.D." after his name.
- Joan Jerard, the staff veterinarian, complained that the database was not password protected, and that anyone could get into it and tamper with employee information.
- Several of the employees ignored Jamie's request that they write in full sentences and instead lifted bulleted lists and fragments from their résumés.
- Some workers wrote sarcastic, fictionalized, or exaggerated "bio-narratives" that were almost useless to Jamie as she began putting together a proposal bid for a contract with the City Parks & Recreation Department.
- Most employees did not understand what Jamie wanted in the "bio" section, and she was swamped with calls and questions. In a follow-up e-mail, she told everyone to provide the number of years they had been employed at the company and to list the other achievements (i.e., publications, awards, promotions, etc.) they had accomplished in their careers related to the work they did at the company.

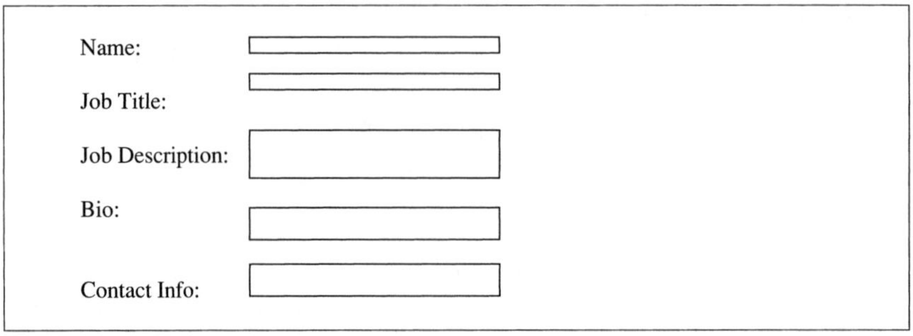

FIGURE A.1.1   Database forms should have clearly defined fields so that users know how to enter information correctly.

- Some of the biographies and job descriptions were full of grammatical errors and misspellings.
- Several staff members simply copied their résumés into the "job description" field, forcing Jamie to format all of their information from scratch, and then call them for bio material.

Questions

1. What could Jamie have done to get employees to submit more consistent written information for her database?
2. How could Jamie redesign her Web form to elicit the chunks of information she needs?
3. What kinds of instructions could she provide for the employees?
4. How can Jamie address Dr. Jerard's concerns about information security?
5. How could Jamie emphasize the need for grammatical consistency?
6. Is it possible for Jamie's employee database to be completed *without* some editing, reworking, and revision on her part? Why or why not?

Activities

Design a Web form for Jamie with a clear and simple set of instructions. This can be done either informally, as a class exercise, or formally, as a graded assignment.

1. Provide helpful fields for the form (do not worry about coding, although if you are studying CGI form development, this would be a good exercise for a mock-up database form). Employees should be able to type in information for Jamie's database. (Getting started: She would need fields for First Name, Last Name, Job Title, Years Employed at AR-Inc., Job Description, employee biographical information, etc.)
2. Write a new set of instructions or guidelines for Jamie to use, so that her database Web form will be more helpful to workers as they compose and revise their job descriptions and biographical information.

3. Assign each member of the class an Alligator Rescue, Inc. job title. As a class, develop a list of data fields and a set of instructions for writing biographical and descriptive sections of each employee record.

4. Have each class member, in the role of a company employee, provide his or her own information for the company database.

5. Discuss/describe the ways information wranglers must deal with multisource texts in the workplace. How consistent was the information the "employees" provided? What differences do you see in the style and format used by each person?

CASE 2: ELECTRONIC COMMUNICATION, FAQs, AND INFORMATIONAL WEB SITES

Carrie Fishbach, a second-year student at Sunnydale University, sent an e-mail to her history professor apologizing for missing class, asking what she missed, and requesting any assignment that would be due the following day. Professor Snyder, upon receiving Carrie's message among several dozen other e-mails requesting everything from complete transcripts of class lectures to deadline extensions and make-up quizzes, fired off the following e-mail to Carrie:

Dear Ms. Fishbach:

In the future, please compose your e-mails to me and other faculty on this campus in a more formal and polite manner—e-mail abbreviations such as "u" for "you" are immature and inappropriate in an academic context. Your request for a recap of the class lecture is simply too time-consuming. Please note that the class Web site (of which I provided you a printed copy on the first day of class) includes a syllabus that provides (1) a full schedule of all reading and writing assignments for the semester; (2) a full set of the course policies, including the number of absences allowed; (3) the "no make-up" policy; (4) the reminder that faculty can reasonably be expected to respond to e-mail within two working days; and (5) an explanation concerning the reasons that professors cannot be expected to write out full transcripts of the entire class lecture and discussion in e-mail. When you miss class, you should get lecture notes from a classmate as students have done for centuries, and you should always check the syllabus for assignments, whether you miss class or not.

If you have relevant questions based upon the assigned reading or class lectures, please take advantage of my office hours, or call me for an appointment.

Yours,
Dr. Rudy Snyder
Professor of History
Sunnydale University

Carrie was almost in tears as she arrived in her advisor's office, complaining bitterly that her professor had "flamed her" and that she was being horribly mistreated. The advisor tried to explain to the distraught young woman that the professor had most likely seen Carrie's demanding e-mail as a kind of "flame" in itself.

Questions

1. Analyze this communication problem in terms of possible problems in the professor's class Web site.
2. Suggest ways that Professor Snyder can improve the class Web site to clarify the e-mail policies and procedures.
3. Suggest ways Sunnydale U. can provide guidance to students for using e-mail to communicate with faculty.

4. Discuss ideas for an informational Web site for students at Sunnydale U. that will help them understand the best ways to communicate with their professors in e-mail.

5. Search your own school's campus Web site for help pages that assist students with everyday campus life. Do the instructions and advice truly reflect your experiences as a student at your school? Why? What would improve these pages? Are these pages designed to impress Web site visitors (such as parents and school benefactors), or to truly help students navigate everyday challenges at school?

Activities

1. Create a Frequently Asked Questions Web page to help students understand how to practice good e-mail "netiquette" at Sunnydale U.

2. In a group or as a class, create a student-friendly Web site and write a set of instructions for students at your own school, helping them to understand how to make effective use of the following kinds of online services. Your pages might include these topics:

> How to apply for admission
> How to register for classes online
> How to communicate effectively with professors using campus e-mail
> How to deal with "spam" or other kinds of unwanted e-mail in your campus account
> How to access and use online campus library resources
> How to manage a campus meal plan account
> How to balance homework and computer-gaming time (studies show that computer gaming has adverse effects on grade point averages)

3. Brainstorm more ideas for creating help and advice Web pages that would be useful for students at your school.

4. If possible, canvas fellow students around campus to find out (a) if they actually use the help pages that are already provided on the campus Web sites, and (b) what kinds of student-centered advice and information they would like to access online.

CASE 3: LOCAL IDENTITY AND MARKETING

Create a real or mock-up home page in which you use text and graphics to reflect (or create) an identity for a company, organization, or institution that does not already have a Web site.

- The page should create an online home and identity.
- The home page should use graphical elements—pictures, photographs, color scheme, etc.—to create visual identity.
- The home page should use consistent and readable typographical elements (text fonts) that create identity or that are consistent with typographical styles already used by the organization, such as letterhead, signs, business cards, and other printed material. If the organization logo employs an unusual typeface, consider using a graphics program to create some flash or graphics elements that employ this text face. Most browsers will default to either Times New Roman or Arial:

  This is Times New Roman, a serif *font*

  This is Arial, a sans serif *font*

  Serif refers to the horizontal line segments that decorate the tops and bottoms of letters. **Sans serif** means "without serif." (See Figure A.3.1.)
- The home page should have an organized and pleasant layout. Elements should be visually balanced and logically organized on the screen.
- The page should provide a clear portal. Its graphics, color scheme, links, and visual layout should indicate to a visitor the overall breadth and depth of the site (see Figure A.3.2). Often the depth of a site can be signaled by the textual elements you choose when constructing linked menus:

  Showing breadth: Indicate the number of "top end" categories introduced by subportal pages—Web pages that anchor or introduce categories of

Figure A.3.1   Fonts (typefaces) are designed for different reading tasks. The *Times New Roman* font employs serifs, which help readers' eyes glide smoothly along the lines of text on a page or screen. The *Arial* font is without ("sans") serifs and tends to force a reader's eyes to slow down and take note. It is typically a headline or banner font, and should be used sparingly in text-heavy Web writing.

Main Item	<H1>Text<H1>		**Main Item**
Sub Item	<H2>Text<H2>		**Sub Item**
	Sub-sub Item	[Normal Text]	Sub-sub Item
	Sub-sub Item	[Normal Text]	Sub-sub Item
	Sub-sub Item	[Normal Text]	Sub-sub Item

FIGURE A.3.2 Help readers visualize the depth and breadth of your site by using hierarchies to organize menus, site maps, and directories.

Web resources on a site (see "shallow and wide" versus "narrow and deep" Web architecture, Chapter 3).

Showing depth: Indicate or preview the depth of various sections, the amount of materials or resources visitors can expect to find, and how many clicks into the site they might need to locate them.

- With HTML or a WYSIWYG Web editing program, you can use tables and alignments to put design elements into an organized layout on the screen. Experiment with different patterns and arrangements of the text and graphics on your page. First try it without using tables or frames and watch what happens to the arrangement of your screen elements as you resize the browser window. Then use tables to place elements on the page where you would like them (you can set the features of your tables so that the borders and lines are invisible). (See Figures A.3.3 and A.3.4.)

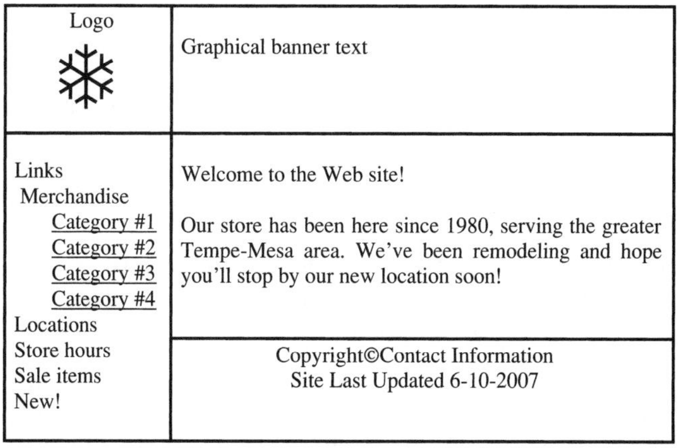

Logo ❄	Graphical banner text
Links Merchandise Category #1 Category #2 Category #3 Category #4 Locations Store hours Sale items New!	Welcome to the Web site! Our store has been here since 1980, serving the greater Tempe-Mesa area. We've been remodeling and hope you'll stop by our new location soon!
	Copyright©Contact Information Site Last Updated 6-10-2007

FIGURE A.3.3 Sample draft: Experiment with frames to arrange text and graphics on the page.

Some Web Table Arrangements

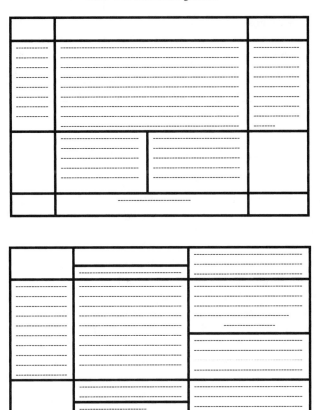

FIGURE A.3.4   Tables and other kinds of space-holders create uniform formatting for text and images. Looking at a number of Web sites, discuss the benefits and drawbacks to the arrangements of columns, banners, navigation links, images, and text on the screen.

Questions

As a group or in class, discuss which elements of the sample page draft seem to work well and which do not. Do your classmates agree on the elements they like and those they dislike? Why do you think that is?

1. Because the computer screen is organized in rows and columns of pixels, graphical and textual elements have to be partitioned and organized by means of these coordinates (even image maps must be coded, either by hand or with a WYSIWYG editor, by using the X-Y axis). Discuss ways to use rectangular spaces on the screen to organize large amounts of text and other data.

2. Looking at some of the Web sites you believe to be graphically exciting, discuss ways the digital artists have resisted the confines of the rectangular X-Y axis paradigm.

CASE 4: TRADITION, BRANDING, AND PUBLIC RELATIONS

Using a search engine, look for Web sites that belong to local historic buildings, monuments, statues, parks, galleries, or small museums—historic and community sites that are not funded with huge Web budgets. (Note: National historic museums and monuments tend to have huge, elaborate, well-funded Web sites—avoid those for purposes of this case.) Start with special landmarks, ones that you like and are familiar with. Think about community parks, local heroes, and even small archaeological digs. Keep several browser windows open and answer the following questions about three or four historic landmark Web sites.

Questions

1. Is the written content sparse or incomplete? If so, what could be added? Does the site depend more heavily on graphics and photos than on written material? Why or why not? What is the level of commercialism? Does it seem appropriate? Too much? Not enough? Why?
2. How strong is the writing? How would you characterize the writing? What kinds of stylistic choices could have made it more interesting to read? For example, does the writing style suggest that the site has been developed with children in mind? Adults? Specialists? Hobbyists? Others?
3. What kinds of words and phrases seem to be common among these kinds of Web sites? Do the different historic/monument sites organize their informational text in similar ways? What kinds of links and topics do they use?
4. Does the site include historic narrative writing? How readable or interesting is it? Could it be improved? Why or why not?
5. How heavily does the site rely on outside links for information? Is the official site closely affiliated with local, state, or national government? Are there links to government Web sites?

Activities

Use your favorite search engine or your city's Chamber of Commerce Web site to find a local historic building, monument, statue, park, gallery, or small museum whose Web site could use help, some small official Web site whose writing could be "punched up" for readers to enjoy. Try to incorporate the following strategies:

1. Develop a brisk, interesting narrative that quickly explains what the historic site is and why it has been preserved and made available to the public.
2. Do some preliminary research on the subject—don't just rely on the Web for your historic narrative. (This element of the assignment is crucial, because writing for the Web should involve more than just moving bits of text around from one site to another. Sources of information should be cited and listed properly, using MLA or APA research manual style.) If possible, visit the monument and collect brochures, booklets, and the titles of good books on the subject.

3. Create some informational written text about the historic site or gallery that Web visitors can enjoy reading, while at the same time gaining insight into the subject. Try to strike a balance between "official mission statement" style and "interesting historical narrative" style.

4. Optional: For smaller Web sites, construct an entirely new site with a new, fresh look and feel, incorporating links to your narratives. If possible, work with the graphical elements that curators/managers of the old site seemed to think appropriate and representative of the historical place in their care.

CASE 5: TASK-ORIENTED WEB SITE

Your company's technical writing team has worked to organize a trip to London, England, to attend the International Professional Communication Conference. Your group has been asked to create a Web site providing information and help for the trip. A memo was circulated, giving general information, but it proved confusing for most employees interested in the trip:

Date: April 1
To: Technical Writers and Web Teams, Robidoux International Corp.
From: Veronica Lodge
Re: Conference in England!

Roberta Reed in Human Resources has confirmed that travel financing has been approved for this year's International Professional Communication Conference. Those planning to attend should pick up travel forms from Roberta as soon as possible and submit them to Sandra at the HR main desk before May 1. The conference is July 10–13, so all who are going will need to clear this with their immediate supervisors and section managers. Make sure your passports haven't expired! Also, see the IPCC Web site about accommodations, or talk to Roberta (more information will be coming soon). Costs for travel and conference hotel accommodations will be covered by the company, but those wishing to extend their stay in the UK for travel/vacation will need to make additional arrangements. See Roberta for suggestions!

See you all in jolly old England!
VL

Because most of the technical writers at your company are not experienced with conference attendance and travel, the memorandum caused a flurry of questions and more than a little confusion. As a result, Veronica, Roberta, and Sandra have asked your Web writing group to create a modest Web site that is "not just a bunch of links" to IPCC Web sites. Instead, the site should include the following pages that will *specifically* help the people you work with who are interested in participating.

Discuss the kinds of content that should be provided for the following pages:

- Deadlines for application to participate
- Travel expense information
- Company travel policies
- Passport information and help
- E-mail list or discussion board for employees who want to organize additional sightseeing outings and excursions
- Travel ticketing information
- Accommodation information

- Tips for travel in the United Kingdom
- Sightseeing opportunities
- Additional travel options
- Links to relevant outside Web sites, including any downloadable schedules and information on the Web site for the International Professional Communication Conference

What additional pages and information should be provided on this site?

Activities

1. Choose one or more of the pages listed above and create a draft of the specific information that should be provided.
2. Submit a proposal and outline for a Web site that provides travel information for a campus, business, or community group trip. Summarize the information you plan to include, the layout and organization you recommend, the kinds of links you feel are appropriate, appropriate contact information, and any graphical elements you think are helpful. Make sure that the site has a "take-down" schedule so that outdated information does not remain online after the trip is over.

CASE 6: HOBBY OR SPECIAL INTEREST WEB SITE

This case is designed to help you write for an information-heavy Web site. The assigned content could be saved in any word-processing program and placed into a simple, multiple-page site, or perhaps into a site constructed using frames. The architecture, while important to organizing and making the information readily available, is secondary to the actual text (and perhaps digital images) the writer is expected to produce.

Provide a detailed proposal that justifies a web site focusing on one of your hobbies or special interests and explains its elements. If you are having trouble generating ideas for your site, you may want to refer to the Web Plan assignment located at the end of Chapter 2. Example topics might be:

Local frisbee golf courses and events	Local Welsh Corgi rescue organization
25th anniversary Blues Brothers film fest	Wildlife in the city: Kansas City, Missouri
My best friend's wedding	Fashion on campus: well-dressed nerds

You may wish to use the following worksheet to create your proposal. After writing down your ideas for the Web site, submit your proposal for feedback from the instructor or from peers, and provide feedback to others regarding their ideas. Feedback should be constructive and helpful so that the Web site can be as attractive and useful for its intended visitors as possible.

Note: Pages with asterisks (∗) are required; the rest are optional.

Proposal Worksheet

Subject: _____

Your level of knowledge about this subject could best be classified as:

_____ *Professional*

_____ *Master*

_____ *Expert*

_____ *Advanced*

_____ *Intermediate—Amateur*

_____ *Novice*

Three main reasons to create a Web site on this topic:

1. _____

2. _____

3. _____

Three main reasons people will want to visit the site (i.e., what will it offer?):

1. _____

2. _____

3. _____

Describe the primary audience of Web visitors for whom you will create this site:

_____

_____

_____

_____

_____

_____

*Home Page

Describe how you will provide the following elements for the home page of your site, including the sources of information you intend to use and methods for crediting or citing those sources.

   Statement of Purpose

   Image(s)

   Establish persona

   Establish "look and feel"

   Color scheme and design

   Contact information

   Links to other pages

   Other subject-specific home page information

*"About Us" Page (should be at least 250 words)

   Establish identity

   Provide important definitions

   Provide relevant biographical information

*Links Page

At least 25 links to Web sites related to the subject/theme of your site. Each link should tell your visitors where the link will take them and what kind of site it is.

Links Checklist:

- *Links should be titled and annotated.*
- *Links should be organized by subheadings.*
- *Each link must have:*

   Title (name) of Web site

   Owner of Web site

   URL clearly appearing and properly linked to the Web site (preferably opening in new window)

   Brief description of Web site

Remember: Links are primarily provided for your visitors so use associative thinking to look for sites they would be interested in, for the same (or similar) reasons they have come to your site. Links might take them to resources, products, services, shopping, barter, trade, supplies, instructions, demonstrations, competitions, conventions, research databases, etc.

*Detailed Instructions Page

Help them out! Write a text-heavy page of at least 500 words of instructions and information that will be helpful to the primary audience of this Web site. (Note: This is not a FAQ page.)

*Site Map

A page that provides links to all other pages in the site in an organized way that reflects the structure of the information/Web pages.

*Identification Footers

Copyright, date the site was last updated, and contact information should appear on every page, preferably at the bottom.

Other

What other kinds of pages do you see a need for?

_____   _____

_____   _____

_____   _____

CASE 7: TERMS AND CONDITIONS OF USE FOR ONLINE COMMERCE OR COMMUNITY SITES

Call up several "terms and conditions" Web pages posted online at sites that provide interactive services. (An easy way to do this is to type "terms of service," including quotation marks, into your favorite Web search engine.) Choose one that is 10 to 20 screens in length.

Questions

1. Look closely at each section on the terms of use page in Figure A.7.1. Is it easy to tell which parts seem to be important for visitors to know and understand, and which parts seem to be posted simply to protect the Web site owners from complaints or lawsuits?
2. List the sections that seem vitally important for customers and Web site users to know and understand. Give one or two reasons explaining why they are more important *from the user's point of view* than other sections seem to be.
3. From the Web site's home page, how many clicks and false leads does it take to find the legal terms and conditions of use?

Activities

Either alone or with a team, prepare a summary Web page that provides a synopsis of the important terms of service shown in Figure A.7.1 (or your instructor may assign a different, similar terms of service Web document).

1. Make sure the synopsis is as free as possible from confusing legal terminology. The page should give visitors the main information and also any "stealth terms" you may unearth as you comb through the document. *Stealth terms* means hidden information that could trick users into making uncomfortable choices. That is, can you find any terms that could cause problems for users? For example, could someone lose access, data, or even money by breaching some rule or condition that is not obvious?
2. Search for information important for visitors to know and understand. Try to keep the information concise and specific, limited to only two or three screens from beginning to end.
3. Make sure that the page you create clearly states that it is no more than a *summary* of the main important terms and conditions and that the page is clearly *linked* to the complete terms and conditions of use.

SERVICE AGREEMENT

(**YOUR FICTIONAL WEB COMPANY NAME GOES HERE**), HEREUNTO REFERRED TO AS "__(shortened version of company name)_____," PROVIDES SERVICES TO YOU ON THIS SITE ("SERVICES") AND INCLUDE PROPRIETARY MATERIALS, THE USE OF WHICH IS SUBJECT TO THE TERMS AND CONDITIONS OF THIS END-USER AGREEMENT, AS AMENDED FROM TIME TO TIME UPON NOTICE FROM _____, WHICH NOTICE MAY BE PROVIDED TO YOU ON THE PAGES THROUGH WHICH YOU ACCESS OR USE THE SERVICES. PROCEEDING WITH THE USE OF THE SERVICES, OR THE CONTINUED USE OF THE SERVICES AFTER RECEIVING NOTICE OF ANY CHANGES, CONSTITUTES YOUR ASSENT TO AND ACCEPTANCE OF THE END-USER AGREEMENT AND EXHIBIT A HERETO. IF YOU DO NOT AGREE WITH ALL THE TERMS, YOU MUST NOT USE THE SERVICES!

(**YOUR FICTIONAL WEB COMPANY NAME GOES HERE**) END-USER SERVICES AGREEMENT

This End-User Services Agreement ("Agreement") is an agreement between you, an individual or an individual acting on behalf of your employer, a corporation, partnership, or other legal entity that will be using _____'s services ("User"), _____ Incorporated, a Missouri corporation located at ___(company street address)___ ("Company"), and the owner of the Web site through which you have requested Everyone.net's services ("Client"). Everyone.net's services, as described below in Section 2 and Exhibit A hereto (the "Services"), include proprietary materials, the use of which is subject to the terms and conditions of this Agreement.

1. ACKNOWLEDGMENT AND ACCEPTANCE OF AGREEMENT The Services, provided by Company on behalf of Client, are provided to User under the terms and conditions of this Agreement and Exhibit A hereto, any amendments to this Agreement and/or Exhibit A, and any operating rules or policies that may be published from time to time by Company and Client, all of which are hereby incorporated by reference. This Agreement comprises the entire agreement between User and Company and supersedes any prior agreements pertaining to the subject matter contained herein.
2. DESCRIPTION OF SERVICES
Company, on behalf of Client, is providing User with any or all of the following services: (a) writing tools; (b) writing discussion groups; (c) speaking engagement queries; (d) web design consultation estimates, and (e) any other services which

(Continued)

Figure A.7.1 Terms of use.

Company may elect to provide on behalf of Client in the future. These Services are provided to User at the discretion of Client, and Company has no obligation to provide the Services directly to User. Company does not charge User for the Services (though Company may do so at any time in the future), but may charge for additional services User may elect to obtain. Company and Client also reserve the right to modify or discontinue, temporarily or permanently, the Services with or without notice to User. User agrees that Company, Client, and their third party service providers shall not be liable to User or any third party for any modification or discontinuance of the Services.

3. USER'S REGISTRATION OBLIGATIONS

User must be at least thirteen (13) years old to register for the Services. In consideration of use of the Services, User agrees to: (a) provide true, accurate, current, and complete information about User as prompted by the registration form; and (b) to maintain and update this information to keep it true, accurate, current, and complete. If any information provided by User ("Registration Data") is untrue, inaccurate, not current, or incomplete, Company and Client have the right to terminate User's account and refuse any and all current and/or future use of the Services.

4. USE OF REGISTRATION DATA

User acknowledges that Registration Data is to be shared between Company and Client. Company and Client agree not to contact User if User informs Company of User's preference not to be contacted. Company shall inform Client if User states a preference not to be contacted. However, Company shall not be responsible or liable if Client contacts User, permits a third party to contact User, or provides or discloses User's Registration Data to any third party.

—(**YOUR FICTIONAL WEB COMPANY NAME GOES HERE**) services

FIGURE A.7.1   *(Continued)*.

CASE 8: SCRIPT FOR DIGITAL VIDEO MINI-DEMO

Professor Claire de Lune had put some assignment materials on her campus Web site but wanted to personalize the materials for her class. She thought it would be fun to include short (30 to 60 seconds) videos explaining grammatical, mechanical, and stylistic concepts.

At first, her plan was to simply turn on the video recording equipment and ad-lib her way through the explanations and demonstrations. Soon, however, she discovered that she occasionally stammered or stumbled over words and sentences. She repeated herself or indulged in too many verbal pauses (such as "um-m-m," "well," "like," "ya know," "uh"). The videos she produced were easy to upload and run, but she didn't like the way they looked or the way she had explained things.

Dr. de Lune decided that her videos needed to be planned more carefully. She turned this project into a class assignment. Asking her students to work in pairs or small teams, she gave each team a grammatical or stylistic concept to work with. Each team created a short script (30 to 90 seconds) for her to follow. They then created some visual supports with various common computer software on the classroom computers. The visuals included various kinds of sentence patterns, metaphors, imagery, analogies, and other components of written English.

Questions

1. Name some topics and concepts you have seen successfully presented as short lectures or demonstrations in your college classes.
2. Which of the topics or concepts do you think could be converted into a short video suitable for an educational Web site?
3. What kinds of writing challenges are involved in producing a video?
4. What happens when visual elements and the narration don't correlate (fit together) very well?
5. What happens when visual elements are played on the screen with no narration?
6. What happens when the only visual element is the "talking head" of one person?
7. What kinds of visual aids could a writer suggest for a 30- to 60-second educational video?

Activities

Alone or with a partner, choose a subject (either from the following list or a different topic that interests you) and write a short video script (30 to 90 seconds) for an educational Web video that introduces the main concept. You may decide to give specific video scene directions or simply focus on the narrator's spoken lines. Remember that your brief script should only *introduce* the topic. Present the main terms and ideas and pique viewers' interest.

Displacement theory (Physics)	Subject-verb agreement (English grammar)	Maslow's Hierarchy of Needs (Psychology)
JFK's televised assassination (History)	Assonance and alliteration (Poetry)	Laws of thermodynamics (Physics)
Hegelian dialectic (Philosophy)	Negative capability (Literature)	The Bill of Rights (Justice studies)
Product liability (Tort law)	Détente (Political science)	Pointillism (Art)
Liminal space (Anthropology)	Mitosis (Biology)	Perspective (Graphic art)
Time signatures (Music)	Placebo effect (Medicine)	Laminitis (Veterinary medicine)
Schematic diagrams (Electronic technology)	Feature creepism (Engineering design)	Holy Grail (Mythology)
Transubstantiation (Theology)	TQM (Business management)	Film noir (Film studies)

Index of Basic XHTML Tags

Item	Command	Description	Display
Document type	<HTM></HTML>	Hypertext markup language*	Beginning and end of HTML document*
Title	<TITLE></TITLE>	Title of page	Title shown for bookmarks and meta-searches (look at the title bar of the browser)
Header	<HEAD></HEAD>	Title shown on the page	Header contains meta tags and title information
Body	<BODY></BODY>	Body/text of the page	Contents of the page are inside body tags
Bold	<B></B>	Bold text	Text appears bold
Italic	<I></I>	Italic text	Text is italic
Paragraph	<P></P>	New paragraph	Start and finish of a paragraph
Hard return	 	Hard return	Start a new line/space
Center	<CENTER></CENTER>	Center items	You can center anything
Blinking	<BLINK></BLINK>	Blinking text	Text will blink (flash)
Font colors	<FONT COLOR="#FFFFFF"></FONT>	Colored font	Text will show in color
Font size	<FONT SIZE=+1></FONT>	Font size	Change text size

*You might want to precede the <html> document type tag with the following !doctype tag, to tell browsers which type of XHTML encoding is in use. This particular tag stipulates that the "transitional" version of XHTML is in use:

<! DOCTYPE HTML PUBLIC "-//W3C//DTD HTML 4.01 Transitional//EN" "http://www.w3.org/TR/html4/loose.dtd">

Meta Tags (Used in Header: Do Not Appear in Browser Display)		
Search engine meta tag	Provides content information for search engines	Search engine displays content information
`<meta name="description" content="content goes here" />`		
Search engine meta tag	Provides keywords for searches	Search engine finds page through keyword searches
`<meta name="keywords" content="keywords go here" />`		
Browser meta tag	Sets language for the page	Page displays in English
`<meta http-equiv="Content-Language" content="en" />`		
Browser meta tag: char set tag	Designates the character set for the page	Page displays in the standard character set for English and other European languages
`<meta http-equiv="Content-Type" content="text/html; charset=iso-8859-1" />`		
Browser meta tag: refresh tag	Causes the page to refresh or reload	Page refreshes after 10 seconds
`<meta http-equiv="Refresh" content="10" />`		
Browser meta tag: redirect tag	Refreshes and redirects the browser	After 10 seconds the browser will be redirected to the designated Web site
`<meta http-equiv="Refresh" content="10; URL=http://www.firstgov.gov" />`		
Browser meta tag: meta cache	Instructs the browser not to cache the page	Page will not be cached by the browser
`<meta http-equiv="pragma" CONTENT="no-cache" />`		
CREATING LINKS		
Link	Link text to a different Web page	Click on underlined text to go to another page
`<A HREF="Newpage.html">New Page</A>`		

Image	Display an image	An image appears on the page	
<A HREF="Picture.gif">Picture</A>			
Image link	Link an image to another Web page	Image is linked to another Web page	
<A HREF="newpage.html"><IMG SRC="pageimage.gif"></A>			
Image link to e-mail	Image link to e-mail account	Click on the image and the e-mail box comes up	
<A HREF="mailto:youremail@here"><IMG SRC="yourimage.jpg"></A>			

Tables			
Begin table	<TABLE></TABLE>	Begining and end of table	Statements to start and end the table
Table row	<TR></TR>	Beginning and end of table row	Table row
Table data	<TD></TD>	New cell	Sets off a new cell within a table row
Color background	<TD COLOR="#FFCCCC"></TD>	Background color	Color in a cell
Colored font	<FONT COLOR="#CCCCFF"></FONT>	Colored font	Text is in color
Cell spacing	<TABLE CELLSPACING=# />	Cell space	Sets amount of space between table cells
Cell padding	<TABLE CELLPADDING=# />	Cell padding	Sets amount of space between a cell's border and its contents
Cell alignment	<TR VALIGN=?> or <TD VALIGN=?>	Cell alignment	Sets alignment for cell(s) (left, center, or right)
Table width	<TABLE WIDTH=300></TABLE>	Sets table width in % or in pixels	Make the table width only 300 pixels
No border	<TABLE BORDER=0></TABLE>	No border	Table has no borders
Table border	<TABLE BORDER=# />	Table border	Sets width of border around table cells

Add Text or Background Color to the Page	
Red = #FF0000	Black = #000000
White = #FFFFFF	Gray = #CC9999
Blue = #0000FF	Green = #00FF00
Light blue = #00FFFF	Yellow = #FFFF66
Light blue = #00CCFF	Purple = #CC33FF

EXERCISE

If you have not already done so, create a Web page using the XHTML code exercise in Chapter 1. Save it to your disk or desktop.

If you have access to a WYSIWYG editor, open a page you created using HTML code and a plain text editor (like the exercise in Chapter 1). Explore the various features of the software by experimenting with the page attributes such as background color, text size, fonts, tables, and bulleted lists. Save your page and view the source code (usually you can click "View" on the menu bar and choose "Source" or "Page source"). Identify as many tags and attributes as you can and make changes as you wish. If your editor has an HTML editing mode (look for a tab or button), make some changes in the heading size, table cells, or colors of the page by using HTML tags. Save your work and view your page in the browser (you may need to click on the "Refresh" button).

For tutorials and practice using HTML and XHTML code, visit some popular Web development sites such as the following:

Lycos Webmonkey beginner's HTML site: *http://hotwired.lycos.com/webmonkey/*
W3Schools Internet developers portal, hosted and updated by Refsnes Data: *http://www.w3schools.com*
National Center for Supercomputing Applications (NCSA) at the University of Illinois at Urbana-Champaign *http://archive.ncsa.uiuc.edu/General/Internet/WWW/HTMLprinter.html*
World Wide Web Consortium (W3C), Dave Raggett's "Getting Started with HTML": *http://www.w3.org/MarkUp/Guide/*
Oxford Brookes University HTML Primer: *http://www.w3c.rl.ac.uk/primers/html/htmlprimer.htm*

Note: These sites are popular and well known, but the Internet is a fickle resource, and some links may have changed or disappeared during the process of this book's publication.

For XHTML tutorials visit the W3 Schools web site: *http://www.w3.org/MarkUp/Guide*

Glossary of Terms for Web Writers

Adware: A program that is installed at the same time as a shareware program or other downloaded software. Adware usually continues to generate advertising even when the user is not running the originally desired program (*see also:* Spyware).

Alias: A short, easy-to-remember name created for use in place of a longer, more complicated name; commonly used in e-mail applications. Also referred to as a *nickname*.

Archives: A searchable, organized site containing a large number of files, possibly acquired over time, and often publicly accessible.

ARPANET: Advanced Research Projects Agency Network. The precursor to the Internet, it was a network developed in the late 1960s and early 1970s by the U.S. Department of Defense. As an experiment in wide area networking (WAN), ARPANET was developed with the goal of being robust enough to survive a nuclear war. Part of the experiment was to study how distributed, noncentralized electronic information networks work.

ASCII: ASCII (American Standard Code for Information Interchange) is the de facto worldwide standard for the code numbers used by computers to represent all the capital and lowercase Latin letters, numbers, punctuation, etc. There are 128 standard ASCII codes, each of which can be represented by a 7-digit binary number: 0000000 through 1111111. ASCII files or "plain text format" files are text (letters, numbers, punctuation) without any special formatting like bold or italics. Every computer can open an ASCII file, and most word processing programs can make and save ASCII files.

Attachment: A file sent along with an e-mail message. If the attached file is encoded, transmitted, and decoded properly, the receiver of the e-mail should be able to open the file and view the document in its original form. Attachments can be rendered unusable because of differences in hardware or software configurations between a sender and a receiver.

Bandwidth: Usually measured in bits per second, bandwidth determines the rate at which information can be sent through your connection. The greater the bandwidth, the more information that can be sent in a given amount of time.

Banner: A graphic element, usually spanning the top of a Web page. Banners can be used to title the page, head a new section, present a company's or advertiser's message, or provide a link to another page.

Bit: Binary DigIT, a single-digit number in base-2 (in other words, either a 1 or a 0); the smallest unit of computerized data.

Blog: Short for Web log, an online journal or diary. Updating a blog is called *blogging* and someone who maintains a blog is a *blogger*. Blogs are typically updated daily using online software or services that allow people with little or no technical background to update and maintain the blog. Blogs are usually arranged in reverse chronological order, with the most recent posts heading the page.

Branding: Marketing shorthand for creating brand recognition. Typical methods employ a name, term, logo, slogan, sign, symbol, design, or some combination of these to establish recognition and brand loyalty.

Browser: A software application used for accessing and displaying Web site content on the computer screen. Mosaic was the first popular browser; newer browser programs include Mozilla, Opera, Netscape, and Internet Explorer.

Bulletin board system or service (BBS): A computer dial-up meeting and announcement system for posting to discussion boards, uploading and downloading files, and generally obtaining online information and services. BBS also refers to a congregation of users gathered electronically by modem, where each person can post messages. They began as informal communities but now include political, commercial, adult, gaming, and many other categories. There are thousands of BBSs around the world, many of which are very small, running on personal computers with special software and one or two phone lines.

Byte: A set of bits that represents a single ASCII character (i.e., letter, number, symbol, punctuation mark). Usually there are 8 bits in a byte, sometimes more, depending on how the measurement is being made.

CERN: Conseil Européen pour la Recherche Nucléaire. The European Particle Physics Laboratory in Geneva, Switzerland.

Chunking: The division of written material into small segments or chunks. Screens are hard on the eyes and have limited size, so chunks have to be small. Creating logical chunks of information that can be assembled easily by database or active server programming helps make Web page displays consistent and readable.

Client: (1) A customer; someone who pays for a technical writer's services. (2) A software program that is used to contact and obtain data from a server software program on another computer, often across a great distance. Commonly used clients include chat programs, Web browsers, and e-mail programs.

CMC: Computer-Mediated Communication. Refers to human-to-human communication in e-mail, chat, Web posting groups, etc.

Codex: A paper, vellum, or papyrus manuscript that is sewn together in the form of a book, with a spine and often a cover. The codex form replaced the scroll as the most common form of manuscript in the first century A.D. Occasionally, when texts of substantial length are available in both print and electronic form, the electronic form will be referred to as the *online* version and the paper form will be referred to as the *print* or the *codex* version.

Connectivity: In computer lingo, the ability of a program or device to link with other programs and devices. For example, a program that can import and manipulate data from a wide variety of other programs and can export information in many different formats is said to have good connectivity. A device or program that has difficulty linking into a network or translating data from other machines is said to have poor connectivity.

Cyberspace: A term coined by William Gibson in his science fiction novel *Neuromancer* (1984) to describe the interconnected world of computer technologies and the society that gathers around—and in a sense within—them. Today, cyberspace is often used interchangeably with "the Internet" and all of the computers and networks that it encompasses.

Data: Factual units of information represented in a readable language (such as numbers, characters, images, or audible recordings) on a durable medium. Data on their own carry no meaning. Empirical data are facts collected and recorded through observations or experiences.

Database: A collection of information stored in a computer medium that can be easily searched, accessed, and manipulated. A database also stores metadata, i.e., data about data. The term *database* is often erroneously referred to as a synonym for a database management system (DBMS). They are not the same thing. A database is a store of data that describe entities and the relationships between the entities. A database management system is the software mechanism for managing that data.

Data stream: A continuous stream of data elements being transmitted, or intended for transmission, in character or binary-digit form, using a defined format; an ordered sequence of data being electronically transmitted over a data link.

Deep linking: The practice of linking to a page one or more layers "inside" another Web site, bypassing the home page of the site.

Directory/subdirectory: A unit of organization for storing information on a computer. Within a directory, you can store subdirectories and files. Most PC and Macintosh computers use the folder as an icon to represent directories and subdirectories (*see also:* Folder).

Discourse community: A group or subculture whose members use a particular style of language—such as members of a particle physics consortium, a genetics think-tank, a religious denomination, or Mötley Crüe fans. Each discourse community has unwritten rules about what can be said and how it should be said. Most of us move among different discourse communities daily.

Document: (1) When used in reference to the World Wide Web, any file containing text, media, or hyperlinks that can be transferred from an HTTP server to a client program, typically a browser. Many browsers can locate and call up nonhypertext files by opening the application associated with those files. For example, Web browsers now can locate a .doc file and signal your word processing program to open and display the file. (2) In the broadest sense, any container of coherent information that has been assembled for human understanding. For technical writers, a document usually refers to a discrete, complete textual artifact that records information. Typical documents include procedural guidelines, annual reports, contract proposals, policy guides, agreements, correspondence, and technical manuals.

Domain name: The unique name that identifies an Internet site. Domain names always have two or more parts, separated by dots. The part on the left is the more specific name chosen by the site owners. The part on the right is more general and indicates the category of site. For example, the domain kcur.org indicates the site is owned by KCUR public radio in Kansas City and that it is the site of a nonprofit organization. Although there are many sites with the .org extension, only one of them is named kcur.org.

Download: (1) Transferring data (usually a file) from another computer to the computer you are using. Technically, when we say that we are "going to visit" a Web site, what we really mean is that we will download the Web site's data files to our own computer, where these files are stored in a temporary file (sometimes called a *cache*) and displayed on the screen in a browser. (2) Copying a file from another computer (or system) to one's own. From the computer user's point of view, to download a file is to send a request to another computer (often a server) by means of electronic protocols—such as File Transfer Protocol (FTP) or HyperText Transfer Protocol (HTTP)—for a file, which is then stored and displayed on one's own computer. (3) The opposite of upload (*see also:* Upload).

Driver: A software application that tells the computer how to operate an external device, such as a printer, CD burner, or scanner. The driver acts as an interface between the computer operating system (such as Windows or Macintosh), and the hardware device. Each hardware component usually requires a driver, and the driver is usually furnished by the manufacturer.

Electronic data transfer (EDT): Transmitting information over a network. An EDT system receives data electronically from various outside sources (often buyers and/or suppliers) and sometimes edits and reformats this data before displaying it.

Experiential cognition: In experiential cognition "patterns of information are perceived and assimilated and the appropriate responses generated without apparent effort or delay. Experiential thought is essential to skilled behavior. It appears to flow naturally, but years of experience and training may be required to make it possible" (Norman, 1993).

External link: A link that points to a page outside the currently displayed Web site. Lacking any other visual cues that we have called up a different site, we can often recognize an external link because it is an "absolute" URL address (e.g., *http://www.z. com/index.html*), rather than a "relative" link, or one that simply points to another file in the same directory as the one already called up (e.g., nextpage.html).

FAQ: Frequently Asked Questions. Web pages that list and answer the most common questions on a particular subject. FAQs are usually written by people who have grown tired of answering the same questions over and over. Sophisticated, well-written Web sites have less need of these pages when they respond to frequent questions by pushing much-needed information to the front end (home page, or main nodes) of the Web site where visitors can easily find it.

Feature creepism: The tendency for designers or engineers to add more capability, functions, and features to a product, even though no such features were planned in the design specifications. Feature creepism often results when novice programmers fail to understand industrial constraints such as resource budgeting and deadlines. It can also cause schedule slip, development cost increases, and product cost increases.

Flame: A personal, derogatory, and frequently crude message posted to an online discussion community such as a newsgroup, discussion board, or e-mail list. Flaming was once considered an argumentative art form, but the term now refers to strongly worded insults. While unfriendly, a remark such as, "You are uninformed and wrong-headed" is not a flame. Rather, a flame might contain comments like "Only a moronic idiot like you would come up with such a wretched idea."

Folder: Another way to refer to a named storage area (on a computer) that contains files and other subfolders. In a URL a single part of the path to a page can be the name of a folder. For example, in *http://www.mysite/sample/test.htm*, "/sample/" points to a folder (directory) named "sample" inside the "mysite" domain directory (*see also:* Directory/subdirectory).

Frames: A term used to describe the viewing and layout style of a Web site. Frames are a technique used to divide the screen into multiple windows. Each window is called a *frame* and can contain its own separate Web page. Usually these separate frames appear seamless and are designed to function easily together on the screen. The advantage of frames is that one window can be scrolled or changed while other windows remain fixed for such purposes as keeping a menu in view all the time.

FTP: File Transfer Protocol. A method of connecting to another computer via the Internet for the purpose of transferring files from one computer to another.

Genre: A type of literature, rhetoric, art, or communication marked by certain shared features or conventions. For example, the three broadest categories of literary genre include poetry, drama, and fiction. These general genres are often subdivided into more specific genres. For instance, precise examples of genres might include murder mysteries, romantic comedies, film noir, sonnets, lyric poetry, epics, tragedies, etc.

Gopher: Predecessor of the search engine, Gopher is/was a widely successful method of making menus of digitized material available over the Internet. Gopher is a client and server style of program, which requires that the user have a Gopher client program. Although Gopher spread rapidly across the globe in only a couple of years, it has been largely supplanted by hypertext file servers, also called the *World Wide Web* (WWW). There are still thousands of Gopher servers on the Internet, and they may remain in use by some users and providers for quite some time.

Graphical user interface (GUI): A graphical display format that presents an environment used to navigate the computer screen.

Host: Any computer on a network that is configured to provide services made available to other computers on the network. It is quite common to have one host machine provide several services, such as SMTP (e-mail service) and HTTP (Web service).

HTML: Hypertext Markup Language. The coded set of tags, symbols, and syntactical patterns that create Web page (HTML) files.

HTTP: Hypertext Transfer Protocol. The digital protocol for moving hypertext files across the Internet. Requires an HTTP client (browser) program on the receiving end and an HTTP server program on the file-storage end.

Human-computer interface (HCI): Sometimes referred to as user interface. The visual display and physical "contact zones" where the user interacts with the computer. HCI is also used in reference to human-computer interaction, the study of how people interact with computers and to what extent computers are (or are not) developed for successful interaction with humans.

Hyperlink/link: An image or portion of text on a Web page that is linked to another Web page, either on the same site or another Web site. Clicking on the link will signal the browser to call up another Web page or to display another section of the same page. Words or phrases that serve as links are usually underlined or appear in a different color from the body text (or both). Images that serve as links may change color or shape as the cursor passes over them (or at the very least, the cursor arrow should turn into the familiar hyperlink hand).

Hypertext: Text on a Web page that is linked to another Web page. Sometimes refers generically to any document "marked up" in HTML and containing hyperlinks.

Icon: A small graphic symbol on the computer screen that represents a function or file type.

Image map: An image containing one or more coded regions, called *hotspots,* which are assigned hyperlinks. Typically, an image map gives users visual cues about the information made available by clicking on each part of the image. For example, a geographical map could be coded into an image map by assigning hotspot sections to each conventional region of interest on the map.

Information management: An ambiguous term covering the various stages of information processing from production to storage and retrieval to dissemination. Information can be moved around from internal or external sources and in any format. Includes creating/collecting, capturing, registering, classifying, indexing, storing, retrieving, and disposing of records, and developing strategies to manage records.

Intellectual property (IP): Property that enjoys legal protection and stems from the exercise of the mind. Content of the human intellect deemed to be unique and original and to have marketplace value, and thus to warrant protection under the law. Intellectual property protections generally fall into four categories: copyright (for literary works, art, photography, and music), trademarks (for company and product names and logos), patents (for inventions and processes), or trade secrets (for recipes, computer programming code, and some kinds of processes). Concern over defining and protecting intellectual property on the Internet has brought this area of the law under intense scrutiny, and many Internet IP issues will probably remain unstable and undecided for decades to come.

Internal link: (1) Link to another page belonging to the same Web site. (2) Link to another section of the same page.

Internet: A worldwide network of computer networks; the vast collection of interconnected networks that all use the TCP/IP protocols. Initially developed as a self-healing data-sharing network for the U.S. military called ARPANET in the late 1960s and early 1970s, but now in popular use as a file-download and e-mail conduit.

Internet Relay Chat (IRC): A protocol that allows users to converse with others in real time. IRC is structured as a network of servers, each of which accepts connections from client programs. It was developed in 1988 by J. Oikarinen in Finland. Many servers around the world are interconnected to allow hundreds of thousands of users to chat at the same time, either in *channels* (also called *chat rooms*) or one-on-one in private message windows. Special IRC clients are necessary to connect but are available online for free.

Intranet: A private network that uses Internet protocols and common Internet applications (such as Web browsers) to emulate the public Internet. Intranets on local area networks and high-speed wide area networks provide higher levels of privacy and security compared with the public Internet.

Inverted pyramid: The way most traditional hard news stories are diagrammed. The most important facts—who, what, where, when, why—should be in the lead (first) and following paragraphs; the least important information—details, background, general interest, analysis—at the end so that the editor can cut from the bottom as space is needed.

ISO: Founded in 1946, ISO is an international federation of national standards organizations from over 100 countries. ISO is a word, not an abbreviation, derived from the Greek *isos,* "equal," found in terms such as *isometric* and *isonomy*. It was created in an attempt to avoid creating even more abbreviations for the members' national languages (e.g., IOS for International Organization for Standardization in English or OIN for Organisation Internationale de Normalisation in French).

ISP: Internet service provider. A company that provides access to the Internet for a fee.

Java/JavaScript: Java is a programming language that is specifically designed for writing programs that can be downloaded to your computer through the Internet and immediately run without fear of corruption or interference with other programs or files on your computer. JavaScript is related to the Java programming language, but is merely a set of commands that can be embedded into a Web site's HTML to enable enhanced interactivity.

Kilobyte: 1,024 (2 to the 10th power) bytes; often rounded off to one thousand bytes. Example: A 720K diskette can hold approximately 720,000 bytes (or characters) of digitized data.

Layout: A rendition that shows the relative positions of various elements (e.g., headline, photo, logo, body copy, etc.) of a page of advertising, a Web page, or a book's design, from text paragraphs and illustrations to chapter titles and page numbers. Layout is one of the most important elements of Web design and one of the most difficult. HTML, the code in which Web documents are written, was designed to present images and text in a spartan, no-nonsense manner. Preparing Web documents that lay out text and images effectively usually involves powerful WYSIWYG editing software; a working, informed knowledge of HTML and possibly other Web coding languages; and a keen sense of the levels of control users will have "at the other end" when their browser displays a Web site.

Local area network (LAN): A computer network that covers a relatively small area, or a nonpublic data communications network confined to a limited geographic area (usually within a few miles). A LAN is used to provide communication between specific, designated computers and peripherals. The area served may consist of a single building, a cluster of buildings, or a campus-type arrangement. A system of LANs can be connected over any distance through telephone lines and radio waves, creating a wide area network (WAN).

Megabyte: A unit of measure for data storage. One megabyte is equivalent to 1,024 kilobytes, 1,048,576 bytes, or 8,388,608 bits.

Menu: On-screen element of the display or graphical user interface. A menu often consists of a set of linked button graphics or of in-site linked text.

Meta tags: HTML tags that hold information in the header of a Web page, providing information that is not displayed in the browser window. Common meta tags provide information to search engines, such as keyword and description tags. Other meta tags provide style settings for the page, such as language and character sets.

Mouseover: A Web page element created with JavaScript that triggers a change when the cursor passes over (mouses over) some visual item (sometimes referred to as a *rollover image*).

MUD: Multi-User Dimension (or Multi-User Dungeon). A text-based online simulation environment used for either gaming or chatting. Different versions include MOO (MUD Object-Oriented), MUSH (Multi-User Shared Hallucination), and MUCK (Multi-User Chat Kingdom).

Multimedia: Integration of more than one form of information; refers to the delivery of information that combines different content formats—video, audio, still images, graphics, animation, text, etc. Multimedia software presents information in many different graphical, sound, and textual contexts.

Navigation bar: A set of buttons or textual links, usually aligned either horizontally or vertically on a Web page and visible on every page for easy navigation.

Operating system: The general-purpose controlling program that gives the computer the ability to run other programs. Operating systems perform basic tasks, such as recognizing input from the keyboard; sending output to the display screen; keeping track of files and directories on the disk; and controlling peripheral devices such as printers, external CD burners, scanners, and floppy disk drives. The most familiar platforms are Microsoft Windows and Apple's Mac OSX.

Packet: Any block of data sent over a network. Each packet contains information about the sender and the receiver, and error-control information, in addition to the actual message. Packets may be fixed- or variable-length, and they will be reassembled if necessary when they reach their destination. *Packet* is a generic term used to describe units of data at all levels of the protocol stack, but computer programmers use it specifically to describe application data units.

Platform: The framework of hardware and/or software on a computer that allows software to run. Typical platforms include a computer's operating system, the architecture on which it runs.

Reflective cognition: Reflective cognition "requires the ability to store temporary results, to make inferences from stored knowledge, and to follow chains of reasoning backward and forward, sometimes backtracking when a promising line of thought proves to be unfruitful" (Norman, 1993).

Rhetorical purpose: Throughout this book, the term *purpose* must be seen as possibly having two meanings: The "purpose" for writing can refer both to the writer's intrinsic *motivation* for producing a text, while at the same time indicating the *desired result* of a written piece. For example, a writer might submit an online article about river conservation for the purpose (motivation) of expressing concern about a local pollution hazard, while at the same time having the purpose (goal) of alerting local protest groups to take action and prevent further damage to the water table.

RTFM: "Read the F****** Manual" (sometimes mercifully translated as "Read the friendly manual"). A gentle suggestion to users who ask questions they could have answered themselves with a little research. Sometimes an expression of frustration with support materials from companies that have not yet hired a professional technical writer, as in, "Given the quality of the writing, it's no wonder more people don't RTFM."

Search engine: Computer programs that search local databases and the Internet for records that match a specific request. In a database, search engines search specified fields (author, title, keywords, dates, etc.) of each record in the database. On the Internet, Web-enabled "robots" crawl about the Web indexing sites, usually looking at URLs, meta tags in HTML headers, or text in the document itself.

Server: A computer on a network that provides services or resources to client computers by sharing its resources; a computer that stores all information and runs software designed to perform the critical functions for its services and resource-sharing functions. For example, a Web server would store all files related to a Web site (or multiple Web sites) and perform all work necessary for hosting the Web site.

Site map: A Web page providing a visual, hyperlinked diagram, index, or outline of a Web site's content. It allows users to navigate through the entire site. Typically, site maps divide the Web site's information into increasingly specific subject areas.

Spyware: Small, hidden programs that send out browser data, download advertising scripts, and work other kinds of hacking mischief on a personal computer (*see also:* Adware).

Table: Rows and columns of cells on a page used to organize the layout and arrange data systematically. In most WYSIWYG editors, you can place anything in a table cell, including text, graphics, and forms.

Tag: A piece of text that describes or "marks up" the formatting of a unit of data, or element, in HTML or XML. The tag is distinguishable as markup (as opposed to data) because it is surrounded by angle brackets (< and >). For example, the element <U>Welcome!</U> has the start tag <U> and the end tag </U>, which enclose the data "Welcome!" When used in an HTML file (Web page), the tags signal the browser to display the data with an underline.

TALK: A UNIX command that enables users to talk in real time similar to Internet relay chat. Users on UNIX systems can use a command to locate someone on the server. When the command is executed, the screen splits in half. If the party being "paged" responds to the message at the bottom of his or her screen, the two users can have a text-based conversation.

Upload: To transmit a file of data electronically from one computer to another computer. Opposite of "download."

URL: Uniform (or Universal) Resource Locator. The unique address of a document or a resource on the Internet, which calls up that particular file when entered into the address field of a browser.

Usenet: A worldwide network of thousands of UNIX systems with a decentralized administration. The Usenet contains more than 14,000 forums, called *newsgroups,* which cover every imaginable interest group. Newsgroups can be thought of as public-access bulletin boards. Users can access them via the Web, using their preferred Internet browser, or via newsgroup reader software.

Web page: A document whose text and other data have been marked up in HTML and can be displayed in a browser window. A Web page is usually part of a collection of documents collectively referred to as a Web site.

Web site: A collection of Web pages linked together in some organizational pattern with a common theme or subject. Usually Web sites provide text, graphics, and audio files as well as connections (hypertext links, hyperlinks, or just links) to other Web sites on the Internet. Frequently Web sites are the front end or interface display for a searchable database of information (often provided by active server pages or other data-organizing programming tools).

Web surfing: To explore a random sequence of Web sites by means of hyperlinks, search engines, and "guessed" URLs. Similar to the concept of "channel-surfing," the practice of frequently changing television channels with a remote control.

Wide area network (WAN): (1) A computer network that connects systems in a large geographical area, usually consisting of two or more LANs. A network connecting computers within very large areas, such as states, countries, and the world. The term predates the current Internet, but still applies to large national and international corporations featuring secure or encrypted systems that do not connect to public Internet servers. (2) A system of local area networks (LANs), connected over any distance, but either partially or entirely closed off from general Internet access.

World Wide Web (WWW): A global system of Internet servers that uses hypertext transfer protocol (HTTP) to transfer specially formatted documents from one place to another. The documents are formatted in a language called HTML (HyperText Mark-up Language) that supports hyperlinks to other documents, as well as graphics, audio, and video files. The user can jump from one document to another simply by clicking on hyperlinks. Originally created by researchers at CERN (Centre Européen pour a Recherche Nucléaire), the European Laboratory for Particle Physics, to facilitate sharing research information. Not all Internet servers are part of the World Wide Web. However, loosely used, WWW (or the Web) refers to the whole constellation of resources that can be accessed using Gopher, FTP, HTTP, Telnet, Usenet, WAIS, and other tools.

WYSIWYG: "What You See Is What You Get." A WYSIWYG editor is a program used for creating documents or Web pages with an easy interface that generates HTML tags automatically. The page designer can see the text and graphics in the way users will see them, rather than having to hard-code all of the symbols and tags.

DOCUMENTS IN A DIGITAL WORLD: FILE FORMATS

The following is a list of common file types used on the Web. The list is not definitive, but covers many of the types of text, image, video, sound, and hypertext files your computer typically downloads when you are visiting Web sites. As with most Internet/computer technologies, digital text and media file types are often replaced by new generations of digitized formats.

.ASP   Active Server Pages, coding that enables Web pages to be dynamically created using HTML, scripts, and reusable ActiveX server components. Typically, ASP sites use one or more scripts (small embedded programs) that are processed on a Microsoft Web server before the pages are called up and displayed in the browser window.

.AVI   Audio/Video Interleave, a video file format used by Video for Windows.

.BMP   Windows BITMAP format, a common image file type.

.DOC   Word-processed document file created in Microsoft Word.

.EXE   Executable program (or self-extracting archive file).

.GIF   Graphic Interchange Format. A common format for images on the Web.

.HTML   HyperText Markup Language/HyperText Markup. Web page file type (some WYSIWYG editors use .HTM).

.JPG/JPEG   Joint Photographic Experts Group format. A commonly used file format for images on the World Wide Web. Uses compressed data, and usually takes up less disk space. Sometimes sacrifices some image quality to do this.

.JSP   Java Server Pages, normal HTML pages with Java code pieces embedded in them. Usually they are used for controlling the content or appearance of Web pages through the use of servlets, small programs that run on the Web server to modify pages before they are sent to the browser.

.MID   Musical Instrument Digital Interface or "MIDI" files, another sound file format made from orchestrated digital sound files.

.MOV   Movie file format, typically developed for Apple's QuickTime viewer.

.MPG/MPEG   Moving Pictures Expert Group format. An international standard format for video compression and desktop movie presentation.

.MP3	MPEG audio layer 3 format. Compressed audio format that is popular for downloading sound and music files.
.PDF	Portable Document Format. A type of formatting that enables files to be viewed on a variety of computers regardless of the program originally used to create them. While PDF files must be viewed using a separate application and can sometimes download slowly, they do have an edge over HTML because publishers can design complicated layouts using any typefaces and graphics, and still remain confident that the end user will view the same layout that the publisher has created.
.PHP	Hypertext Preprocessor, a programming language that allows dynamic content that interacts with databases. Typically PHP is used for developing Web-based software applications.
.RTF	Rich Text Format. A method of encoding text formatting and document structure using the ASCII character set.
.SGML	Standard Generalized Markup Language, a system for organizing and tagging elements of a document; HTML (hypertext markup language) was built upon the ISO SGML standards.
.TIF/.TIFF	Tagged Information File Format, another type of image file. Usually these are large high-quality images; the format is preferred by desktop publishers and others who are dealing in high-resolution print images.
.TXT	File extension for a plain TeXT file. ASCII compatible, plaintext is stripped of the extra formatting symbols and codes that different word processing programs often add into the background invisibly.
.WAV	Sound file format, for Windows standard waveform sound files.
.WPS	Various Microsoft Works file formats. Used in the Works word processor, spreadsheet, database, and communications suite of applications. (Also .BPS, .WKS, .BKS, .WDB, .BDB, .WCM, or .BCM.)
.XLS	Microsoft Excel spreadsheet text files.
.XML	Stands for eXtensible Markup Language, a standard for creating markup languages. XML is not a fixed set of elements like HTML. It is a metalanguage, enabling authors to define their own tags.

References and Suggested Reading: Writing, Web Design, Web Writing Theory

D

I. Quick Reference for Writers

Sammons, Martha C. *The Internet Writer's Handbook*. Pearson Longman, 2004.

II. Design and Coding: Learning to Design and Build Web Sites

Batschelet, Margaret W. *XHTML/CSS Basics for Web Writers*. Prentice Hall, 2006.

Cederholm, Dan. *Bulletproof Web Design: Improving Flexibility and Protecting Against Worst-Case Scenarios with XHTML and CSS*. New Riders Press, 2005.

Johnson-Eilola, Johndan. *Designing Effective Web Sites: A Concise Guide*. Houghton Mifflin, 2001.

Krug, Steve. *Don't Make Me Think: A Common Sense Approach to Web Usability*. New Riders Press, 2005.

Lopuck, Lisa. *Web Design for Dummies*. Hungry Minds, 2001.

Nielsen, Jakob. *Designing Web Usability: The Practice of Simplicity*. New Riders Press, 1999.

Williams, Robin. *Web Design Workshop*. Peachpit Press, 2001.

III. Theory: Ideas and Discussion

Aarseth, Espen. *Cybertext: Perspectives on Ergodic Literature*. Baltimore: Johns Hopkins University Press, 1997.

Beason, Larry. "Ethos and Error: How Business People React to Errors." *College Composition and Communication* 53, 11 (2001): 33–64.

Bereano, Philip. "Technology and Human Freedom." In M. D. Ermann, M. B. Williams, and C. Gutierrez (Eds.), *Computers, Ethics, & Society*. New York: Oxford University Press, 1990, pp. 278–284.

Berners-Lee, Tim. *Weaving the Web: The Original Design and Ultimate Destiny of the World Wide Web*. New York: Collins, 2000.

197

Carroll, John M., and Mary B. Rosson. "Paradox of the Active User." In *Interfacing Thought: Cognitive Aspects of Human-Computer Interaction*. Cambridge, MA: MIT Press, 1987, pp. 80–111.

Cialdini, Robert. *Influence: The Psychology of Persuasion*. New York: William Morrow, 1984, 1993.

Ellul, Jacques. *The Technological Society*. (J. Wilkinson, Trans.) New York: Alfred A. Knopf. 1964/1976 (Original work published 1954).

Feenberg, Andrew. *Critical Theory of Technology*. New York: Oxford University Press, 1991.

Gackenbach, Jayne (Ed.) *Psychology and the Internet: Intrapersonal, Interpersonal and Transpersonal Implications*. New York: Academic Press, 1998.

Gill, Karamjit S. (Ed.) *Human-Machine Symbiosis: The Foundations of Human-Centred Systems of Design*. London: Springer, 1996.

Haas, Christina. *Writing Technology: Studies on the Materiality of Literacy*. Mahwah, NJ: Lawrence Erlbaum, 1996.

Hauben, Michael, and Ronda Hauben. *Netizens: On the History and Impact of Usenet and the Internet*. Los Alamitos, CA: IEEE Computer Society Press, 1997.

Hawisher, Gail, and C. Selfe (Eds.) *Passions, Pedagogies, and 21st Century Technologies*. Logan, UT: Utah State University Press, 1999.

Johnson-Eilola, Johndan. *Nostalgic Angels: Rearticulating Hypertext Writing*. Norwood, NJ: Ablex, 1997.

Lanham, Richard A. *The Electronic Word: Democracy, Technology, and the Arts*. University of Chicago Press; reissue edition, 1995.

Latour, Bruno. *We Have Never Been Modern*. (Catherine Porter, Trans.) New York: Harvester, 1993 (original work published 1991).

Lévy, Pierre. *Becoming Virtual: Reality in the Digital Age*. (R. Bononno, Trans.) New York: Plenum Trade, 1998.

Marin, Irwin C. "Emotional WorkLoad: Its Operationalization, Measurement, and Consideration in the Design of Human-Computer Interfaces." In Y. Anzai, K. Ogawa, and H. Mori (Eds.), *Symbiosis of Human and Artifact*. Amsterdam: Elsevier Science, 1995, pp. 871–875.

Murray, Denise E. *Knowledge Machines: Language and Information in a Technological Society*. New York: Longman, 1995.

Norman, Donald A. *The Design of Everyday Things*. New York: Basic Books, 1998, 2002.

Norman, Donald. *Things That Make Us Smart: Defending Human Attributes in the Age of the Machine*. Reading, MA: Perseus, 1993.

Porter, James E. *Rhetorical Ethics and Internetworked Writing*. Greenwich, CT: Ablex, 1998.

Postman, Neil. *Technopoly: The Surrender of Culture to Technology*. New York: Alfred A. Knopf, 1992.

Raskin, Jef. *The Humane Interface: New Directions for Designing Interactive Systems*. Reading, MA: Addison-Wesley, 2000.

Rheingold, Howard. *The Virtual Community: Homesteading on the Electronic Frontier*. New York: HarperCollins, 1993.

Snyder, Ilana (Ed.) *Page to Screen: Taking Literacy into the Electronic Era*. New York: Routledge, 1998.

Stone, Allucquère R. *The War of Desire and Technology at the Close of the Mechanical Age*. Cambridge, MA: MIT Press, 1996.

Sullivan, Patricia, and Jennie Dautermann (Eds.), *Electronic Literacies in the Workplace: Technologies of Writing*. Urbana, Illinois: NCTE, 1996.

Tapscott, Don. *Growing Up Digital: The Rise of the Net Generation*. New York: McGraw-Hill, 1998.

Vaske, Jerry J., and Charles E. Grantham. *Socializing the Human-Computer Environment*. Norwood, NJ: Ablex, 1990.

Welch, Kathleen. *Electric Rhetoric: Classical Rhetoric, Oralism, and a New Literacy*. Cambridge, MA: MIT Press, 1999.

Zinsser, William. *On Writing Well: An Informal Guide to Writing Nonfiction*. New York: HarperCollins, 1980, 2006.

Index